SERIES EDITOR ᴇᴍɪʟ ᴋɪʀᴄʜɴᴇʀ

forthcoming titles

The new Eastern Question
ANDREW COTTEY

The emerging European security system
EMIL KIRCHNER AND JAMES SPERLING

Seeking asylum: Germany and migration into Europe
BARBARA MARSHALL

Turkey's relations with a changing Europe
MELTEM MUFTULER

Democratic theory and the European Union
ALBERT WEALE

GREECE IN A CHANGING EUROPE

στην Αγάπη και την Ευγενία

to Nina, Christopher and Emily

KEVIN FEATHERSTONE
& KOSTAS IFANTIS
EDITORS

GREECE
IN A CHANGING EUROPE

Between European integration
and Balkan disintegration?

MANCHESTER UNIVERSITY PRESS
Manchester and New York

distributed exclusively in the USA and Canada by St. Martin's Press

Published by Manchester University Press
Oxford Road, Manchester M13 9NR, UK
and Room 400, 175 Fifth Avenue, New York, NY 10010, USA

Distributed exclusively in the USA and Canada
by St. Martin's Press, Inc., 175 Fifth Avenue, New York, NY 10010, USA

British Library Cataloguing-in-Publication Data
A catalogue record is available from the British Library

Library of Congress Cataloging-in-Publication Data
Greece in a changing Europe : between European integration and Balkan disintegration? / edited by Kevin Featherstone and Kostas Ifantis.
    p.   cm.
   "Conference held at the London School of Economics on 16–17 June 1994. The conference had the title 'Greece in a changing Europe'"—CIP front matter.
   Includes index.
   ISBN 0–7190–4766–8 (hardback)
   1. Greece—Foreign relations—1974– —Congresses.   2. European Union—Greece—Congresses.   3. Greece—Foreign relations—Balkan Peninsula—Congresses.   4. Balkan Peninsula—Foreign relations—Greece—Congresses.   I. Featherstone, Kevin.
II. Ifantis, Kostas.
DF854.G725   1996
327.495—dc20   95–37791

ISBN 0 7190 4766 8 hardback

First published in 1996

00 99 98 97 96   10 9 8 7 6 5 4 3 2 1

Typeset in Great Britain
by Northern Phototypesetting Co Ltd, Bolton
Printed in Great Britain
by Biddles Limited, Guildford and King's Lynn

CONTENTS

List of figures and tables   *page* vi
Notes on contributors   vii
List of abbreviations   viii
Series editor's foreword   ix
Preface and acknowledgements   x

PART I **Themes and context**   1

1   Introduction   *Kevin Featherstone*   3

2   Greek political culture and foreign policy   *James Pettifer*   17
    Comment by Loukas Tsoukalis Is Greece an awkward partner?   24

PART II **Greece and the European Union**   31

3   Contradictions in the Europeanisation process   *Panayiotis Ioakimidis*   33

4   Greek fiscal policy and the European Union   *George Tridimas*   53

5   Greece and economic and monetary union   *George Michalopoulos*   72

PART III **Greece and the minorities issue**   93

6   The international protection of minorities in Greece   *Christos L. Rozakis*   95

7   Citizenship and the protection of minorities   *Stephanos Stavros*   117

PART IV **Greece and the new security agenda**   129

8   A Greek view of Balkan developments   *Thanos Veremis*   131
    Comment by Jonathan Eyal A western view of Greece's Balkan policy   142

9   Greece and the USA after the Cold War   *Kostas Ifantis*   147

10 Greek foreign policy priorities for the 1990s
    Theodore A. Couloumbis & Prodromos Yannas   160

Index   176

Figures and Tables

Figures

4.1	Public sector expenditure, revenue and deficit	58
4.2	Public expenditure shares	59
4.3	Revenue shares	60
4.4	International Comparisons. Government expenditure, revenue and deficit for Greece and the EU	62
4.5a	Public Sector Borrowing Requirements by source of finance	63
4.5b	Public Sector Borrowing Requirements by fiscal authority	64
5.1	CPI and wage inflation in Greece (1984–94)	74
10.1	Greece's security profile	165

Tables

4.1	Long-run trends of the Greek economy	54
4.2	Net receipts from the EU	55
4.3	International comparisons	62
5.1	Economic indicators, Greece (1980–94)	74
5.2	Public finance in Greece (1986–93)	76
5.3	Convergence indicators for selected EU countries	77
5.4	Real effective exchange rate, various definitions	80
5.5	Prices and monetary indicators in Greece (1988–93)	81
5.6	Inflation and economic growth in Greece and the EU	83
5.7	Convergence programme (1994–99)	84

Theodore A. Couloumbis is Professor of International Relations, Department of Political Science and Public Administration, University of Athens and President of the Hellenic Foundation for European and Foreign Policy.

Jonathan Eyal is Director of Studies, Royal United Services Institute, London.

Kevin Featherstone is Professor of European Politics and Jean Monnet Chairholder in European Integration Studies, Department of European Studies, University of Bradford.

Kostas Ifantis is Lecturer in International Politics, School of Social and Historical Studies, University of Portsmouth.

Panayiotis Ioakimidis is Associate Professor of European Studies, Department of Political Science and Public Administration, University of Athens.

George Michalopoulos is Senior Research Fellow in the Department of European Studies, University of Bradford.

James Pettifer is a Senior Associate Member of St Antony's College, Oxford.

Christos L. Rozakis is Professor of International Law, Department of Law, University of Athens.

Stephanos Stavros is a member of the legal staff, European Commission on Human Rights, Council of Europe, Strasbourg.

George Tridimas is Lecturer in Economics, Department of Economics, University of Reading.

Loukas Tsoukalis is Professor of European Integration, Department of Political Science and Public Administration, University of Athens and Director of the Economics Department, College of Europe, Bruges.

Thanos Veremis is Professor of Modern European History, Department of Political Science and Public Administration, University of Athens and Director of the Hellenic Foundation for European and Foreign Policy.

Prodromos Yannas is a Visiting Lecturer at the Athens University of Economics and Business, and a member of the Faculty of IST-Studies in Athens.

ATA	Automatic Wage Indexation
CFSP	Common Foreign and Security Policy
COPA	Committee of Professional and Agricultural Organisations in the EC (transl. from French)
CPI	Consumer Price Index
CSCE	Conference on Security and Co-operation in Europe
CSF	Community Support Framework
EAGGF	European Agricultural Guidance and Guarantee Fund
EC	European Community
ECU	European Currency Unit
EEC	European Economic Community
EMS	European Monetary System
EMU	Economic and Monetary Union
EPC	European Political Co-operation
ERM	Exchange Rate Mechanism
EU	European Union
FYROM	Former Yugoslav Republic of Macedonia
GDP	Gross Domestic Product
IMF	International Monetary Fund
IMPs	Integrated Mediterranean Programmes
KKE	Communist Party of Greece
MBFRs	Mutual and Balanced Force Reductions
NATO	North Atlantic Treaty Organisation
ND	New Democracy
OAE	Organisation for the Reconstruction of Enterprises
OECD	Organisation for Economic Co-operation and Development
PASEGES	Pan-hellenic Federation of Agricultural Co-operatives (transl. from Greek acronym)
PASOK	Panhellenic Socialist Movement
PSBRs	Public Sector Borrowing Requirements
SEA	Single European Act
SEB	Confederation of Greek Industries
UNICE	Union of Industries in the EC
WEU	Western European Union

SERIES EDITOR'S FOREWORD

The events of 1989 unleashed a number of significant changes in European development, bringing in their wake consequences such as the dismantling of the iron curtain, the transformation of communist regimes, German reunification, dissolution of the Warsaw Pact and the Soviet Union, an end to the cold war syndrome, and the arrival of a host of new states. The consequences of these changes affect nation states, the European Union, and European security and stability. Whilst Europe as a whole has moved from enmity towards friendship and from conflict to co-operation in economic, political and military fields, the internal stability and cohesion of many states has been adversely affected. The result has been civil wars, fragmentation, migration, and economic and social hardship. Parallel to these developments are attempts by the EU for a larger and more integrated entity.

How Europe is responding to these changes and developments and their consequences is the focus of this book series, appropriately entitled, *Europe in change*. Books in this series take both a historical and interdisciplinary perspective in order to compare the post-1989 situation with earlier periods in European history and benefits from the theoretical insights of different disciplines in analysing both events and developments.

It is interesting, and even fitting, that the first book of the series should be about Greece with its long, and important, history of continuity and change. The adaptation required by EU membership and changing circumstances in the Balkans and Eastern Europe pose the most recent challenges to Greece. This collection edited by Kevin Featherstone and Kostas Ifantis provides a timely and interesting analysis of post-1989 internal and external developments in Greece. It will make an important contribution to our understanding of Greece, Greek–EU relations and the study of South Eastern Europe.

Emil J. Kirchner
October 1995

PREFACE AND ACKNOWLEDGEMENTS

Greek foreign policy is faced with an important transition. It is obliged to respond to major new pressures emanating from three spheres: the European Union, the Balkans and the international system after the end of the Cold War. The study of how Greek foreign policy is adapting to these pressures helps to illuminate not only the particular case of Greece, but also to some extent the general nature of European Union membership and the wider character of the conflict in the Balkans. Consideration of Greek foreign policy is thus both timely and significant.

This book is the outcome of a large conference held at the London School of Economics on 16–17 June 1994. The conference had the title, 'Greece in a Changing Europe: Opportunities and Constraints'. With the exception of the chapter by Michalopoulos, each of the other chapters in this volume stem from papers presented at the conference.

The conference was chaired by the book's two editors. They received, however, crucial help and support from several other individuals and from relevant educational bodies. Dr Spiros Economides (LSE) acted as the local organiser for the conference. Professor Thanos Veremis (Athens, then on leave at St Antony's, Oxford) and Dr Nikos Papadakis (ELEMEP) served as academic advisers for the conference programme. Dr Papadakis also gave other helpful logistical advice. Dr Howard Machin gave a warm welcome to the conference on behalf of the LSE. His staff afforded invaluable and highly efficient help with the conference arrangements: none more so than Patricia Fearnley. Finally, Dimitris Karas has been a source of continuing encouragement to both of us. We would like to express our gratitude to each of these colleagues.

The conference could not have been held without the generous financial support extended by The Hellenic Foundation, The London Hellenic Society and The North Atlantic Treaty Organisation. In this respect, we would like to record our deepest appreciation to Mr S. J. Fafalios, Mr J. Ad. Hadjipateras and Dr Spyros Philipas. In addition, the University of Bradford, University of Portsmouth, University Association for Contemporary European Studies, Political Studies Association and ELIAMEP each gave further assistance to the conference organisation.

Several colleagues enhanced the conference proceedings by making various academic contributions, notably as chairs or discussants: (in chronological order) Professor Helen Wallace, David Marsh, Andreas Andrianopoulos, Dr Georgios Markopouliotis, Professor Nicos Mouzelis, Dr Mark Mazower, Dr Jane Cowan, Dimitris Katsoudas, Georgios Papandreou, Dr Spiros Economides and Professor Richard Clogg. We would like to record our thanks to each of them.

Inevitably, the organisation of a conference such as this and the preparation of the current volume involved a major commitment of our own time and energy. This made demands on our respective partners. We would like to thank our wives for their forbearance and to dedicate this volume to them: Agapi and Nina.

Kevin Featherstone
Kostas Ifantis
December 1994

PART I

Themes and context

$\mathcal{K}$EVIN $\mathcal{F}$EATHERSTONE

1

Introduction

This volume addresses three important dimensions of current international concern: first, the future of the European integration process and the pressures towards a 'multi-speed' Europe; second, the tensions and ramifications of the crisis in the Balkans; and finally the implications of the end of the Cold War for small Western European states. The common focus across all three dimensions is the changing foreign policy of Greece in the 1990s.

The magnitude of change that Greek foreign policy has faced in recent years is undeniable. As with other nations, conditions and assumptions which were accepted for several decades have been fundamentally revised. Policy has had to adapt to a new, and rapidly changing, environment. Greece represents an exceptional case, however. The conjunction of the pressures emanating from the international, European and Balkan environments have created a highly complex challenge to Greek foreign policy. Greece is the only Balkan member of the European Union and the only stable liberal democracy in the region.

Adaptation has certainly proved difficult. Greece has been subject to mounting international criticism for its stance in relation to both the European Union (before 1993, the European Economic Community, then the European Community; here the EU throughout the book), and the Balkans. The image and reputation of Greece has been tarnished, as the international press reports criticism of her policies throughout the world. Consideration of Greek foreign policy is thus both unusually timely and significant, in both the European Union and Balkan contexts.

To set the context for the specialist chapters that follow, this introduction offers a brief survey of how the three dimensions of change identified above have impinged on Greek foreign policy and domestic politics. It does not attempt to give equal attention to each dimension, let alone their various aspects. With respect to the first dimension, the introduction begins by considering the form of Greek participation in the EU and the implications of membership for Greece. It evaluates the extent to which Greece is an exceptional EU member, taking into account the various criticisms made of it. It also highlights certain impacts of membership on Greek foreign policy and domestic politics. Turning to the wider environments prompting foreign policy change, the introduction then considers the consequences of the developments in the international system, together with changes in the Balkans, for contemporary Greek foreign policy. The intention in this brief survey is to portray the three dimensions of change affecting Greek foreign policy and to highlight the major themes raised in the subsequent chapters.

What kind of EU member is Greece?

Greece's membership of the EU has always had a controversial aspect to it (Verney 1987). Even in domestic terms, the entry bid in the 1970s championed by Constantine Karamanlis (Prime Minister and leader of the centre-right New Democracy party) was opposed vociferously by both PASOK (Socialists) and the Communists; a domestic polarisation which was not matched in the cases of Portugal or Spain, but one which did rival in intensity, if not in form, that of Britain and, more recently, Denmark. After entry, Andreas Papandreou (as Premier and leader of PASOK) attempted a UK-style renegotiation of the conditions of membership, and only increased economic aid from the EU helped his Government to adjust to the demands. However, his Government never felt able to place itself wholeheartedly at the core of an EU consensus on the proper course for the Community to follow. Throughout the 1980s, PASOK had distanced itself from its partners on common foreign policy stances, and it remained ambivalent on questions involving further transfers of national sovereignty.

By the start of the 1990s, Greek membership of the EU was based on a peculiar paradox. As Ioakimidis explains in his chapter, in general terms, the majority of the Greek public favoured 'deeper' European integration and political elites had also shifted in this direction, though divisions remain. Yet Greek membership became more controversial to her EU partners. International press reports gave very negative views on Greek policies and performance in London, Paris and Brussels.

Such criticism combined two dimensions: Greece's position in the EU and Greece's position in the Balkans. Both were intertwined and reinforced each other. A momentum built up behind such journalistic reports. A perspective was formed on Greece's membership of the EU which established a predisposition to see all fresh actions by her in a damning light. Moreover, this momentum seemed largely uncontrollable by Athens; a feature which was deeply damaging to her position. Greek leaders have often succumbed to paranoia in the past, in response to foreign pressures, but on this occasion concern over the spread of such criticism seemed justified, insofar as the criticism was itself exaggerated.

So, what kind of EU member is Greece? The chapters by Ioakimidis, Michalopoulos and Tridimas give a more substantial answer to this question. Here, at the outset of the study, several summary points can be addressed. First, criticism of Greece often focuses on the level of EU aid she receives: Greece is seen as a 'bottomless pit' into which European money has been poured, but with little return in terms of an improved economic performance by her.

The statistics on EU aid can be interpreted in various ways. In isolation, the absolute levels of aid are impressive: in 1993, Greece received some 5,147.9 m. ECU (c.$6,027m) in payments from the EU budget (OJ C327; 24 November 1994). For a small nation like Greece such sums were significant; they represented approximately $16.5m per day. Greece was far from being the largest recipient of EU money, however. France, Italy, Spain, and Germany each received larger amounts. However, in relative terms, this meant that with less than 3 per cent of the EU's total population, Greece received 8 per cent of total payments from the EU budget. With broadly comparable populations, Portugal received 5.3 per cent and Belgium 3.8 per cent of total payments. Yet notions of a 'fair' distribution are only partially relevant when considering allocations from the EU budget. For example, despite being the poorest EU member-state, Greece actually paid more into the EU budget in 1993 than did Portugal. Indeed, Portugal received substantially more money from the EU under the (ESF) European Regional Development Fund (ERDF) and the European Social Fund than did Greece. The larger payments to Greece were mainly under the Common Agricultural Policy (CAP) (the EAGGF sections) – by far the largest section of the EU budget – where Greek farmers received much more than their counterparts in Portugal. This imbalance has an effect on the targeting of aid for infrastructure projects and, presumably, its impact on growth.

In any event, it is hardly surprising that as the poorest EU member-state, Greece received a disproportionate share of available aid. The reality is, however, that the total 'pot of gold' distributed by the EU is not that large. Indeed, the total EU budget is little more than 1 per cent of the total GDP of its member-states, or barely over 2 per cent of its member-states' public expenditure. As a means of reducing the inequalities in the economic well-being of its member-states, the EU budget is thus woefully inadequate. EU aid can only be expected to have an effect at the margin.

In sum, it is an exaggeration to assert that EU money has been 'poured' into Greece; in real terms, there is not so much to pour. In isolation, EU transfers do offer important help to a small state like Greece. Yet the level of aid given to Greece reflects its relative poverty, and the type of aid received reflects the peculiarities of EU policies. Greece receives more under agriculture; Portugal more under the regional and social funds. Across the EU member-states, money from Brussels is only approximately distributed on grounds of equity or economic need.

However, the performance of the Greek economy over the last decade or so has been very poor; indeed, to such an extent that it has led to a deterioration in Greece's relative position in Europe. These matters are fully discussed by Tridimas and Michalopoulos in their chapters. In particular, the problem of over-consumption by the State persists. The EU's Monetary Committee produced a scathing analysis in March 1992 of the Mitsotakis Government's domestic economic management. This followed an agreement the previous year on a ECU 2 billion loan from the EU to provide medium term financial assistance to Greece, to help it with EMU (Economic and Monetary Union) convergence. The first tranche was paid in March 1991, but the next two instalments were dependent on Greece meeting certain conditions in its economic performance. Greece was advised in 1992 that it was so far off target that the second tranche of ECU 600 million would not be forthcoming, should it be requested. To avoid this humiliation, the Mitsotakis Government delayed the application. The fiscal crisis of the State threatens Greek interests in the EU: it will be extremely difficult for Greece to meet the Maastricht Treaty's convergence criteria for participation in the final stage of economic and monetary union. In this, though, Greece is not alone: the same might be said for Italy and Belgium, two of the original founders of the EU.

Putting these different aspects together, the main point here would appear to be that it is the poor performance of the Greek economy that threatens to relegate Greece to membership of an outer circle or a slow lane in the European integration process. In other words, it is not so much that EU money has been poured in with little effect, rather it is the more general domestic mismanagement of the State's own resources (and monetary policy) that retards Greece's progress. EU membership has not overcome long-term features of the clientelistic state, which serves as a cultural obstacle to Greek participation in the EU's inner core. The deepening of the European integration process serves to expose such obstacles and differentiates not only Greece, but also Italy and Spain, from the EU's core. The poor economic performance of these countries creates the justification for a 'multi-speed' Europe.

The second type of criticism levelled against Greece concerns the extent to which it implements or abides by EU rules. This aspect is very difficult to measure, but some general indication is available via the EU Commission's annual monitoring of the application of European law. Its 1994 report showed the number of infringement proceedings initiated by the Commission against member-states (OJ C 154: 6 June 1994). In 1993, some 125 cases had been initiated against Greece, the same number that had been started against Portugal. Both countries shared the position of being the target for the highest number of infringement proceedings. Both countries have fared very similarly in recent years; in 1990, however, Portugal had performed much worse than Greece, whilst in 1989 the reverse had been true. In 1993, after Greece and Portugal, came Germany, Italy and Spain. In 1992, Italy, Spain and Portugal each performed worse than Greece. Moreover, the classification of suspected infringements relating to the single market showed that, for 1991 and 1992, 9.4 per cent and 11.5 per cent respectively of all cases concerned Greece. However, Germany,

France, Italy and Spain each had worse records. Thus, in these respects, Greece has not been exceptional in infringing EU laws and its position can be compared to that of several other countries.

Two further measures of legal rectitude are available. First, it is worth looking at the record of member-states in implementing EU directives. Elsewhere, Frangakis has reported that, for EU legislation originating in the period 1962–92, out of a total of 1,087 directives Greece had implemented 960, that is 88.3 per cent (Frangakis 1994: 184). This was the lowest rate of compliance in the EU. However, Greece was only marginally behind Luxembourg (88.4 per cent), Italy (89.1 per cent), Portugal (89.2 per cent) and Germany (89.9 per cent). Another indication is gained from the progress being made to implement single European market legislation. In this respect, Greece has also recently been the worst case in the EU, but again the range of differentiation between member-states has been very small. By 14 September 1994, Greece had transposed 80.4 per cent of the single market legislation, marginally behind Germany (80.6 per cent), but somewhat below the EU average of 88.8 per cent. The EU trend has fluctuated between countries over time, however.

A third area of criticism of Greece is the suggestion that it adopts policy positions outside the general EU consensus, thus putting itself out on a limb. This charge has several dimensions to it. The first concerns foreign policy initiatives under the European Political Co-operation Process (EPC) and the Common Foreign and Security Policy of the EU. Several examples of a divergence in general foreign policy orientation can be cited from PASOK's early years in power after 1981. More recently, the divergences have appeared on specific issues concerning Greece's relations with her neighbours: the response to the crisis in the former Yugoslavia, the recognition of the Former Yugoslav Republic of Macedonia (FYROM), disputes with Albania over the rights of the predominantly ethnic Greek population in its southern provinces and negotiations with Turkey over long-standing disputes in the Aegean and in Cyprus. These issues are discussed in the chapters by Veremis, Eyal and Couloumbis. A long-term shift can, however, be noted. In the last years of the Cold War, Papandreou maintained a residual opposition to embracing pro-American policy positions. By the early 1990s, however, foreign policy disagreements between Greece and her EU partners have focused on more immediate issues arising from instability on Greece's borders. A clear conflict of national interest has appeared, prompted by different strategic perceptions.

The most severe divergence occurred at the start of Greece's tenure as President of the EU Council in the first half of 1994, when the Papandreou Government imposed a unilateral trade embargo on FYROM. Greece's partners were outraged by what they saw as an inflammatory action. Athens, by contrast, saw it as a means of breaking the deadlocked negotiations with Skopje. The EU Commission took the unprecedented step of referring the case to the EU's Court of Justice in Luxembourg. At the end of June 1994, the Court refused the Commission's request for an emergency interim ruling ordering Athens to end

the blockade. The effect of the decision was to favour greatly the Greek Government's position and to help it resist the pressure from its partners.

In the current Balkan crisis there are a number of conflicts of interest
between Greece and its EU partners. Some of these are particularly acute. As
Eyal and Veremis point out in their chapters, the Greek positions on the crisis
have had their own legitimate justification. Indeed, in some respects, they have
been vindicated in the light of subsequent events. Moreover, it would be misleading to assume a unanimity of view amongst Greece's EU partners on the
Balkan crisis. The EU is a long way from establishing a truly common foreign
policy and the EPC and CFSP (Common Foreign and Security Policy) processes
have continued to sustain a diversity of views. The Greek case can be seen as
being symptomatic of a wider foreign policy disunity.

A second dimension of Greece being judged to be outside an EU consensus
concerns opinions on the future deepening of the European integration
process. The weak position of Greece in relation to EMU has already been
noted. Yet, in other respects, since the late 1980s, successive Greek governments
have in fact gone along with all major EU initiatives in economic and social
policy, as well as of institutional reform. The Maastricht Treaty was passed
speedily and with relatively little opposition in the Greek parliament. Both
major parties – PASOK and ND – vied with each other in the October 1993 elections to present themselves as the more pro-European (Featherstone 1994).
Even Andonis Samaras's breakaway party from ND, Politiki Anoiksi, which is
hawkish on Greece's Balkans policy, accepts the need for a deepening of the
European integration process. In this respect, thus far it has been barely distin-
guishable from ND. For all three parties there remain ambiguities over the commitment to a specifically federal EU, but ND and PASOK support further
institutional reform to increase democracy at the EU level. Indeed, the Papandreou Government launched an initiative in this area during its presidency of
the EU in early 1993. All three parties seek to resist Greece being consigned to a
slow lane of European integration – despite the EMU difficulties – and wish to be
at the heart of Europe. It is only on the far left fringe in which Europe still creates divisions. Whilst the more moderate Synaspismos and the Greek Left party
support further EU integration, the larger KKE (Communist Party of Greece)
has reverted to a hardline denunciation. Their April 1993 Congress agreed a
new statement on Europe, which roundly condemned the Maastricht Treaty.
The KKE currently has just nine seats in the 300-member Greek parliament,
however.

Thus, in many respects, Greece has been closer to the EU's mainstream
thinking than several of its partners: notably, the UK and Denmark. This represents a significant shift since the mid-1980s, when Greece was as troublesome
as its two northern partners. All three, for example, had opposed the convening
of the Inter-Governmental Conference (IGC) in 1985 to negotiate the Single
European Act (SEA). Currently, Greek exceptionalism refers to its membership
of a group of weaker states that are very unlikely to be able to join in EMU for

some time to come, and to its assertion of its rights in the Balkans. Only in the latter case can the Greek position be termed unique.

To return to the earlier question: what kind of EU member is Greece? The brief survey offered above suggests some important points of distinction. Greek exceptionalism needs careful qualification. First, the allocation of EU money to Greece is not particularly exceptional. Moreover, the total amount could only be expected to have a marginal effect on the level of Greece's economic disparity with the rest of the EU. The prime economic factor causing difficulties for Greece in the EU is the more general domestic fiscal crisis and high level of inflation, which threaten to leave Greece outside any early moves to EMU, as Michalopoulos indicates. The solution to this problem requires radical changes in long-standing clientelistic traditions in the Greek State and a change in popular expectations. It is also a situation faced elsewhere, however, notably in Italy. Secondly, Greece is not exceptional in its record of non-compliance or infringement of EU law. Finally, Greece is exceptional in its current stance on the Balkans, but in the great swathe of other EU policies it is supportive of the general consensus favouring a deepening of integration. Added together, these creates quite a different picture of Greece as an EU member; not so much the awkward partner, but a supporter – albeit as one of the weaker economies, uniquely threatened by a civil war on its doorstep. Stabilisation of the situation in the former Yugoslavia and of Greece's relations with Skopje might significantly transform the international image of Athens by reducing its exceptionalism.

The consequences of EU membership

The changing form of European integration creates problems for anyone attempting an academic analysis. In particular, the impact of membership on the policies and constraints of its constituent states is inadequately understood. European integration in the 1990s penetrates widely into domestic politics and foreign policy, changing policy agendas. Moreover, the perceptions of the conditions of membership vary between different domestic polities. The EU has several different 'faces'. Viewed through the lens of Greek politics, the EU is a force for modernisation, for raising of standards, for better public financing alongside fiscal discipline and for economic liberalisation. In this respect, a similar image of the EU is identified by Italian politicians and voters; indeed, the economic liberalisation identified with the EU is sometimes seen there as having contributed to the recent revolution in Italian politics. It contrasts sharply with the impression many voters in Britain and Denmark have of 'Brussels', a label used pejoratively to stress the anonymity and distance of the Commission from its grass roots.

In the foreign policy domain, the image of the EU in Greece has a noticeably different character from that which exists in economic or social affairs. As already noted, recent Greek governments have diverged from their EU partners on policy towards the Balkans and Turkey. In foreign policy matters Greece's EU partners are seen as being out-of-touch, reckless, and/or hypocritical. At the very least, EU membership acts as a constraint on Greece's policy towards its near neighbours, as Athens has to respond to pressure for common positions, whilst trying to assert its sovereign rights. In other respects, though, EU membership also strengthens the foreign policy position of Greece, notably in relation to Turkey.

This peculiar mix of images represents, in large part, the perception of EU membership in the Greek polity and the recognition of its consequences. At this point it is instructive to consider the domestic consequences of Greece's membership of the EU. At home, the deepening of the European integration process since 1985 has, in the Greek case, coincided with a continuing debate over the nature and role of the State. Indeed, two major domestic issues have dominated each Greek election since 1985: the economic responsibility of the State and the clientelistic practices of the 'party-state' (Featherstone 1994a). Both issues have provoked fierce debate over the need to reform; to break the log-jam of deep-rooted traditions seen as impeding 'good' governance. Reform of the State's economic role is directly related to the consequences of European integration.

The role of the State suffers from a dual tradition of dependency. As a 'peripheral' nation, the State has been dependent, both economically and militarily, on external powers, whilst at home, social institutions and voters have been dependent on state paternalism and the allocation of favours. The State has been placed at a crucial intersection: dependent on foreign support, but faced with insatiable demands for its support and resources at home. In the immediate post-war period, Britain and then the USA were Greece's major external patrons, but membership of the EU since 1981 has shifted Greek dependency to a body whose common policies have become increasingly pervasive and penetrating in domestic society. As Ioakimidis notes in his chapter, today EU membership challenges the traditional relationship in Greece between the State and economy, and even the State and society. The new patron reaches parts of the Greek system older patrons could not or did not seek to change.

The terms and conditions of EU membership have confronted long-established traditions within the Greek political system. For many years, parliament played a minimal role in foreign policy matters in general, and EU issues in particular. By June 1990, however, the parties had agreed – in a new climate that sought greater transparency – to establish a parliamentary committee on European integration, composed of twelve national and twelve European parliamentarians, headed by a vice-president of the national parliament. It is to consider institutional issues arising from EU membership, co-operation between the national and the European Parliament, the incorporation of European legislation and EU issues arising from the work of other national parliamentary committees (Tsinisizelis, 1995).

For its part, EU membership has challenged the long-term problems of public administration in Greece. These can be summarised as poor co-ordination, a defensiveness towards new external demands and an inflexibility in its operation. Personnel continue to be appointed on the basis of political favours and party commitment, rather than on technical merit. Yet, there is some evidence that EU membership has prompted a more open style of policy-making (Tsinisizelis 1995). The Ministry of the National Economy remains the key actor on EU economic policy (with foreign and security policy matters handled by the foreign ministry and the Prime Minister's Office), but it liaises – perhaps increasingly so – with experts from other ministries and those from outside government. Decision-making remains tightly controlled, nevertheless, and is typically dominated by the general authority of the Prime Minister. The Single European Act, for example, is understood never to have been discussed by the Greek cabinet as a body. It is likely, however, that the nature of the Maastricht Treaty and the diverse agenda for the Inter-Governmental Conference planned for 1996 will necessitate a broader approach within the governmental structure.

The ability of national Governments to maintain narrow control – to act as 'gatekeepers' between the domestic and the European spheres – is increasingly undermined by the terms of the European integration process itself. If not pluralistic, the policy process has to be more corporatist, at least. For example, close co-ordination is required between the Government and agricultural lobbies (such as PASEGES which is a member of COPA, the EU-level lobby organisation), the main trade union organisations (GSEE and ADEDY, both members of the European Trades Union Confederation, ETUC) and big business represented in SEB (Federation of Greek Industries and a participator in UNICE, the EU employers organisation).

Within the domestic party system, the endogenous movement for economic de-regulation in Greece was crucially strengthened by international, and specifically European, pressures (Featherstone 1994b). For ND in the mid-1980s, EU membership reinforced the shift away from state paternalism and ideological vagueness towards a more defined neo-liberal stance, along the lines of other centre-right parties in the EU. EU membership 'Europeanised' ND – to use the phrase adopted by Ioakimidis – as a party that could speak warmly of the 'social market economy' and of 'the Thatcher experiment', both alien to the Greek tradition. The ND manifesto of 1985 and its 1989 programme (with the slogan of Liberty–Creation–Social Protection) expressed the shift. This ideological shift was undoubtedly the result of a range of factors: it imported the predominant international centre-right philosophy, and it may even have occurred without EU entry. Yet, the political environment created by EU membership – the cross-national networks and the new EU policy norms – also made a significant impact on how the party redefined itself in the opposition years of the 1980s. For ND modernisation would come via less regulation, paralleling the philosophy of the single European market programme of 1985.

The impact of EU membership has probably been most profound in the case of PASOK, although its relevant ideological shift in domestic policy came somewhat later. In the 1980s, PASOK's public sector strategy had fallen well short of its proclaimed socialist ideals. Its extension of state intervention lacked the coherence and consistency that some of its earlier statements had promised. Nevertheless, PASOK increased public spending and consumption, running up exceptionally high public deficits. In its last years in office it was accused of profligacy and irresponsibility in charge of the public purse, summarised by the opposition taunt against the Finance Minister: *Tsovola, dhos ta ola* ('Tsovolas, give it all away'). This was an independent domestic strategy seen by many as an attempt to buy popularity. Even so, its 1989 election manifesto recognised the need for a gradual liberalisation of market mechanisms and, in its last years in office, PASOK had been obliged to allow the operation of private radio and television stations, breaking the traditional state monopoly.

By the time of the 1993 election, the centre ground of economic policy debate had shifted significantly from that of the 1980s. The Right continued to espouse free market economics and PASOK more fully committed itself to less statism, leaving the little-reformed KKE more isolated than for many years. PASOK's programme combined less statism with an emphasis on social solidarity. It echoed the policies put forward by the French socialists after 1984 or the British Labour Party after 1987. Unemployment, Papandreou told Parliament, 'cannot be fought by increasing the public sector, but through growth'. Moreover, 'Privatisation is not incompatible with our policies so long as it does not lead to private monopolies, or damage national interests.' PASOK's economic philosophy had undergone a significant change; moreover 'Europe' had been used as a dominant pretext for the shift. The Party's 1989 programme and campaign publicity emphasised the need to adapt to the demands of the Single European Market. Its 1993 programme went even further in stressing the national interest in adapting to 'the challenges of a united Europe'. As with ND, other pressures behind the shift were relevant – in this case, the tarnished image of past statism and the desire to appear forward-looking – but the consequences of a changing form of European integration were often cited and highlighted.

European integration has in recent years posed as a major challenge to the Greek State tradition and those who have sought to uphold it. It would not be an exaggeration to assert that a faltering endogenous momentum for economic liberalisation was crucially helped and strengthened by the obligation to follow EU policies – notably the Single Market and EMU convergence – which upheld similar policy principles. Seen from the viewpoint of domestic Greek politics, therefore, EU membership and the Commission appear as both modernising and liberalising agents (as they do elsewhere in southern Europe).

Greece and the evolving international system

The 'deepening' of the European integration process could by itself have been assumed to have had a major impact on Greek domestic politics and foreign policy in the first part of the 1990s. However, two further dimensions of change also brought their own consequences for the country. The conjunction of all three sets of changes transformed the overall context of Greek foreign policy and created major difficulties for the achievement of its interests, as Couloumbis explains in his chapter.

The Civil War in the former Yugoslavia has already been noted as having provoked a serious clash of interests and policy between Greece and her EU partners. Seen from Athens, the conflagration in the former Yugoslavia has had the potential to spread more widely in the Balkans, as neighbouring powers might be brought in to protect their respective interests. Intervention by the EU, and indeed the UN, is viewed as having, on occasions, exacerbated this danger by its impetuous and even reckless nature. Veremis in his chapter discusses these matters in detail. The risk to Greek interests is the active participation of Turkey in the conflict in Bosnia, the possibility of its support (and/or that of Bulgaria) for the Skopje regime and the provocations emanating from Albania in its treatment of the ethnic Greek population within its borders. The collapse of the former Yugoslavia has made the Greek neighbourhood very threatening.

After almost forty years of relative stability on its northern borders, Greek foreign policy has to re-focus its attention on crises very close to home. The Cold War and the repressive regimes circled across its northern borders had maintained a relative peace. Now, earlier tensions have re-emerged, with a renewed attention to issues of self-determination and the rights of ethnic populations. Foreign critics have highlighted alleged abuses of the human rights of several minorities within Greece: Jehovah's Witnesses, far Left activists sympathising with the Skopje regime and Muslims in Thrace. The chapters by Stavros and Rozakis give extensive attention to these matters as issues of the legal protection of individual rights within Greece. To foreign critics and campaign groups, these cases have been equated with abuses elsewhere in the region. By most current measures this would be seen as an exaggeration. Yet, the Greek dilemma is that whilst it boasts of being the only stable democracy in the region, it establishes for itself a higher moral code by which its domestic actions might be judged. Despite feeling itself to be surrounded by threats within the Balkans, more is expected of it.

The background reality is that Greece is one of the most homogeneous societies within the EU. Judged in terms of its ethnic composition, its linguistic usage and its religious faith, Greek society has many large majorities and very few minorities. Greece has not faced regionalist demands for secession or separatism. Instead, there has been a strong and pervasive sense of what it is to be Greek, as a means of distinction from foreigners. This sense of identity carries with it certain dangers in terms of the small minorities that do exist within her borders. The sense of national identity has had an important inclusive character. The *ethnos* (nation) has assumed social primacy; indeed, it has had a supremacy over notions of individual rights and the scope for dissent, as Stavros argues in his chapter. Elsewhere, Pollis has taken a more extreme view on this matter (1992) and Pettifer, in this volume, sees a greater heterogeneity.

The demand for recognition by FYROM in 1992–93 is a case in point. The demand conflicted with the Greek preference for the maintenance of Yugoslav unity and threatened further instability. More particularly, it inflamed the sensitivities of almost all Greeks by its use of the title Macedonia. To Greeks the title denotes an exclusive and integral part of their own history and culture, dating back to Alexander the Great. Successive Greek governments have objected to the use by the Skopje regime of the star of Vergina (a Greek symbol), official maps, currency notes and articles in the constitution which suggest irredentist claims over Greek territory. The UN and the EU had agreed to a temporary compromise – the use of the FYROM title – but by the end of 1994 a permanent solution still seemed a long way off.

The end of the Cold War has transformed the wider European landscape. In the early years of the post-1974 Greek regime, political controversy surrounded Greek participation in NATO and an exclusive identification with Western interests. In the 1980s, PASOK's foreign policy sought to promote detente and ameliorate inter-block conflict. This also involved, however, various actions regarded by Washington as being anti-American. PASOK also sought to establish new openings to the Middle East and the Third World. Now the Cold war has ended, the position of Greece *vis-à-vis* Washington and Moscow has changed, as Couloumbis and Ifantis point out in their chapters.

Relations with the US have a much better air about them than before. Clinton and Papandreou have been able to put the bilateral relations on a more positive footing than in the period of Reagan and Bush, as Ifantis details. As individual leaders, Clinton is probably better disposed to closer relations with Greece and on his part Papandreou was much warmer to Washington after 1993 than he was before 1989. More substantively, however, it is in the US interest to avoid offending long-term allies in an unstable and important region, whilst for Papandreou, the US cannot so easily be portrayed as a demon after it has just won the Cold War and the old regimes of Eastern Europe have been exposed as oppressive to international audiences.

The context of Greece's relations with the US has changed, but interests may be not have moved significantly closer to convergence. The interpretation of how to deal with the crisis in the former Yugoslavia differs between the two sides, whilst Greco-Turkish relations continue to pose problems for Athens in its dealings with Washington. Greece's relations with the US are undergoing a significant transition after the end of the Cold War, but it still faces a difficult task in re-defining its needs and expectations. Couloumbis addresses this subject in his wide-ranging chapter.

The end of the Cold War also presents new opportunities for Greece in its future relations with Moscow and the constituent elements of the former Soviet Union. Traditional cultural affinities have re-emerged, notably in relation to the Orthodox religion, whilst Moscow's view of how to handle the Yugoslav crisis appears closer to the Greek position than that of many Western governments. Again, a new agenda has opened up for Greek foreign policy, albeit one set within the context of small state diplomacy.

This brief survey has introduced the theme of three dimensions of change affecting Greek foreign policy and domestic politics in the 1990s. They represent a unique conjunction and place Greek foreign policy in probably its most important transition since the end of the Greek Civil War (1946–49). The other major period of transition for Greek foreign policy – the return of democracy in 1974 after the seventh-year dictatorship of the Colonels – provided a new European vocation for Greece and also prompted sustained criticism of too close a tie with Washington. Yet, the readjustment by Greece at that time was within a stable international and Balkan setting. Moreover, Greece was to join a relatively stable European body which had not yet acquired the far-reaching objectives of the 1980s and 1990s. In the mid-1990s, however, the external world has undergone a more dramatic shift; one in which Greek foreign policy must adapt to three interlocking environments of change.

The impact of these three sets of changes on Greece displays some general differentiation. First, the impact of EU membership in economic and social policy is as a strong modernising and liberalising force, revising state-economy and state-society relations. 'Europe' represents a progressive momentum, setting standards and raising new aspirations. By contrast, the current crises in the Balkans impinge on Greek politics in the manner of the 'shock of the old': reawakening long term fears and tensions. The Balkan crises raise a different kind of politics, traditional in character if not in setting. Politics that are characterised by ethnicity, by minority rights and, indeed, by national rights. In this context, Balkan nations – Greece included – view the present on the basis of dominant historical legacies. Finally, changes in the international system, notably the end of the Cold War and of bipolarity, release Greek foreign policy from the constraint of support for the West. They provide an opportunity to place relations with Washington and Moscow on a new footing. These changes may also represent the final nail in the coffin for the post-Civil War settlement in Greece, lessening the Communist/anti-Communist cleavage, after a prolonged transition or 'death' since 1974.

The differential nature of how these changes affect the Greek polity provides a fascinating backdrop to this study. It represents a complex mix of pressures that impinges into the domestic political arena in terms of policy agendas and political behaviour: between, loosely, modernisation and traditionalism, or more simply, continuity and change. Greek foreign policy has been placed in a new setting. The analysis of how it adapts or fails to adapt will be crucial to understanding the position of Greece in the EU, the Balkans and the international system in the 1990s. Ultimately, such an analysis should be of interest not only to specialists in Greek affairs, but also to those sensitive to a 'multi-speed Europe', the nature of the current Balkan crisis and the character of the international system.

References

Featherstone, K. (1994), 'The Challenge of Liberalization: Parties and the State in Greece after the 1993 Elections', *Democratization*, 1:2, 280–294.

Featherstone, K. (1994), 'Political Parties', in P. Kazakos and P. C. Ioakimidis, (eds.), Greece and EC Membership Evaluated, London, Pinter.

Frangakis, N. (1994), 'Law Harmonization', in P. Kazakos and P. C. Ioakimidis, eds., *Greece and EC Membership Evaluated*, London, Pinter.

0.J. C154, *Official Journal of the European Communities*, Luxembourg, 6 June 1994.

O.J. C327, *Official Journal of the European Communities*, Luxembourg, 24 November 1994.

Pollis, A. (1992), 'Greek National Identity: Religious Minorities, Rights and European Norms', *Journal of Modern Greek Studies*, 10:2, 171–195.

Tsinisizelis, M. J. (1995), 'Greece in the European Union: A Preliminary Political Institutional Balance Sheet', unpublished paper, University of Athens.

Verney, S. (1987), 'Greece and the European Community', in K. Featherstone and D. K. Katsoudas, (eds.), *Political Change in Greece: Before and After the Colonels*. London, Croom Helm.

JAMES PETTIFER

2

Greek political culture and foreign policy

In terms of the dominant element in the political culture of the Greek elite and population as a whole, commitment to Europe is central. In a recent public opinion poll, Greece recorded the highest percentage of popular support for European integration and the Maastricht Treaty processes of all European countries.[1] But it is also an unquestionable fact that among the leadership of the European countries that are members of the EU, Greece is seen as the most difficult and problematic member, a nation that in 1994 had been taken to court by the European Commission over its blockade of the FYROM, and has been subject to regular criticism in the most influential quality press organs in Germany, France, the United Kingdom and elsewhere.[2] There appears, to most independent observers, to be an irreconcilable gap between the perceived enthusiasm of the Greek people and the Greek political elite for the EU, and the incapacity of Greek Governments to behave in a *communitaire* fashion.

Key to the Greek government's current behaviour are the uncertainties concomitant with the development of the Balkan crisis and with increasing Greek economic dependence on the EU. Although Greece has a number of independent foreign policy positions on general world problems, and an influential lobby in Washington, in practice the most important work takes place on issues connected with the Mediterranean and Balkan neighbours, and within an EU framework. Within this framework, very traditional problems, such as the relationship with Turkey, have in general terms been absorbed for many years within the national security framework inherited from the Cold War in institutions such as NATO.

It may appear presumptuous, in some senses, for non-Greeks to comment on the relationship between popular political culture and foreign policy, as many Greeks quite rightly see misunderstanding of the nature of the Greek cultural and political identity as one of the main problems affecting Greek–EU relations at present. When Greece joined the EU, after the end of the dictatorship 1974, there was a substantial element of Philhellenist affirmation in the minds of important European leaders of the time, such as the French President, Mr Valèry Giscard d'Estaing, coupled with monumental ignorance of actual Greek social and economic conditions by lower ranking officials and northern European populations generally.[3] Greece was seen by these committed Philhellenists as the source of most civilisation in Europe at an intellectual level, and deserving privileged treatment within the Union in its drive to re-establish democracy. But this perspective was never shared by the northern European countries, where the 'Roman' vision of the EU, that excluded the more nationalist concerns of the Greek people, always predominated. Put in schematic terms, the Roman vision was universalist and federalist, striving for a Europe without frontiers and for ultimate political and economic unity. But at the very time that the 'Roman' view received its fullest articulation so far, under the Maastricht Treaty, the reality dawned that Greece has no shared land frontier with other members of the EU and actually has great instability on its doorstep: the war in ex-Yugoslavia, the conflict with Skopje and the increasingly bad relations with Albania.

A feature of Greek political culture that is often misunderstood by outsiders is the diversity and heterogeneity of the sources of the modern Greek identity. There is often a polar opposition – as can be seen in much recent and generally hostile foreign press comment on Greece – between the idealised Philhellenism of the elite and the confused and economically backward modern Greek reality. The elite perception depended to a large extent on the tradition of a classical education involving study of the ancient Greek language and culture that fewer and fewer members of the northern political caste now enjoy. The technocratic modernism of the 1980s has bred its own elite, but one personified in the values of media empires such as that of Rupert Murdoch. This new elite sees the inherited classical political culture as not only irrelevant and antiquated, but sometimes giving rise to left-leaning criticism of existing societies through its embodiment of traditional humanist values. According to this outlook, Plato's Guardians have little place in the world of the computer and Star Wars. The Greeks are seen as thinking of themselves as heirs to Alexander the Great or Pericles, yet being unable to conduct properly many of the basic functions of a modern state.

Apart from the patronising and inaccurate perceptions of at least some aspects of modern Greece which this psychology reflects, it also is blind to many of the most powerful forces in Greek society and culture. These forces determine political attitudes at a popular level and also affect foreign policy formulation in the case of the governing party. The major determinants to which the northern European critics of the Greek policy-makers are very often effectively blind include, most importantly, the influence of the Orthodox Church, the influence of legitimate nationalist feeling in such matters as relations with Turkey and Cyprus and the frustration wrought by outside manipulation of Greek foreign and security policy in the recent past. Furthermore northern

Europeans often seem wholly ignorant of the trauma of internal upheaval such as the Civil War (1944–1949) and the Colonels' dictatorship and the fact that whole segments of the Hellenic population come from families who were refugees from hostile surrounding countries well within living memory. For all these reasons, many Greeks are exceptionally sensitive to any prospect of a repeat of such bitter and humiliating experiences. The sum effect of recent history has been to cloak Greeks in a conservative and defensive frame of mind, resistant to the modernism of the period of capitalist triumph, or the different, but equally modernistic, integrationist agenda in the EU.

The character of this conservatism and resistance to modernist technocratic ideology has not been very well understood outside Greece, nor by some sections of the Greek elite itself. The generally heterogeneous ethnic composition of most of Greece has led to an assumption of complete homogeneity, aided by the dominant role of the Greek Orthodox Church in national religious life. This has run counter to not only the dominant right wing cultural agenda of the American oriented international media – exemplified by the poor image of Greece portrayed by the Murdoch press and CNN – but also the liberal agenda of multiculturalism exemplified by the attitudes of most fellow EU members. Sometimes the two meet, as in the way *The Times* of London has taken up the cause of the Slav-speakers of northern Greece and has used the issue as a symbol of Greek social and cultural intolerance. The fact that the Church is seen domestically as a normal part of the Greek identity, thanks mostly to its positive role in the struggle for national independence going back to the early nineteenth century and before, is irrelevant to these foreign commentators.

There is, therefore, a very large constituency within Greek public opinion who, at one level, may well share the general aspiration for a successful internationalist integration of Greece within EU processes and foreign policy. Nevertheless they may also have an inherited political culture with a very strong nationalist content, derived from civil and national conflicts in the recent past, which, in practice, has a far stronger emotional and practical force than anything emanating from Brussels or Strasbourg. As the ideology of federalism has become more pervasive among the Greek policy-making elite – particularly in the diplomatic service – this contradiction has grown in importance.

In practice, however, the theorists and practitioners of Greek foreign policy have generally had no option but to recognise this conservative and nationalist reality over the post-war years. It is worth remembering that although the generally hostile media image of Greece over the problem of Macedonian recognition (*see* Ch. 8), has centred on a foreign policy issue, this is by no means the first time since the Second World War that major differences between Greece and its most important allies have arisen in this way. The disputes with the West over Cyprus in the 1950s and 1960s have many common characteristics with the divergence of opinion over FYROM, where legitimately held views of an elected Government in Athens, overwhelmingly backed by Greek public opinion, seemed to be treated with the weight of a mere client state rather than an independent country. The cultural assumptions made in much of northern Europe are that Greece should change its policy over Macedonia because it is indebted to the EU for financial support and for attaining a much higher standard of living than would otherwise have been achieved. The political leaders of the previous generation no doubt felt the same way when they argued with Athens Governments over thirty years ago that conformity to Western and NATO policy over Cyprus was required in exchange for the NATO security umbrella or, prior to that, military support for the Right in the Greek Civil War. If Greece was able to resist these pressures for policy change over Cyprus during the height of the Cold War, when major international security issues were at stake, it must be extremely unlikely that the EU leaders in the 1990s will be any more successful in inhibiting traditional Greek nationalist concerns over Macedonia when the Cold War is over and financial constraints are the only means of pressure open to the EU.

A traditional nationalist outlook may, however, carry a high cost in terms of Greek foreign policy and international influence generally. In a sense this is already the case in respect of the international image of Greece and the perception of Greek interests in the minds of opinion formers in the West. A major, and critical, international public relations battle was lost when Yugoslavia began to break up and FYROM first emerged. Greek Government public relations were extraordinarily inept in this period, allowing the small group of ex-communists around President Kiro Gligorov in Skopje to capture the international media agenda and dictate the context in which the Macedonia problem was discussed. Greek government organs almost totally failed between 1992 and 1994 to point out to the world the increasingly undemocratic and repressive nature of the Skopje regime, its undemocratic electoral system and its poor treatment of national minorities, including, in particular, the Albanians.[4] Critically, the Skopje Government was able to gain recognition and sympathy for its preferred choice of name for the new republic. Additionally, it accrued other forms of international support, particularly in key international financial institutions like the World Bank and the International Monetary Fund (IMF) as the Greek case went almost by default in the international media. The legitimate Greek national interest was never clearly or effectively articulated in this period. It is difficult to avoid the conclusion that part of the reason for this was the uncritical assumption by Athens policy-makers that the European integration process embodied in Maastricht would evolve rapidly, leading automatically to an effective common foreign policy and hence avoid the need for Greek leaders to defend their own national interests. Ironically in the diaspora, the situation was slightly different. In the US the Greek lobby was very successful in the publicity war against the FYROM protagonists in marked contrast to Europe, where the 'Europeanist' ideology was paramount.

In contrast to the lack of impact in Europe, at home the reverse process took hold of the political culture, in an essentially populist way. To a significant extent it appeared as if whole sections of the Greek elite did not clearly realise that, in the metaphorical sense, letting the nationalist genie out of the bottle might be more difficult than corking it back up again. The passions released by domestic publicity campaigns were profound and often irrational, based on partial readings of Greek history, some going back to the ancient world and others to the Civil War period with the characterisation of all the Slav-speaking minority in northern Greece as entirely pro-communist. The incapacity of all the elite to understand the growth of new and legitimate Balkan nationalism in the aftermath of the end of communism in Eastern Europe in 1989 was equally remarkable, as was the adherence to a concept of 'Yugoslavia', long after the word had ceased to carry any real meaning.[5] Thus the federalist thinking of the dominant element in Athens in these years was, in many ways, the worst of both worlds for the country: a negative perception of Greek national interests within Europe, and a burgeoning sense of nationalism within Greece, particularly over the Balkan issues.

The war and associated conflicts in the Balkans have, therefore, begun to change Greek political culture in fundamental ways, particularly at a populist level. One of the main causes for the disintegration of the ND Government in 1992–93 was the breakaway movement of Politiki Anoiksi, 'Political Spring', a faction founded by the ex-ND Foreign Minister Antonio Samaras, which campaigned on a strongly nationalist platform. Although the party gained very limited support in the Autumn 1993 general election, and has not appeared to flourish since, the seeds which it planted may well grow. Even if they do not grow in terms of 'Political Spring' becoming a major party, the effect on the political culture has been profound. It has been an axiom of the present PASOK Government that the circumstances for a similar internal split over national issues will not be allowed to exist and, although the traditionalist nationalist element in PASOK is smaller than in ND, it has been assuaged, in policy terms, by the blockade of the Skopje border and the assurance that policy concessions to northern European EU pressures are extremely unlikely. It seems that Andreas Papandreou watched the Mitsotakis Government disintegrate over this issue and had no wish to see a similar fate overtake his own. The victory for Greece in the European court case over this issue in the summer of 1994 makes concessions even more unlikely. Nationalism has entered the political culture, via the Samaras breakaway, in a manner which has fractured the solidarity of the elite discourse on modernisation and identity within Europe, making resistance to populist pressures by the federalists in the Greek diplomatic service and foreign ministry very difficult.

Another fundamental change in the political culture engendered by instability in the Balkans is the extension of the political influence of the Church. Given the increasing importance of religion in almost all Balkan countries, this phenomenon may well have far reaching effects in Greece. In the past, the Church has generally seen PASOK Governments as an object of cultural opposition; a secularist party with only a weak, if any, commitment to the position of the Church in national life and an enemy likely to champion changes in social legislation of which the Church disapproves. But in the current conflict with both Tirana and Skopje, the PASOK Government enjoys very warm relations with the Church. This relationship appeared to be endorsed by the joint secular-clerical organisation of the huge Macedonia demonstration in Thessaloniki in February 1994, one of the largest political demonstrations ever held in Greek history. The blockade of the border and the generally firm stands taken over Balkan issues in the last six months have found favour with the traditionally irredentist-influenced northern bishops and, as a result, PASOK enjoys unusual support in these quarters. Given the difficulties which the previous PASOK Government had over relations with the Church, it is very unlikely that this change in the political culture will be resisted by the current Government. It gives Andreas Papandreou a priceless asset in his ambition to leave his party as the natural government of Greece.

In this context a key indicator in future politics is likely to be the degree to which the government begins to involve itself in the fate of the Greek minorities in the surrounding countries.[6] The unsatisfactory treatment of the Greek minority in Turkey, for instance, has not generally been taken up as an issue by Athens Governments in recent years, at least in terms of international media projection. The 'ethnic cleansing' of Turkish-governed islands like Imbros has not been highlighted, despite the severe human rights violations suffered by resident Greeks. Until recently, the struggle for human rights for the Greek minority in Albania was largely confined to Vorio Epirot organisations and the Church. It therefore remains to be seen how far the present Government will actually go to defend the minority if the current worsening trend of violations continues.[7]

It also remains to be seen how these tensions and contradictions can be contained by the Greek political elite who are responsible for evolution and implementation of foreign policy. Many outside factors are clearly involved. If, for instance, the Maastricht process falters and the Inter-Governmental Conference that is to be held in 1996 fails to reach agreement on a viable federalist agenda, many problems will be solved for Greek policy-makers. The key issue is likely to be how far the growth of nationalism elsewhere in Europe destroys the ambitions of the integrationalists. If it does so, the strong policy stands taken by recent Greek Governments on nationalist issues will not be out of keeping with what is happening elsewhere in Europe, and Greek–EU differences can probably be contained within manageable limits. But notwithstanding this possibility, given the rapid growth of nationalist feeling in most European countries, it is likely that a debate at popular level on the merits of the EU itself will begin in Greece.[8]

In this debate the degree of commitment to the European ideal will be measured not simply in economic terms, but also in terms of cultural identity. An important factor will be the capacity of the Greek Government to overcome the communications and public relations disasters of the past and project internationally, and in a competent way, the legitimate national interests of the Greek people. It remains to be seen how far the evolution of a new nationalist cultural identity and more active involvements in the Balkan conflicts will prevent effective Greek participation in an integrationalist Europe.

Notes

1 *Athens News,* 30 September 1993.
2 *See,* for example, *The Times* London, Response to the Helsinki Watch report on the Slav–Macedonian issue, 20 August 1994.
3 J. Pettifer, *The Greeks – Land and People since the War,* (London, Viking/Penguin, 1993/94), p. 231 ff.
4 Minority Rights Group Report, *The Southern Balkans,* (London, 1994).
5 The term is still used widely by the Greek media, even in 1994, and on road signs and in public announcements.
6 As far as I am aware, the only recent reportage of this issue has taken place outside Greece. *See,* for instance, *East European Newsletter,* (London, throughout 1993–94).
7 The recent deterioration of Athens–Tirana relations bears this out (November 1994).
8 In terms of the settlement with the Skopje government over the flag and the so-called 'small package' issues in 1995, it is noticeable how irrelevant the EU was to the whole process. The United States' backing of the Greek position led to a major setback for the ambitions of the Gligorov government. In addition, the deal was a particularly serious defeat of German diplomacy.

Is Greece an awkward partner?

Introduction

There has been strong criticism of Greek policies in other European countries, criticism which has been expressed both in official statements and comments made in the mass media. In recent years, Greece has often been presented as the black sheep of the EU and several commentators have gone so far as to question the ability of the country to continue as a full and active member of the Union. Criticism has tended to concentrate on two main issues, namely the state of the economy and Greece's Balkan policy. This commentary will deal with the two issues in turn in an attempt to understand and broadly explain the nature of the problem and the policies pursued; to explain but not necessarily to justify.

Economic Failure

Despite all the new pillars erected by the architects of the Maastricht treaty, the question of economics still remains the key element of European integration, and hence the main factor to determine the success or failure of a member-country's participation in the Union. On the basis of virtually any macroeconomic indicator, Greece seems to diverge significantly from the rest of the EU in that its performance is worse than the others in controlling inflation, the government deficit, and so on (Spraos 1993; Alogoskoufis 1993; Papademos 1993). This observation applies to all four convergence criteria referred to in the new Treaty as a pre-condition to progress to the third and final phase of economic and monetary union.

Alas, the data provide no consolation for those who would look for a trade-off between real growth and macroeconomic stability. Unlike the experience of the other so-called cohesion countries, the growth performance of the Greek economy has not been good either. As for unemployment, the figures for Greece have admittedly been better than for the Union average; but this is largely due to the traditional ploy of Greek governments of simply adding to the number of those (under)employed in the wider public sector. This can hardly be a sustainable form of policy in times of growing public deficits.

The Greek economy has not performed well since accession to the EU in 1981. There are a number of factors which account for this negative performance. The first is related to the high degree of external protection given to the Greek economy prior to accession, which was almost entirely of a non-tariff form and which had clearly survived the old association agreement signed with the EEC back in 1961. The exposure to an intensely competitive environment forced upon Greece through membership of the EU required a major effort of adjustment which promised to be both long and painful. It has been precisely this kind of adjustment which has been strongly resisted by the Greek political class and society at large.

The period of EU membership has been characterised by an intensification of the domestic political struggle in Greece, which has also manifested itself increasingly in populist slogans and policies. In the 1980s, a highly inefficient welfare system and increasingly redistributive policies were largely financed through borrowing, thus leading to a very rapid growth of public debt. Intermittent efforts at macroeconomic stabilisation were abandoned mid-way for electoral purposes.

The combination of high inflation rates and large government deficits, coupled with continuing uncertainty with respect to the basic rules of the economic game and the line separating the private from the public sector, largely account for the negative economic climate, the low level of investment and the progressive worsening of the international competitiveness of the Greek economy during this period. On the other hand, the most effective form of economic redistribution achieved by allegedly socially conscious governments has been at the expense of future generations which, of course, do not have as yet the right to vote.

Greece's negative economic performance and most particularly the manifest inability of successive governments to provide macroeconomic stability are closely related to the persistence of patron–client relations as the main distinguishing feature of the political system. In this and many other respects, the process of modernisation has proved extremely slow. The comparison with Spain and Portugal, where democracy was restored at about the same time as in Greece, is not very encouraging (Gunther *et al.* 1995).

On the other hand, two recent developments are likely to have a decisive, long-term effect on the role which the Greek State can play in the economy. External liberalisation, essentially the product of EU membership, has created an open economy which in turn severely constrains the ability of governments to influence the allocation of domestic resources and the distribution of wealth on the basis of political favouritism and non-transparency. The rapid indebtedness of the public sector is the other reason why governments are now unable to deliver the goods to which much of their electorate has long been accustomed. Both developments are in the process of undermining the system of patron–client relations, and we may have witnessed so far only the beginning of this process.

The relatively low credibility which Greece seems to enjoy in the EU has much to do with economics. A major net recipient of EU funds, Greece has also had recourse twice in recent years to the loan facilities of the EU and has failed to meet the conditions imposed in terms of macroeconomic stabilisation. A serious improvement on the economic front seems to be therefore a precondition for Greece's recovery of its lost credibility in Europe.

Balkan insecurity

Greece has so far failed to pursue a coherent Balkan policy. At the same time, it has failed to act as a stabilising force in the region. Instead, it has allowed itself to become part of Balkan politics, which it should have tried to avoid at all costs. This failure has undoubtedly much to do with the sweeping nature of the changes that have occurred in the region since 1989. It is also linked to Greece's own inadequacies and most particularly to the interplay between foreign policy and domestic politics. In mitigation, however, this is not the entire explanation. Greece's failure to play a stabilising role in the Balkans is also due to an important external factor. The policies pursued by its main European partners have not only undermined a potentially stabilising role for Greece; they have, in fact, directly contributed to Greece's sense of insecurity.

Greece is a country with a strong national identity, and the emphasis is on distinctness from other nations. History, language and religion place Greece in a category all of its own inside the Union, without this implying that there is an obvious affinity with its Balkan neighbours. Unlike the Scandinavians, the Slavs or even the descendants of the Latins, the Greeks do not belong to any wider family of nations. A long history and the role of the diaspora point perhaps to some resemblance of Greece with Israel. True, such factors as, for example, the alleged historical continuity of the nation may be sometimes heavily overplayed in the domestic debate, yet a complete dismissal of those factors by rational models of politics can be almost equally dangerous and misleading.

Greece is a relatively small country in a traditionally turbulent neighbourhood. The region has a long history of conflict which has continued to this day. More recently, and particularly since the turn of the century, new nation-states emerged from the decline and collapse of the Ottoman empire. National frontiers are thus relatively recent and not universally accepted; and ethnic minorities, the remnant of the old Balkan mosaic, have been traditionally linked to irredentist policies. Since the 1920s, when its own irredentist ambitions ended in disaster, Greece has been fundamentally a status quo country with a strong perception of external threat. The image which most Greeks have of their country is that of a fort being surrounded by real and potential enemies. This perception of threat, combined with the strong Western orientation of its elites, explains why Greece has repeatedly tried to escape from the harsh reality imposed on it by geography.

The third important characteristic is that Greece is a country of individuals, with little respect for the State and its institutions. There are several historical explanations for this attitude. The existence of a strong national identity is closely related to history and culture and not to the organised public expression of the nation. Compromise is almost a dirty word in the Greek vocabulary and exaggeration is an in-built element of domestic political discourse. It is no surprise that the mixture of all those elements can be sometimes explosive.

On the other hand, a strong national identity, combined with little respect for the State and a feeling of insecurity related to perceived external threats, can produce a strange combination of attitudes and policies which are at times plainly contradictory. Greece generally feels comfortable and proud to be a member of the EU. Unlike several of its partners, it appears to have no major difficulties with transfers of sovereignty to Brussels. This, therefore, explains why Greece has, after some initial doubts and hesitations, landed itself in the federalist camp, giving its support to measures which would strengthen the powers of both the Commission and the European Parliament.

The irony is that Greece is mostly interested in something that the EU is not apparently ready to provide as yet, namely a system of collective security. Such a system of collective security was offered to Greece by NATO; but in practice it only applied in the case of aggression from the Warsaw Pact countries on its northern frontier, and not against Turkey which, although a formal ally, is generally considered by Greeks as the source of the main external threat. An analogous situation exists in the context of the EU and this has occasionally caused tension between Greece and its European partners; even more so when Greece has felt abandoned by them on important issues of foreign policy.

With the end of the Cold War and the collapse of communist regimes in its northern Balkan neighbours, Greece was presented with a set of major opportunities and risks. Given its relative economic weight, its democratic experience and its membership of the EU and NATO, Greece had the possibility of playing a leading role in the emerging new system of regional interdependence; at least as long as the Pandora's box containing the old, undying worms of irredentism and ethnic conflict remained closed.

In the event, Greece misplayed its hand. It tried to prevent, to the exclusion of more rational policies, the break up of Yugoslavia. Admittedly it was fearful of the consequences of unleashing the ethnic rivalries contained by the old Titoist regime. In particular, it was seriously concerned about the problems which were expected to arise from the independence of what has been temporarily called the Former Yugoslav Republic of Macedonia.

The forces ready to tear Yugoslavia apart could not be contained for long. As that country's disintegration has brought with it a long, bloody war, whilst also reviving the old ghosts of modern Balkan history, so the sense of insecurity felt by Greeks has increased. The threat of war spilling over the old Yugoslav border, the major economic implications of being cut off from its land connections with Western Europe, the irredentism in Skopje (perhaps unavoidable in the process of nation-building out of a mosaic of ethnic groups, yet no less provocative), and the potential for the persecution of the Greek minority in Albania, were all new and frightening images that now had to be added to the old constant of Greek foreign policy, namely the perception of a Turkish threat.

Faced with a host of real and sometimes imagined problems, Greece has proved unable to establish an order of priorities for its foreign policy. Its reaction has been highly emotional, often exaggerated and perhaps even irrational.

The explanation lies mainly in the interaction between foreign policy and Greek domestic politics (Clogg 1993; Wallden 1994). A sensationalist press and a minority of super-patriots have played on the general feeling of insecurity that has been heightened by increasing instability in the region. The political class became a prisoner of its own rhetoric, thus contributing to the vicious circle. At this hour of turmoil in the Balkans there has been a painful shortage of states-men who could rise above historical rivalries.

There was a similar shortage of good leadership in most other European countries, considering that the responsibility of Greece's European partners for the growing instability in the Balkan region cannot be overstated. The prema-ture recognition of the independence of Slovenia and Croatia, without any seri-ous consideration being given to the need for an overall, lasting settlement which would also deal effectively with the problem of ethnic minorities con-tributed greatly to the tragic events in former Yugoslavia (although admittedly the problem did not apply to Slovenia). Moreover, this error of judgement was exacerbated following the even more irresponsible act of recognition of the independence of Bosnia, which defied both history and the current balance of power in the country.

At the same time, the indifference, coupled with sheer contempt, with which Greek concerns and fears, not always imaginary, were often treated by Greece's partners were not the best examples of the kind of solidarity on which a common foreign and security policy of the EU should be based. Even though Athens must carry its fair share of responsibility for recent developments, the experience of being chastised by paternalistic Europeans for not behaving like civilised Scandinavians in the Balkans confirmed to Greeks the profound igno-rance of their partners of the history and the realities of the region.

Descriptions of the Greek political scene in terms of a cheap soap opera or a farce have often appeared in European newspapers. It would, indeed, be diffi-cult to pretend that the functioning of the Greek political system does not con-stitute a cause for concern. However, given the inconsistent, if not disastrous, nature of the policies pursued by Greece's partners in respect of the Yugoslav conflict and the wide range of problems facing European countries and institu-tions, the visitor from Mars might wonder whether the authors of such articles were under the impression that, in contrast to the admittedly poor Greek show, they were watching Shakespeare at home. A certain degree of humility, self-crit-icism and the ability to listen to one's partners remain essential elements of the European construction. We still have much to learn.

References

Alogoskoufis, George (1993), 'Budgetary adjustment and competitiveness', in L. Tsoukalis (ed), Greece in the European Community. The Challenge of Adjustment (in Greek), Athens, Papazissis.

Clogg, Richard (1993), 'Greece and the Balkans in the 1990s', in H. Psomiades and S. Thomadakis (eds.), *Greece, the New Europe, and the Changing International Order*, New York, Pella.

Gunther, R., Diamandouros, N. and Puhle, H.-J. (eds.) (1995), *The Politics of Democratic Consolidation. Southern Europe in Comparative Perspective*, Baltimore, Johns Hopkins University Press.

Papademos, Lucas (1993), 'European Monetary Union and Greek Economic Policy', in H. Psomiades and S. Thomadakis (eds.), *Greece, the New Europe, and the Changing International Order*, New York, Pella.

Spraos, John (1993), 'Macroeconomic Policy in an Open Economy', in L. Tsoukalis (ed), *Greece in the European Community: The Challenge of Adjustment* (in Greek), Athens, Papazissis.

Tsoukalis, Loukas (1993), *The New European Economy, Second Revised Edition*, Oxford, Oxford University Press.

Wallace, Helen (1994), *European Governance in Turbulent Times*, in S. Bulmer and A. Scott (eds.), *Economic and Political Integration in Europe*, Oxford-Cambridge Massachusetts, Blackwell.

Wallden, Sotiris (1994), *The Macedonian Problem and the Balkans 1991–1994: The Impasses of Greek Policy* (in Greek), Athens, Themelio.

PART II

Greece and the European Union

P.C. IOAKIMIDIS

3

Contradictions between policy and performance

The Europeanisation process

EU membership is now widely recognised as an important factor in shaping a nation's political scene. It tends to blur the distinction between domestic politics and external foreign policy and to create new patterns of political behaviour. It encourages new institutional and administrative structures and interactions by redistributing power and competencies and reorienting political objectives. Membership has redefined territorial political relations, produced new governmental networks, given rise to new demands and pressures and has provoked new ideological tensions and conflicts.[1] All these tendencies are encapsulated in the term 'Europeanisation'. According to the writer, R. Ladrech: 'Europeanisation is an incremental process reorienting the direction and shape of politics to the degree that EU political and economic dynamics become part of the organisational logic of national politics and policy-making.'[2]

Europeanisation does not merely imply a rhetorical ideological commitment to the objectives of the integration process. It involves the internalisation of the inner logic, norms and dynamics of the EU into the domestic policy formulation process. It entails the willingness and capacity of governments to define and execute national policies by placing them in the wider context of EU objectives. In other words, the phenomenon of the Europeanisation of the domestic political environment does not occur simply because the political elites or, for that matter, the society at large have come to exhibit attachment to 'the lofty ideals of European integration.' Europeanisation dictates that the imperatives, logic and norms of the EU become intrinsically absorbed into domestic policy, to the extent that the distinction between European and domestic policy requirements progressively ceases to exist.[3]

The ideological acceptance of the objectives of European integration undoubtedly constitutes a vital precondition for the Europeanisation process,

as defined above, to take hold. It would, of course, be wrong to assume that
rhetorical advocacy of European integration automatically denotes the internalisation of all EU logic, discipline and behaviour. The Greek case suggests that
a discrepancy might well exist between the rhetorical adherence to the integration logic and the actual behaviour in terms of defining objectives and carrying
out policies.

The nature of the Europeanisation process

In the case of Greece, it will be argued that the Europeanisation phenomenon
has taken the form of what could be termed asynchronic and autarkic Europeanisation. Asynchronic Europeanisation implies that certain important components of the State's political system have become rapidly and extensively
Europeanised, while other vital elements of government and administration
have failed to move as quickly. The consequence of this asymmetric and unbal-
anced Europeanisation is the generation of systemic tensions and conflicts
between the Europeanised parts on the one hand and the less developed in this
respect on the other.

While asynchronic describes the pace and intensity of Europeanisation, the
nature and content of the phenomenon can be said to be autarkic. This means
that the political system and elites seek to internalise European inputs and logic
as a means of fostering their continued control in terms of structural stability
and practices, ideological attitudes, policy objectives, resources and orientations, rather than as a means of changing or adapting to the new environmental conditions and new dynamics generated by EU membership.

The Greek domestic political environment is undergoing a process of Europeanisation characterised by these two forms. The asynchronic nature of the
process tends to produce a dualistic system of structural, organisational and
behavioural patterns which works to split Greek society, on the one hand, into
the modern, European section quite ready to internalise the European inputs
and logic of action and, on the other, into the hellenocentric, traditional section
which either resists, rejects or, at best, hesitantly accepts the need for change.[4]

The autarkic nature of the Europeanisation process primarily concerns the
political actors and, in particular, the leading political elites. It appears that
these elites are inclined to interpret Europeanisation in the rather narrow perspective of accepting the need to broaden the legitimacy of the political system,
but then agreeing to scarcely any change in the fundamental structural archi-
tecture of the system or in its basic political objectives. Thus European logic
enters the system and stimulates pressures, even quite severe pressures, and
demand for change, yet these pressures are fiercely resisted by the political elites
and actors themselves.

One can therefore argue at this general level that Greece will have to overcome the asynchronic and autarkic nature of Europeanisation to date in order

to be able to adapt smoothly to the requirements of integration over the course of the remainder of the decade. As long as Europeanisation is prevented from spreading synchronically and adaptively, the political and societal system will continue to be under stress and the contradiction of having a country advocating deeper integration and yet performing in a seemingly un-European manner will persist.

The stages in the Europeanisation process

The start of the Europeanisation process can be traced back to 1975, the year when Greece submitted its application to become a full institutional member of the EU. Greece had been an associate member of the EU since 1961 and a country striving to become 'European', i.e. modern and Western, ever since the foundation of the modern Greek State in 1833.[5] The Europeanisation as defined above commenced with the launching of the application for full membership in 1975 in the wake of the collapse of the military dictatorship and the re-establishment of the democratic institutions.[6]

The Europeanisation process can be divided into two broad chronological phases; the first which spans the period between 1975 and 1985; that is the period between the launching of the bid for full membership and the termination of the transitional period for full accession. This phase came to a close in 1985, not only in the formal sense with the expiry of the transitional arrangements laid down in the Act of the Accession, but in a more substantive sense as well. The year 1985 saw clearly the beginning of the end of the agonizing process in which the political implications of joining the EU, and Greece's role in its development, gained ideological acceptance. The request for a special loan to support the ailing Greek economy put by the Greek Government to the EU in October 1985 can be taken as ushering in the second phase of the Europeanisation process and as a turning point in resolving the ideological dilemma of the integration process. It is evident that the first phase of Europeanisation embraces the period prior to formal accession (1975–1980) and the first five years following the formal accession (1981–1985). These two distinct chronological periods are however treated as a single, unified phase because they were shaped by identical concerns, dynamics and conflicts, they posed almost the same type of problems and produced broadly identical consequences.[7]

The first phase (1975–1985)

During the first phase, the Europeanisation process affected the domestic political environment in a number of ways, the most important and identifiable of which can be viewed at three levels.

a   It contributed to the consolidation of the newly-founded democratic institutions.

b   It generated pressures which led to administrative adjustments so that the country could cope with the requirements of Community membership.

c   It underpinned the external political orientation of the country.

Before however discussing these, it is important to begin by recording that one of the principal features of the first phase was that a sizeable section of the Greek body politic, including PASOK, which from 1977 emerged as the main opposition party and from October 1981 as the governing party, opposed both Greece's institutional participation in the EU and the process of European integration being pursued by the European States.[8] Inevitably this opposition implied resistance to the Europeanisation process, at least to the most important and penetrating aspects of it.

The divisive nature of Greece's design to join the EU and of its perceived position in it, at least until 1985, did not offer the most propitious conditions for the Europeanisation process to penetrate the political and institutional systems. Thus the main political debate, especially during the period 1975–1981, focused principally on the political merits and ideological dimension of accession rather than on the practical decisions needed to absorb the shock of accession and transform the institutional and administrative system into flexible and effective instruments capable of responding to EU policy requirements. It is quite indicative in this respect that, during this period, no worthwhile study dealing with the practical implications of accession for the Greek economy, society or political system was undertaken, while several books focusing on the general, ideological aspects of capitalist integration were published.[9] Furthermore the overriding political emphasis placed by the conservative forces to EU membership was its ability to stabilise the democratic political framework and this overshadowed the need to make practical, economic and technocratic adjustments in order to meet EU policy imperatives.

The second sub-period of the first phase of the Europeanisation process (1981–1985) was marked by the largely unsuccessful efforts of PASOK Governments to chart an independent strategy for the socio-economic modernisation of the country. This strategy – termed 'the third road to democratic socialism' in the sense that it differed from the first road (the Soviet) and the second (the social democratic model of Western Europe) – involved, among other initiatives, repudiation of the EU model of formulating and executing policy.[10] In blunt terms, the third road was a deliberate attempt to resist the Europeanisation of Greece's policy content, policy-making and policy implementing and the adjustment process associated with it.

As noted, this resistance took initially the form of outright opposition to Greece's membership of the EU. Upon assuming power, PASOK declared that it intended to explore the possibility of conducting a referendum on Greece's role in the EU with the view of withdrawing the country from the Union.[11] However since the conducting of referenda constituted a constitutional prerogative of the President of the Republic, the Government quickly abandoned this option in favour of a policy aiming at shaping what was referred to as a 'special regime' or 'special relationship' for Greece within the EU.

This 'special regime/relationship' essentially meant that permission would be sought for Greece not to abide by the panoply of EU legislation affecting the functional role and institutional structure of the State. To that end, the Government submitted in March 1982 a memorandum to the EU requesting derogations in the provisions relating to dismantling state monopolies (e.g., the petroleum monopoly), relaxing state controls over sections of the economy and instituting measures entailing substantial restructuring of the state/society relationship (like, for instance, the introduction of VAT).[12] Not surprisingly the EU declined to satisfy these demands, maintaining that Greece's developmental problems could be tackled, not through the suspension, but through the effective application of the community policies.[13] Nonetheless the EU decided to grant Greece additional transitional periods for implementing certain provisions relating to State deregulation and it announced a financial package for supporting the economy, which resulted in the adoption of the Integrated Mediterranean Programmes (IMPs) in 1985[14]

Thus in the period 1983–85 Greece was consciously or unconsciously resisting the adjustment to Europeanisation process in three particular domains:

a   Resistance to the pressures emanating from the EU for redefining the economic role and functions of the State and the latter's relationship with the society. This was exemplified in the refusal to align economic policy with the economic guidelines and trends prevailing in the EU, however vague these might have been. More importantly perhaps, Athens refused to transfer State enterprises of a monopolistic nature to the private sector of the economy and to shed control over economic activities (public procurement, etc). If anything, the opposite seemed to have been the case, causing serious friction with the European Commission. In 1983, for instance, the Government nationalised the leading cement company, Hercules, in contravention of important EU regulations concerning competition policy.[15] More characteristically, in the same year, the Government set up the OAE (Organisation for the Reconstruction of Enterprises) to assist so-called ailing industries of the private sector.[16] This, in effect, resulted in bringing a host of so-called 'problematic' private companies into the public domain, thereby enlarging the scope of the public sector in gross defiance of the EU rules, policy, and dynamics.[17] Predictably enough, this gave rise to a plethora of legal cases involving infringement of EU legislation, some of which were eventually heard by the European Court.[18]

b   Resistance to the Europeanisation of foreign policy objectives and strategies. This is, perhaps, the area of public policy over which Greece has fought most hard to preserve autonomy of action, in disregard to the consensus requirements of European Political Co-operation (EPC).[19] There are numerous examples of such resistance: refusal to go along with the EPC over issues relating East-West conflict, the Middle East, and others. At the same time, Greece appeared to pursue foreign policy initiatives falling evidently outside the framework of EU policy orientation.[20]

c   Refusal to endorse plans for deepening European integration at the institutional level or extending the scope of integration to areas of security and defence. Examples in this case include: opposition to the Genscher–Colombo plan, to the Spinelli plan for European Union and opposition to convening the Inter-Governmental Conference in 1985 to formulate the Single European Act.[21]

Nevertheless, in spite of these deliberate attempts to thwart or restrict the impact of the Europeanisation process, the latter began to percolate down through the politico-economic system. It affected this system in at least three identifiable ways:

a   By consolidating democratic institutions. The decision to join the EU was taken by Greece, first and foremost, on the ground that full institutional membership would contribute to consolidating the newly-founded democratic institutions. It was specifically expected that the EU would provide a safety net to protect the country against attempts at undermining the democratisation process. Numerous studies have demonstrated that EU membership has been a powerful, contributing factor to the smooth transition to democratic politics in Greece.[22] Even before officially entering the EU in 1981, the anticipated adherence provided a strong stimulus to democratic stabilisation. The orderly transfer of governments in 1981 and 1989 confirmed the level of political consolidation that had been achieved.

b   By forcing administrative adjustment. Given the general climate prevailing during the first phase of the Europeanisation process, it is hardly surprising that the only sector of the domestic political structure that was directly penetrated by the ethos of the EU was public administration. Irrespective of the ambivalent attitude towards the EU, Greece's governmental and administrative machinery had to cope with every day negotiating pressures and it had to respond by developing the required structures for European policy-making, policy co-ordinating, and communicating with the European institutions. This machinery found it immensely difficult both to comprehend and deal with a political system like that of the EU, which was based upon a federal model of Germany. Greece, as a unitary, over-centralised State, was not ideally placed to grasp the complexities of this quasi-federal blueprint for policy-making and co-operative institutional bargaining in decision-making. The learning process took almost five years (1981–1985). The Europeanisation of the administration started immediately after Greece's formal accession with the setting up of departments to handle EU negotiations. The Ministry of Foreign Affairs was entrusted with the task of co-ordinating European policy and presenting it to Brussels. Although Greece has not as yet succeeded in moulding an institution-alised, stable system for formulating and co-ordinating European policy, for reasons that cannot be explained here, the administration seems to have progressively acquired the basic skills for handling EU negotiations and has succeeded in internalising EU logic.[23]

c   By consolidating external political orientation. The intention to join the EU during the years before 1981 and actual membership provided a clear signal as to where post-dictatorship Greece intended to travel in terms of foreign allegiances. In time a fundamental political consensus was eventu-ally built regarding Greece's place and role in the international system. In spite of recent concerns over Athens's international leanings, the Euro-peanisation of Greece's external orientation could be viewed as a major development given the country's uncertain geographic position and its oscillation between East and West.[24]

The second phase (1985–present)

The second phase in Greece's Europeanisation process started in 1985. This year has been called a landmark in Greece's evolving position in the EU in that it wit-nessed the end of the transitional stage in not only a formal sense in terms of the Act of Accession, but also in a most substantial political one. In that year, the PASOK Government came to the conclusion that it had to abandon its policy of ambivalence towards the EU, a policy which served to keep the country in a state of suspended animation, with 'one foot in, one foot out', in favour of a policy of active pro-Europeanism. As already noted, the act which marked the virtual break with the previous policy was the decision to seek a special loan from the EU, thereby submitting the economy to the discipline, control, and imperatives of the integration process. Although the EU granted the loan, it imposed stiff conditions. These had the effect of placing the Greek economy, for the first time since accession, in the institutional framework and logic of the EU.[25] This, in effect, meant that the Europeanisation process within Greece's governmental and administrative organs was unblocked and hence it could begin to take its full course.

A number of factors account for PASOK's about-turn on Europe. The flow of considerable financial transfers which had made Greece overly dependent on the EU budget for improving its welfare was certainly a powerful consideration. This could not be ignored, especially as some sectors of the social strata, notably the farmers, who were particularly benefitting from the EU transfers, had come to support enthusiastically the idea of membership.[26] Another factor contribut-ing to the change of orientation was the growing appreciation that, by being an institutional member of the EU, Greece enjoyed significant bargaining power in the regional environment, especially in relation to Turkey.

The about-turn coincided with some immediate political and economic realities. By 1985 the negotiations between Greece and the EU on the Greek memorandum submitted in 1982 had been completed with the adoption of the

IMPs. These, along with the expiry of the formal transitional arrangements, implied that the period of grace, tacitly granted to Greece in respect of not having to complying fully with EU legislation and policies, was also to be terminated. Greece had accordingly to absorb the impact of being a fully-fledged member of the EU system. The Europeanization process could therefore proceed.

The second phase of the Europeanisation process proved important not only for domestic reasons, but also because the EU itself proceeded to institute policies and instruments of decision-making bound to percolate more deeply into the politico-economic systems of its member-states. The adoption of the Single European Act (SEA) with all its institutional innovations, the programme for the establishment of the single internal market and the new Structural policy (first the 'Delors package') introduced in 1988 were all measures directly impacting on national political systems, blurring even further the distinction between the meanings of 'national' and 'European'.[27] From 1985, therefore, the Europeanisation logic began to permeate the whole socio-economic system, whereas until then it was chiefly confined to the bureaucratic structures and limited number of elite groups.

The new problems created by Europeanisation

The Europeanisation of Greek politics essentially revolved around a single, overriding issue: the redefinition of the role, size, scope, functions and morphology of the state. In no other EU member-country has the problem of Europeanizing the role of the state been as difficult and complex to address. The reason for this is quite simple. The Greek State, shaped by special historical, cultural and political factors, the most pervasive of which is the patron–client interaction, has evolved into an over-sized, over-centralised entity. It is therefore highly unresponsive to the environmental pressures and the challenges of adjustment because it is tightly controlled by its political parties and elites.[28] The issue of redefinition has raised four broad problems for Greece to solve:

Redefinition of State/society boundaries
The Europeanisation process has demanded first and foremost from accession, but most forcefully from 1985 onwards, for the redrawing of the boundaries between state and society. This principally involved the ceding of some important state functions to the society and the assumption of some other new functions by the state. It entailed, in more concrete terms, the shedding of the patronising functions, controls, and regulations performed by the Greek State as a direct result of its patron–client system and corporatist structures.[29]

If one looks at the cases concerning misapplication or outright violation of EU law and policies by Greece, one soon realises that most of them centre on the reluctance or overt refusal of the Greek State to relinquish control of public enterprises and other forms of regulated activity and to institute transparency in its dealings with public entities. Nevertheless persistent EU pressure has forced the total or partial abandonment of a wide range of state economic activities. Besides the State monopolies of a commercial nature that had to be liquidated following the Act of Accession's entry into law, other economic entities that were liberalised to a smaller or larger degree include banks, the petroleum monopoly, cement, and shipyards. Pressure has built for reducing state controls on telecommunications, electricity, airlines and other state-owned or state-controlled companies.[30]

Although in line with the worldwide trend for privatization and State deregulation, the Greek case owes more to the Europeanisation process, i.e. to the need to conform to the EU policy requirements, rather than to political or ideological preferences. Only in the years 1992–93, under the ND Government, did a privatisation (*apokratikopiisi*) policy appear to be pursued as a clear political preference. Even this, however, was justified by reference to EU imperatives.[31]

In addition to withdrawing from certain economic activities, the Greek State has come under intense pressure to modify or scrap altogether the tight regulatory regime comprising regulations ranging from the setting of interest rates, the operation of banks, the movement of capital, public procurement, the granting of state subsidies, the establishing of foreign language schools, recruitment into the wider public sector, and so on. Again, the resistance of the Greek State to changing this regulatory regime constituted a very severe source of friction with the European Commission.[32]

It is interesting to note in this context that the two economic stabilisation programmes, agreed between Greece and the EU in 1985 and 1991 respectively and backed up by special community loans, involved a drastic reduction of the role of the state. The first programme, adopted in December 1985, stipulated the abolition of a wide array of state monopolies (concerning the production of matches, salt, petroleum, etc.) as well as the elimination of various export subsidies and the progressive lifting of a host of other state controls upon the economy.[33] The second programme adopted in March 1991,[34] apart from the drastic curtailment of public expenditure, envisaged the reduction of public sector employment (by 10 per cent between 1991 and 1993), the enhancing of the transparency of the public sector's financial accounts, the deregulation of consumer prices of oil products and the freeing up of the labour and service markets, all in order to ensure that Greece participated fully in the internal market.

Seen from the state/society relationship, it is clear that these programmes were not merely designed for economic stabilisation. More than that, they proved to be strategies for the redefinition of the functional morphology of the Greek State, including the latter's liberation from clientelistic encirclement. This is also the reason why the programmes failed to yield the desired results and were ultimately abandoned.

The Problem of policy-planning

The introduction of medium-term policy planning and programming as a systematic instrument of policy-making was also a consequence of the Europeanisation process. True, policy planning had been established in Greece in the early 1960s, but had never been treated seriously or consistently as a policy instrument. In 1983, the Government drew up a five-year development programme which, characteristically, made no specific reference at all to the EU and was never actually implemented.[35]

What prompted the Greek State to embrace policy planning as an operational instrument of government was the establishment of the IMPs in 1985 and the requirement they imposed for presenting integrated programmes to Brussels.[36] Considerably reinforced by the adoption of the new EU structural policy (the 'Delors Packages' of 1988), this requirement contributed radically to changing the process, content, and style of policy-making in Greece. It would not be an overstatement to say that, for the first time, the Greek bureaucracy was compelled to set up bodies and procedures for medium-term planning of operationally enforceable measures. The seven Greek IMPs, the first five-year Community Support Framework (CSF), drawn between 1989–1990, and the second seven-year CSF, drawn between 1993–1994, constitute the first concrete examples in policy planning in modern Greek history. To these one could add perhaps the convergence policy programme submitted to the EU in accordance with the Maastricht Treaty provisions.

Coupled with the need to formulate, on a virtual daily basis, negotiating positions to be presented to EU organs, the compulsory introduction of policy planning as a functional prerequisite for taking advantage of the Union's financial resources has imposed upon Greece requirements which it could hardly fulfil efficiently given its clientelistic underpinnings.

The participation problem

The growing Europeanisation has shaped conditions and raised demands for wider participation in policy-making and policy planning. These have set in motion the process for the progressive de-bureaucratisation of policy-making. It is notable that, on the Greek side, the seven IMPs of 1985 were formulated almost exclusively by the administrative and technocratic personnel of the Ministry of National Economy (MNE), yet the first CSF was drafted in 1989–90 by a much wider group of policy-makers comprising participants from the regions and the private sector of the economy including the trade unions and industrialist organisations. The drafting of the second CSF marked an even further step towards widening participation in policy-making. As was revealed, as many as forty-six private agencies contributed to the framing of an original regional development plan for the second CSF.[37] Even more wider participation was achieved in the policy implementation phase, both from local and regional government bodies and the private economy.

A further aspect of increased participation is that non-state agencies have established various networks of co-operation with corresponding bodies in other member-states as well as channels of influence of the Union policy through direct contacts with the Union's bureaucracy in Brussels.

The transformation of the policy-making process through the introduction of planning and programming, as well as through the widening of the net of participating players, has shaped an environment of interactive policy exchanges between the state and the society to an extent unprecedented in the Greek political process. This, in turn, has given rise to demands for institution-alising the forms of participation, thereby recognising them as a stable, perma-nent feature of the public policy-making process. Thus a persistent demand of the Confederation of Greek Industries (SEB) has been the creation of a Social and Economic Council as an institutional forum linking the state with eco-nomic and social actors in shaping policy.[38]

The decentralisation/redistribution problem

As in virtually all other member-states, the Europeanisation of policy-making in Greece has generated the environmental conditions for a significant territo-rial redistribution of political power and financial and economic resources. Greece, as probably the most over-centralized state in the Union, was con-fronted from 1985 with the task of implementing the increasingly complex EU structural policy based on principles such as programming and partnership, which entailed substantial regional and local involvement in policy-making and policy implementing.[39]

Although the PASOK Government was ideologically predisposed in favour of local decentralisation, the European inputs into policy-making and especially policy implementing processes afforded the impetus for drawing local and regional players into the process. Even though the central authorities (MNE) retained a hegemonic role in policy-making, the policy implementing process, based on the monitoring committees organised at local level in accordance with the principle of partnership, allowed the local/regional authorities to partici-pate actively. More than that, however, it enabled the latter to shift their inter-ests and activities from very petty concerns to wider developmental objectives and, in so doing, to revitalise their role and associate it with a new agenda of action.[40] Furthermore, the monitoring committees evolved into a framework which allowed the local/regional authorities to forge networks of communica-tion, contacts and co-operation with European institutions (such as the Com-mission) and corresponding local/regional bodies in other member-states. This type of networking can be seen as a building block to the development of what has been described as 'multi-level government' in the EU.[41]

In short, the Europeanisation process has thrown up conditions for enhancing the role of the regions, thereby reinforcing the trends towards decen-tralisation unleashed in the early 1980s. The regions have found in the EU's structural policy the resources and communication links to pursue develop-mental strategies of their own. All this has inevitably generated demands for further territorial redistribution of political power; a process clearly working against the Athenocentric model of government. Responding to these demands, PASOK decided to institute a second tier of local administration (elected prefects), thereby complementing the significant institutional innovations in the structure and organisation of local government enacted in the 1980s.

The limits of the Europeanisation process

Although a central consequence of the Europeanisation process involved the redefinition of the role of the State, other components of the political system have also been affected. Parliament, for instance, despite its overall weak position in the political structure, made a belated attempt in 1990 to get to grips with the integration logic by setting up a specialised committee to deal with EU issues. It must however be pointed out that, generally speaking, Parliament has not displayed any great interest in defending those functions and powers which are threatened by the EU. Indeed, it has hardly shown any enthusiasm in becoming involved either in EU policy-making or in scrutinising European legislation.[42]

The impact of the Europeanisation process on the political parties is demonstrated by the split it has caused between the so-called 'Europeanists' and 'traditionalists'. This cross-party schism has grown more apparent in PASOK and less in ND and the other parties (Synaspismos, KKE).[43] The Europeanist faction is mainly composed of political figures who, in one way or another, have become directly exposed to European influences (such as ministers involved in European affairs and members of the European Parliament). The Europeanist group aims at getting the parties to devise a modernising policy which will go beyond rhetorical acceptance of the European logic and thus prove capable of spurring the country's structural adjustment to EU requirements.

The upsurge of nationalism in the Balkans, combined with Greece's difficulties in finding solutions to problems with neighbouring countries, especially FYROM, seem to strengthen the position of the traditionalist group. Yet it would not be an exaggeration to state that the future shape of the political parties may be determined by the struggle between the Europeanists/modernisers on the one hand, and the traditionalists on the other; between, that is, those who argue for the deeper Europeanisation of the Greek political system and those who seek to resist it in the name of safeguarding the traditional values of Hellenism.

The conflict between Europeanists and traditionalists highlights the nature and limits of the Europeanisation process. It highlights first its asynchronic nature. As noted, some sections of society have become extensively drawn into the European logic and have become dependent on European outputs. Yet the Europeanisation process has not proceeded with the speed and the breadth necessary for altering the fundamental nature of the Greek political system in such a way as to make it more responsive to the EU logic and requirements. The questions that must now be answered are: why does the asynchronism exist and why is there this intriguing contradiction in Greece's orientation and performance? The following reasons seem to account for the phenomenon.

The clientelistic system[44]

Albeit to a diminishing degree, the political parties are still, to an extent, locked into clientelistic patterns of political relations which condition their exchanges with the state apparatus and institutions. They still tend to see the state as the instrument for satisfying clientelistic demands; as a mechanism for allocating favours; as a collective patron to their active supporters who become clients of the state bureaucracy[45] – conditions thought essential for retaining electoral support. As recently as April 1994, *Eleftherotypia*, a leading Greek newspaper, denounced *rousfeti* (clientelism/favouritism) practised by Greece's major political parties:

> As the incurable disease perpetuating endemic corruption, mediocrity, dishonesty and incompetence in the administration, as the virus eating away the Greek State, as the obstacle preventing the staffing of the State machinery with competent personnel, the overall consequence being that the latter is not in a position to function effectively and efficiently.[46]

This type of bureaucratic clientelism, as a structural factor underpinning the interactive relationship between state and society, constitutes a significant impediment to deepening the Europeanisation of Greek politics; a process involving as it does the radical rebalancing of relations between the state and the civil society in favour of the latter. Political parties appear unwilling to allow the Europeanisation process to take its full course because that would imply a loss of state resources otherwise available to be dispersed for clientelistic purposes and electoral support. The importance of this was stressed by a Greek analyst who pointed out that 'political parties fight only for the control of the State because the only issue that seems to bring them in conflict is pre-electoral State appointments or, conversely, post-electoral dismissals.'[47]

The subordination of the state apparatus to political parties makes it exceedingly difficult for the European logic to permeate the system. For, apart from taking state resources away from party hands and transferring them to society, Europeanisation means that whatever functions, powers and resources are left to the state apparatus, including EU resources, should be managed in a much more transparent and autonomous way. Thus, in an apparently paradoxical way, the Europeanisation process works at two seemingly contradictory levels: on the one hand, it works for the shrinking of state powers in favour of society yet, on the other, it tends to strengthen the role, competitiveness and independence of the state apparatus against the clientelistic motives of political parties.

Political parties have so far been relatively successful in restraining the Europeanisation process. The failure to curb public deficits and reduce the size of the state pay-roll envisaged by the stabilisation programmes is seen as a consequence of the parties' resolve to retain their grip over the state. It is characteristic in this respect that, as a number of empirical studies have shown,[48] the size of the state gets swollen typically in terms of personnel and resources (i.e. expenditure which results in increased public deficits) in the years in which general elections take place, when the need to satisfy clientelistic pressures are much greater. Not surprisingly, the increased resources the state disposes in those years are not spent on investment projects, but on various consumption type activities: salaries of newly-hired civil servants, in the main. Thus, approached from this angle, the key problem linked to Greece's position in the EU, namely that of achieving greater macroeconomic convergence by slashing public deficits, moves from being one that can be solved in political rather than economic terms. This is why one can not be overly optimistic about the future; parties seem to be trapped in the clientelistic logic.

In short, political parties want the Europeanisation process to proceed, but only to the extent that it does not threaten their control over the state apparatus and their ability to use that apparatus for their own ends. Hence the phenomenon of autarkic Europeanisation. Political parties vow to work for the Europeanisation of the socio-economic system, but it seems only insofar as this process enhances the autarky of the system in terms of allocating clientelistic favours. Viewed in this light, it is clear that the Europeanisation of the Greek political system hinges decisively on the willingness and ability of the political parties to shed the clientelistic practices and transform themselves into modern institutions of policy articulation.

Political culture

Political culture is widely recognised as a crucial determinant of political behaviour and political performance. It is also a complex variable to handle. Viewed from a cultural perspective, Greece emerges clearly as a distinct case in the EU in that it is the only member-state sharing a cultural identity moulded by such disparate elements as Orthodoxy, the Byzantine tradition and classical influences. This cultural blend of rationalism and Eastern sentimentalism represents a mixed blessing. It endows Greece with a rich and creative cultural formation, but at the same time it bestows a culturally volatile system which pulls in opposite directions in external orientation; to the West and the East at the same time.

Moreover, certain cultural syndromes influence behaviour in such a way as to hinder the deeper internalisation of the European logic by the political actors and consequently make Greece's *ensomatosis* (incorporation) in certain respects into the EU appear shaky. Two particular syndromes deserve attention:

a   **The syndrome of the underdog culture.** This important trait of political culture, according to N. Diamantouros who coined the phrase and studied the phenomenon,[49] very much determines the way Greece is inclined to view the outside world. This deep-rooted syndrome contains the notion that the West despises Greece because of 'its glorious historical tradition'. It therefore wishes to humiliate Greece and treats it as an 'inferior entity'. Accordingly, the West is perceived as inherently inimical to Greece's interests and as constantly conspiring to damage them. This notion instinctively drives important strata of the Greek elite often to side with whoever appears to be against or in conflict with the West, irrespective of the merits of the case.[50] This of course hardly forms the ideal basis for Greece's role in the EU process of consensus-building, especially as regards issues of foreign policy.

The deeper implications of this syndrome for Greece's role in the EU concerns its stance towards the very idea of negotiating for the working out of compromises. This syndrome makes Greece doubt, if not reject outright, the logic of rational negotiating, bargaining and compromising over a wide range of issues; thereby rejecting the very logic upon which the EU is built and sustained. Normal negotiating concessions, however innocuous, are sometimes perceived as unacceptable or even humiliating climb downs. Moreover, this syndrome restrains Greece from consistently aligning its foreign policy with EU foreign policy objectives and choices, even though Greece appears to support ardently the idea of developing a fully-fledged common foreign policy.

b   **The syndrome of foreign protection.** A variant of the above syndrome is that of protection. As is well known, Greece had been the object of foreign intervention and, at the same time, foreign protection from the foundation of the modern Greek State. This had left a pervasive legacy and shaped a deep-seated syndrome of protection-seeking, even though 'protection' is condemned as a deleterious phenomenon ending up leading to unacceptable interventions in domestic politics. Yet the mental map of the Greek political class, and the psychological way it looks towards the outside, would seem to be invariably shaped by the protection-seeking syndrome.

More precisely, Greece tends sometimes to view the EU not so much as the arena for the maximisation of Greek interests through hard bargaining and compromise, but as an institution bound to offer protection to it against foreign threats. If one looks closely at how Greece uses the concept of solidarity, one can easily see that, more often than not, the ruling elite tend to interpret it in such a way as to imply protection. This of course leads Greece into the fallacy of expecting too much from the EU in terms of political support in its foreign policy objectives, of which the latter is neither institutionally capable nor politically willing to offer. This results in understandable frustrations on both sides.

Taken together, these two syndromes enter into the Europeanisation process not only as basic parameters shaping political behaviour and performance, but also as powerful factors affecting the definition of foreign policy objectives and choices. The apparent inability of the political elites to translate consistently rhetorical commitment to European integration into political objectives compatible with EU integration logic owes much to these syndromes.

No doubt, these syndromes are greatly compounded by the turbulent geographic situation in which Greece finds itself and the threats and insecurity this situation generates. It is true to say that Greece is the only member-state of the EU which feels intensely threatened by its regional environment; a perception that feeds various vacillations in foreign policy orientation. And this ought to be properly understood by Greece's partners in the EU.

Concluding remarks

As the foregoing analysis shows, EU membership has deeply affected the organisational structure and functional dynamics of the Greek political system. The Europeanisation process has given rise to a new set of problems, created new demands, changed deeply ingrained perceptions and altered the territorial, as well as the institutional balance of power. European logic has entered the policy-making process and shaped extensive interdependencies between Greece and the EU institutional framework. Huge financial flows from the EU budget have contributed to the reorientation of developmental objectives, while pressures for greater nominal convergence have led to the reassessment of macroeconomic policy.

Nevertheless, the Europeanisation process has not yet penetrated to the point of altering the fundamental relationship that binds political parties, state and society together, namely the clientelistic relationship in the broader sense of the term. This relationship results in the subordination of the State apparatus to the parties on the one hand, and on the other, it makes political parties prone to subordination to strong socio-economic interest groups, thereby creating conditions for a corporatist social structure. This in turn means that the restructuring of the relationship and balance between the state and society, which is of fundamental importance for the Europeanisation process, is hampered.

Consequently, a basic prerequisite for the Europeanisation process to be advanced is the modernisation of the political parties; a political process which is under way and is manifested in the conflict between the Europeanists/modernisers and the traditionalists within the two large political parties. The dialectic significance of this process is that, while it is being driven by the Europeanisation process, it serves to reinforce the latter group.

In summary, modernisation of the political parties emerges as an indispensable condition for Greece's adjustment to EU dynamics. Even with less enthusiastic advocacy of European integration than at present, modernised political parties are likely to make a much more important contribution to the adjustment and the Europeanisation processes.

A further prerequisite is, of course, the reorientation of policy objectives, especially in the field of foreign policy; a reorientation likely to result from a change of perceptions towards and within the cultural 'syndromes' that have been discussed. In practical terms, this means that political elites ought to absorb the significance of Greece's participation in the EU as an institutional member and project this significance in a way that would enhance the country's sense of security and self-confidence, discarding the besieged mentality and the notion of impotence in the face of adverse developments in the regional environment. This would allow political parties to overcome the glaring contradiction of advocating deeper integration along federal lines while, at the same time, pursuing policies more compatible with a nationalistic model and less consistent with their pro-integration stance.[51]

Notes:

1 C. Harvie, *The Rise of Regional Europe*, (London, Routledge, 1994); R. O. Keohane and S. Hoffman, (eds.), *The New European Community Decision Making and Institutional Change*, (Boulder, Westview Press, 1994); R. Leonardi (ed.), *The Regions and the European Community The Regional Response to the Single Market in the Underdeveloped Areas*, (London, Frank Cass, 1993); R. A. W. Rhodes, 'The Europeanization of Sub-central Government', *Staatwissenschaften Staatpraxis*, vol. 2, no. 3, 1994 Jahrgang; H. Wallace, W. Wallace, C. Webb (eds.), *Policy-making in the European Community*, (London, John Wiley and Sons, 1977); W. Wallace (ed.), *The Dynamics of European Integration*, (London, RIIA, Pinter, 1990); N. Frangakis *et al.*; *National Administration and Community Law*, (in Greek), (Athens, Sakkoulas, 1993); P. C. Ioakimidis, *The City and European Integration*, (in Greek), (Athens, Themelio, 1994); P. Kazakos and C. Stefanou (eds.), *Greece in the European Community: the First Five Years. Trends, Problems, Prospects*, (in Greek), (Athens, Sakkoulas, 1987).

2 R. Ladrech, 'Europeanization of Domestic Politics and Institutions: the Case of France', *Journal of Common Market Studies*, vol. 32, no. 1, (March 1994).

3 W. Wessels, 'Administrative Interaction', in Wallace, *The Dynamics*, 229–241.

4 See P. Kazakos, *Greece Between Integration and Marginalization*, (in Greek), (Athens, Diaton, 1991).

5 R. Clogg, *A Short History of Modern Greece*, (Cambridge, Cambridge University Press, 1979); N. P. Mouzelis, *Modern Greece Facets of Underdevelopment*, (London, Macmillan, 1978).

6 On Greece's accession, *see* P. C. Ioakimidis, *The Relations between Greece, EEC and the USA*, (in Greek), (Athens, Papazisis, 1979); L. Tsoukalis (ed.), *Greece and the European Community*, (London, Saxon House, 1979); A. Mitsos *et al.*, *Accession to the European Communities*, (in Greek), (Athens, Synchrona Themata, n.d.).

7 On the consequences of this period, see among others T. Gianaitsis, *The Accession to the European Community and the Effects on the Industry and Foreign Trade*, (in Greek), (Athens, Foundation for Mediterranean Studies, 1978); N. Maravegias, *The Accession to the European Community: Effects on the Agricultural Sector*, (in Greek), (Athens, Foundation for the Mediterranean Studies, 1989); A. Mitsos, *The Greek Industry in the International Market*, (in Greek), (Athens, Themelio, 1989); P. Roumeliotis (ed.), *The Integration of the European Community and the Role of Greece. Utopia and Reality*, (in Greek), (Athens, Papazisis, 1985); G. N. Yannopoulos (ed.), *Greece and the EEC*, (London, Macmillan, 1986).

8 On PASOK's views, *see* PASOK, *Greece and the Common Market: The Counter-Arguments*, (Athens, 1976); K. Featherstone, *Socialist Parties and European Integration. A Comparative History*, (Manchester, Manchester University Press, 1988), 170–190; P. Kazakos,

'Socialist Attitudes Toward European Integration in The Eighties'; C. Kariotis (ed.), *The Greek Socialist Experiment. Papandreou's Greece 1981-1989*, (New York, Pella, 1992).

9 There were very few exceptions to that. The Agricultural Bank of Greece (ATE) and the IOBE (Institute of Economic and Industrial Studies) and some foreign research centres sought to fill the vacuum by producing empirical studies.

10 *See* Papandreou's speech in the volume: *Speeches of the Prime Minister, Andreas G. Papandreou 1981–1982.*

11 *Ibid.*, 191.

12 This memorandum is published in *Epitheoresi ton Evropaikon Kinotiton*, 1982, vol. 3.2.

13 The EU response is also contained in the above volume.

14 *See* P. C. Ioakimidis, *The Transformation of the EEC*, (in Greek), (Athens, Papazisis, 1988), 317–332.

15 D. Tonge, 'Greece seizes Control of Major Cement Exporter' and 'New Blow for Greek Business Confidence', *Financial Times*, 15 September 1983. There were, of course, other cases of bringing companies and industrial firms under state control like, for instance, the Skaramanga Shipyards.

16 This was set up by Law 1386/86.

17 P. Kazakos, 'The Regulatory Role of the State in the Economy' in L. Tsoukalis (ed.), *Greece in the European Community: The Challenge of Adjustment*, (Athens, EKEM/Papazisis, 1993).

18 *See* various Commission reports on the implementation of EU law, and Frangakis *National Administration*.

19 C. L. Rozakis, *Greek Foreign Policy and the European Communities. Effects from the Accession 1981–86*, (in Greek), (Athens, Foundation for Mediterranean Studies, 1987); Y. Valinakis, 'Greece in the European Political Co-operation: The First Ten Years', in Tsoukalis, (ed.) *Greece in the European Community*, 249–277.

20 *See* characteristically, V. Walker, 'Greece and Soviet Union Edge Closer Together', *Financial Times*, 18 February 1983; S. J. Nuttal, *European Political Co-operation*, (Oxford, Clarendon Press, 1992).

21 S. Verney, 'From the Special Relationship to Europeanism: PASOK and the European Community, 1981–89', in R. Clogg (ed.), *Greece 1981–89, The Populist Decade*, (London, St. Martin's Press, 1993).

22 Among others see, P. C. Ioakimidis, 'Greece in the EU: Policies, Experiences and Prospects', in H. J. Psomiades and S. B. Thomadakis, *Greece, the New Europe and the Changing International Order*, (New York, Pella, 1993); S. Verney, 'To Be or Not To Be Within The European Community: The Party Debate and Democratic Consolidation in Greece', in G. Pridham (ed.), *Securing Democracy: Political Parties and Democratic Consolidation in Southern Europe*, (London, Routledge, 1990); R. Gillespie, 'The Consolidation of New Democracies', in D. W. Urwin and W. E. Paterson (eds.), *Politics in Western Europe Today*, (London, Longman, 1990); A. Fatouros, 'Political and Institutional Facets of Greece's Integration in the European Community' in Psomiades and Thomadakis, *Greece, the New Europe*, 23–42.

23 On this aspect, see P. C. Ioakimidis, 'The Greek Administration and the Shaping of European Policy' in Tsoukalis, *Greece in the European Community*, 209–230; A. Makrydimitris and A. Passas, *The Greek Administration and the Co-ordination of European Policy*, (in Greek), (Athens, EKEM Working Paper, no. 20, 1993); I. D. Anastopoulos, 'National Administration and European Community: the Required Adjustments of the Greek Administrative System' and N. Skandamis, 'The Community Aspects of the National Administration', both in N. Frangakis *et al.*, *National Administration*.

24 P. C. Ioakimidis, 'Greece in the EU: Policies'; Rozakis, *Greek Foreign Policy*. For a more theoretical analysis, *see* D. Constas, 'Systemic Influences on a Weak, Aligned State in the Post-1974 Era', in D. Constas (ed.), *The Greek Turkish Conflict in the 1990s*, (London,

Macmillan, 1991); Th. Kouloumbis, *Greece and International Developments*, (in Greek), (Thessaloniki, Paratiritis, 1988).

25 *See* Commission Decision 85/594/EEC, *Official Journal of the European Communities*, L373/9, 31 December 1985; 'EEC Sets Tough Terms in Granting Loan to Greece', *Financial Times*, 19 November 1985; *Kerdos*, 6 December 1985.

26 Net financial flows increased from 150m ECUs in 1981 to 1,300m in 1985. See P. C. Ioakimidis, 'The Budgetary Account of Greece's Participation in the EEC (1981-85) and the Prospects for the Future', in Kazakos and Stefanou, (eds.) *Greece in the European Community.* 67–97.

27 W. Wallace (ed.), *The Dynamics of European Integration*, (London, Pinter/RIIA, 1990).

28 On the nature of the Greek State generally see Mouzelis, *Modern Greece*; K. Tsoukalas 'Free Riders in Wonderland', *Helleniki Epitheorisi Politikis Epistimis*, no. 1, (in Greek), (January 1993); K. Tsoukalas, *State Society and Labour in Post-war Greece*, (in Greek), (Athens, Themelio, 1986); S. B. Thomadakis, 'European Economic Integration, the Greek State and the Challenges of the 1990s', in Psomiades and Thomadakis, *Greece, the New Europe*, 351–375.

29 L. T. Katseli writes that 'the pattern of ownership and control identified with State corporatism and the dual institutional structures that have evolved were directly challenged by the integration of the economy into the European Community in 1981....', L. T. Katseli, 'Economic Integration in the Enlarged European Community. Structural Adjustment of the Greek Economy', in C. Bliss and J. Braga de Macedo (eds.), *Unity with Diversity in the European Economy*, (Cambridge, Cambridge University Press, 1990).

30 *See* daily press reports, *Kathemerini, Naftemporiki, Express*, for relevant cases. The most recent one concerns the Olympic Airways, *Express*, 28 April 1994.

31 *Naftemporiki, Kathemerini*, various issues, 1992, 1993.

32 Frangakis *et al.*, *National Administration*.

33 *See* note no. 25.

34 Council Decision of 4 March 1991 concerning an EU loan in favour of the Hellenic Republic (91/136/EEC), *Official Journal of the European Communities*, L66/22, 13 March 1991.

35 *Ipurgion Ethnikis Ikonomias-KEPE, Plan for Economic and Social Development 1983–1987*, (in Greek), (Athens, August 1985).

36 On the IMPs and the Greek State, see F. Papageorgiou and S. Verney, 'Regional Planning and Integrated Mediterranean Programmes in Greece' in Leonardi, *The Regions*, 139–161.

37 Ministry of National Economy, *Regional Development Plan 1994-1999*, (Athens, 1993).

38 Personal interviews and *Express*, (11 November 1993).

39 Commission of the EEC, *Guide for the Reformed EC Structural Funds*, (Brussels, 1989).

40 P. C. Ioakimidis, 'The Implementation of EC Cohesion Policy in Greece: the Tension between Bureaucratic Centralism and Regionalism', Paper presented at the Conference on 'EC Cohesion Policy and National Networks', Centre for European Studies, Nuffield College, Oxford, 2–3 December 1993; S. Verney and F. Papageorgiou, 'Prefecture Councils in Greece: Decentralization in the European Community Context', in Leonardi, *The Regions* 109–138.

41 G. Marks, 'Structural Policy and Multilevel Governance in the EC' in A. W. Cafruny and G. Rosenthal (eds.), *The State of the European Community; the Maastricht Debates and Beyond*, (London, Lynne Rienner, 1993).

42 P. C. Ioakimidis, 'The EC and The Greek Political System: an Overview', in P. Kazakos and P. C. Ioakimidis (eds.), *Greece and EC Membership Evaluated*, (London, Pinter, 1994).

43 See T. Georgakopoulos, 'The Third PASOK Congress; For How Long Together?', *Avgi*, 22 April 1994; P. Kazakos, 'The Meteoric European Step', *Eleftherotypia*, 22 April 1994; S.

Verney, 'PASOK and European Union: the History and Prospects of an Idiosyncratic Relationship', *Eleftherotypia*, 16 April 1994. (all in Greek).

44 See D. A. Sotiropoulos, 'A Colossus with Feet of Clay: the State in Post-Authoritarian Greece', in Psomiades and Thomadakis, *Greece, the New Europe*, 43–56.

45 *Ibid.*, 52.

46 *Eleftherotypia*, 11 April 1994.

47 I. K. Pretenderis in *To Vima*, 15 May 1994. Writing in the newspaper, *Eleftherotypia*, Th. Anastassiadis pointed out that 'today political parties constitute the single most important obstacle to the modernization of the State', *Eleftherotypia*, 20 April 1994. Writing in *Kathemerini*, Ino Afentouli noted that 'the two largest parties are not statist parties; they are clientelistic parties. They think that the State is their own shop and so they strive to control it; for otherwise they would lose their clients', *Kathemerini*, 29 April 1994. Also I. Afentouli, 'The Parties and their Responsibilities', *Kathemerini*, 22 April 1994. Characteristically, a recent analysis of various legislative acts purporting to reform public administration has concluded that the principal concern of both major parties (PASOK and ND) has been 'the reproduction of clientelistic relationships between political authority and society', *see* D. A. Sotiropoulos, 'The Main Parameters of the Greek Bureaucracy', Anti, 13 May 1994. *See also* A. Makridimitris, 'Collective Demands and Administrative Reform: Aspects of Greek Administrative Culture', *Helliniki Epitheorisi Politikis Epistimis*, no. 3 (April 1994).

48 *See*, among others, S. B. Thomadakis, D. B. Seremetis, 'The Greek Electoral-Fiscal Cycle and its Destabilizing Properties', in *Helliniki Epitheorisi Politikis Epistimis 1993*, (in Greek), 48-82; K. Spanou, 'Elections and Public Administration', in Y. Vulgaris, *et. al.*, *Elections and Parties in the 1980s; Developments and Prospects of the Political System*, (in Greek), (Athens, Themelio, 1990).

49 N. Diamantouros, 'Politics and Culture in Greece, 1974–91; An Interpretation', in Clogg, *Greece*, 1–25.

50 *See also* C. Simitis, *Nationalistic Populism or National Strategy?*, (Athens, Gnosi, 1992).

51 See P. Kazakos, 'Tradition and Populism in Foreign Policy', *Eletherotypia*, 9 May, 1994.

4

Greek fiscal policy and the European Union

Introduction

Contrary to many expectations at the time, Greece's economic performance since joining the EU in 1981 has been rather poor, displaying low growth, high inflation and high indebtedness. This is in contrast to the more successful record accomplished during the 1960s and the 1970s, when the performance of the Greek economy had actually outpaced the EU average. Table 4.1 which compares the trends of the Greek economy over the last thirty years with those of other member-states at comparable levels of maturity, shows clearly that Greece has increasingly fallen behind in the objective of catching-up with the EU average. Unlike the 1960s and the 1970s, when the rate of growth of GDP at 8.5 per cent and 4.0 per cent respectively was twice as large as that of the EU and unemployment was sharply declining, the eighties have been characterised by less than half of one per cent growth, increasing unemployment, a rate of inflation almost three times as high as the EU average, a deteriorating current account as a proportion of GDP, and a public sector sinking deeper into debt. What is more, these disappointing trends appear to be endemic to Greece alone. Other less developed members of the EU such as Ireland, Spain and Portugal have achieved considerably superior rates of performance and have moved closer to the European average.

Undoubtedly world-wide economic circumstances and the adverse effect of structural adjustments, precipitated by the abolition of domestic protective and other restrictive practices in advance of falling into line with EU trade policies, are partly responsible for the poor economic performance of Greece. However, many other countries have confronted similarly unfavourable conditions. Indeed, for weaker economies the damage caused by addressing structural problems and other such shocks is partly offset by the transfer arrangements that the EU has put in place in order to reduce the disparities between the advanced and the lagging member-states. As Table 4.2 shows, Greece has been a net beneficiary of the EU Budget. In the period 1981–1992, the net receipts from the EU increased from 9.1 billion drachmas to 815.6 billion, or from less than half a percentage point of GDP to almost 5.5 per cent. Payments from the Structural Fund (Social and Regional), the Integrated Mediterranean Programmes (IMPs) and the European Agricultural Guidance and Guarantee Fund (EAGGF) (which administers the Common Agricultural Policy (CAP)) formed the largest component of those financial benefits, promoting Greece's less developed regions, financing investment in infrastructure and assisting farmers.

Table 4.1 Long-run trends of the Greek economy

	1960–70	1971–80	1981–90	1960–70	1971–80	1980–91
	Per capita growth			Unemployment		
GREECE	8·5	4·0	0·4	5·0[a]	2·2	7·1
EUR 12–	4·6	2·4	1·9	2·3	4·2	9·6
	Inflation			External balance		
GREECE	2·5	13·2	18·3	−3·1	−1·9	−4·4
EUR 12–	3·9	10·7	6·5	0·3	0·0	0·1

	Annual change of real GDP (%)			Budget deficit	
	1961–73	1974–85	1986–90	1981–90	1991–93
GREECE	7·7	2·5	1·6	12·3	15·0
Spain	7·2	1·8	4·5	4·6	5·5
Ireland	4·4	3·8	4·7	8·5	2·2
Portugal	6·9	2·2	4·6	7·9	5·7
EUR 12–	4·8	2·0	3·3	4·4	5·2

	GDP per head*							
	1960	1965	1970	1975	1980	1985	1990	1993
GREECE	36·8	41·1	46·7	51·7	52·6	51·3	47·0	48·8
Spain	62·5	69·1	73·0	79·4	72·0	70·4	74·8	75·6
Ireland	60·6	58·3	58·8	61·9	63·1	64·7	71·1	55·7
Portugal	37·8	41·8	48·4	50·5	53·0	51·3	75·33	60·5
EUR 12–	100	100	100	100	100	100	100	100

Growth:	Average annual percentage change of per capita GDP at 1985 prices
Unemployment:	Average percentage of civilian labour force unemployed
Inflation:	Average annual percentage change of private consumption deflator
External Balance:	Balance on current transactions with the rest of the world as a percentage of GDP
Budget Deficit:	Net borrowing of general government as a percentage of GDP
EUR 12–:	European Union member countries, including West Germany
*:	at current prices in purchasing power standard
a:	1964–70 only

Source: European Economy, various issues

Table 4.2 Net receipts from the EU (% of GDP)

1981	1982	1983	1984	1985	1986	1987	1988	1989	1990	1991	1992
0·5	1·6	2·4	2·2	2·6	3·3	3·9	3·4	4·0	4·5	4·7	5·5

Source: Annual Report of the Governor of the Bank of Greece, various issues.

The unenviable economic performance of Greece has become the cause of tension and concern both in Greece, as living standards have stagnated, and in the EU. In the latter case, Greece's economic decline is imposing a heavy burden on the EU budget, frustrating European efforts towards convergence and thus slowing down the introduction of Economic and Monetary Union (EMU).

Given the current poor state of health of the Greek economy, especially the repeated resort to budgetary deficits, the implications for EMU are a particular cause for concern. EMU and the introduction of a single currency will result in the loss of independent national monetary and exchange rate policy, but that loss cannot be compensated by greater autonomy in the conduct of national budgetary policy. Because budgetary deficits bear on aggregate demand, interest rates and the rate of growth of the money supply, 'excessive' national budgetary deficits will jeopardise monetary stability. In recognition of these threats to stability, the 1991 Maastricht Treaty on European Union has made participation in the EMU conditional on satisfying various convergence criteria, which aim to minimise the differences between member-states in the inflation rates and the size of fiscal deficits. Although in the long run EMU is expected to bring substantial benefits from greater efficiencies in the pattern of production, investment and trade and to enhance macroeconomic stability, the prospect for the immediate future is that pursuit of these aims will strain the Greek economy even further.

This chapter seeks to examine the pattern of fiscal policy in Greece and its link to EU membership. A systematic inquiry requires first an understanding of the role of the State in the economy; this is the subject of the following section. The second section examines the pattern of public finances in Greece for the period 1958–1992, whilst the third concentrates on their structural deficiencies. The fourth section focuses on recent efforts to reform the public sector, while the fifth concludes the paper.

The role of the State in fiscal policy

The deliberate involvement of the Greek Government in the economy, particularly its active pursuit of structural and macroeconomic objectives, was for decades regarded as an unquestioned part of the overall development process. The result was a complex set of controls and interventions in the market mechanism and an enormous expansion of the size of government activities. Lately, however, despite the original successes of the 1960s and the 1970s, the poor economic performance during the late 1980s and 1990s has led to calls for a re-examination of the role of the State in the economy. A consensus on imposing some discipline on its spending profligacy has now emerged. It has, however, yet to be implemented.

During the relatively virtuous decades of the 1950s and 1960s the Greek Government's *modus operandi* in fiscal policy was at least to balance current public expenditure with tax revenue, and to use deficit finance only for investment in infrastructure (which was expected to increase output and future tax revenue). The State, however, also assumed control of certain sectors of activity deemed to be of strategic importance for the development of the economy. Its influence also reached into the financial and foreign exchange markets, where an intricate system of regulations and quantitative and qualitative controls on the lending and borrowing activities of financial institutions began to evolve. Finally, in the goods and labour markets a web of interventions was established, including controls on prices and profit margins, procedures for granting licences, income policies, and minimum wage legislation.

The pace of state intervention has increased since the mid-1970s, for both political and economic reasons. The Greek Government has taken on an increasingly direct and prominent role in the economy by expanding its share of consumption and transfer expenditure, by nationalising private enterprises and by running larger and larger deficits. Recruitment by the public sector and control of ailing firms became part of the policies pursued to contain unemployment, suppress inflation and redistribute income. The pace became frenetic in the 1980s when the Socialist Party, advocating a corporatist state (strong trade unions with the power to centralise wage bargaining) took power. In the pursuit of the protection of jobs and the need to raise the purchasing power of workers, the Government imposed mandatory wage increases in almost all sectors, operated automatic wage indexation from 1982 to 1991, imposed strict controls on firms seeking to lay off redundant workers (requiring them to obtain the authorities' approval) and subordinated commercial and profitability considerations of public enterprises and ailing firms to its social objectives. Moreover, long and destructive strikes were not uncommon, often resulting in the Government yielding to pressure from organised labour and other interest groups. Likewise, the pensions system, which until the 1980s was an insurance mechanism paying benefits based on the record of past contributions, was transformed into an unfunded welfare system where payment of benefits was, to a large extent, unrelated to individual inputs.

If it can be argued that excessive government interference contributed to the recent record of disappointing economic performance, characterised by falling factor productivity, slow income growth, high inflation, and high public sector indebtedness, it is also true that such poor results have meant that the social development targets appear to have been missed as well. Prompted partly by recognition of this spiral and partly by the obligations of the membership of the EU and the Maastricht conditions, some important steps have been taken in the 1990s to reverse Greece's economic decline, particularly by redressing the role of the State and reforming the public sector.

Deregulation and price liberalisation in the financial and in the goods markets got under way first with the stabilisation programme of 1985–87 and has been pursued with renewed vigour since 1991. A more difficult task lies ahead for the proposed privatisation programmes and fiscal policy, since these have often been used as platforms for advancing the electoral chances of the incumbent party. Although it appears that the political parties have come to recognise the urgency of the situation and the need for corrective action, progress in imposing discipline and consolidating the public finances has been slow.

Public expenditure and tax revenue

The impact of fiscal policy is manifested in the size, composition and balance of the two sides of the budget: expenditure and revenue. In surveying the profiles of government expenditure and revenue two broad conclusions emerge:

a   Changes in direction in Greek politics account for significant variations in the trends of the total and the composition of expenditure and revenue, which points to the presence of a partisan link in the use of fiscal instruments.

b   Very rapid increase of expenditure in comparison to the EU, which has not been matched by an increase in revenue.

Figure 4.1 presents the long-term patterns of public expenditure (E) and government revenue (R) in Greece for the period 1958–1992. Both expenditure and revenue display very sharp upward trends, with public expenditure rising from one fifth to more than one half of GDP and tax revenue increasing from 20 per cent to almost 40 per cent of GDP.[1] The considerably faster growth of public expenditure has resulted in a yawning government deficit (D). Perhaps the most striking feature of the latter is the abrupt change in trend experienced at the beginning of the 1980s. The figure shows that, throughout the 1960s and 1970s, the deficit rose gradually from 2 to 6 per cent of GDP. In 1981, however, it more than doubled to almost 13 per cent. Following that, partly as a result and partly as a response to the economic conditions of the time, it continued in a historically unprecedented upward trend reaching an initial peak of 17 per cent of GDP in 1985, which itself was surpassed by another of 20 per cent in 1990. Such figures are unmatched by international standards.

The overall picture is unravelled in Figures 4.2 and 4.3 which trace the different patterns of the various components of expenditure and revenue that prevail during different phases. Figure 4.2 shows the paths of the GDP shares of the principal components of public expenditures; namely government consumption (G), investment (I), transfer expenditures – the sum of subsidies plus

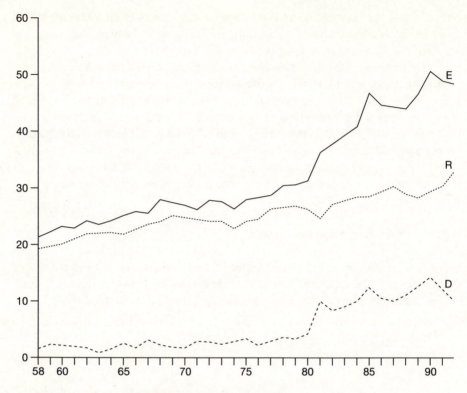

<small>FIG</small> **4.1 Public sector expenditure, revenue and deficit
(per cent of <small>GDP</small> at market prices)**

transfer payments to households – (T), and interest payments on the public debt (Int). Similarly, Figure 4.3 presents the profiles of the shares of the various sources of government revenue: income taxes (D), indirect taxes (I), social security contributions (S), taxes on corporation profits (B), and non-tax sources (O). The figures reveal that major turning points in the growth pattern of individual categories of spending and taxation coincide with major political events like the military coup of 1967, the return to democratic government in 1974, the accession to power of the socialist party in 1981, its re-election in 1985 and the weak coalition governments in the period 1989–90.

In the sub-period 1958–67 the share of public expenditure in <small>GDP</small> increased from 21 per cent in 1958 to 30 per cent in 1967. More than half of this increase took the form of rises in transfer expenditures, while consumption and invest-ment rose only modestly. During the same sub-period, driven by buoyant rev-enue from social security contributions and indirect taxes, the share of tax revenue increased from 20 per cent to 26 per cent of <small>GDP</small>, while the percentage of income taxes has remained virtually constant. In the succeeding sub-period, 1967–74, the growth in consumption and transfer expenditure and indirect taxes declined, while the rate of growth of public investment and income taxes

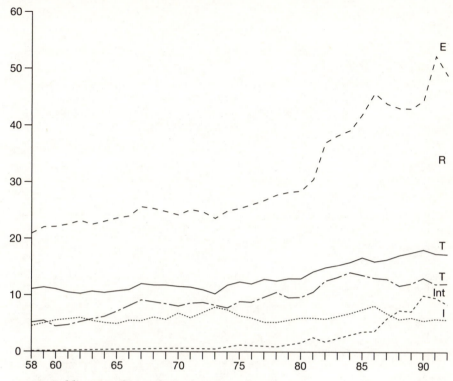

FIG 4.2 **Public expenditure shares (per cent of GDP)**

accelerated. After recording a sharp temporary decline in 1973, the year of the
first oil crisis, the relative shares resumed a persistent upward trend for the rest
of the period (for reasons which differ across the various categories of expenditure and revenue).

In 1974 the new democratic Government had to provide not only for
urgent defence needs (in view of the worsening relations with Turkey and the
invasion of Cyprus), but also for consumption expenditure on administration,
health and education, and transfer payments. Such increases in civilian spending reflected changes in social priorities after the collapse of the dictatorship
and the rapid inflation which increased the cost of provision of public services
and welfare payments. During the same period, tax revenue from direct and
indirect taxes and social security contributions also increased, but their rates of
growth lagged behind those of public expenditure, resulting in a widening
deficit. The same period witnessed the advent of two additional significant
trends. The first was the increase in the share of interest payments on public
debt, which resulted from larger government borrowing (following larger budgetary deficits) and from higher nominal interest rates (following higher inflation rates). Secondly, public investment decreased in an effort to counteract
inflationary pressures.

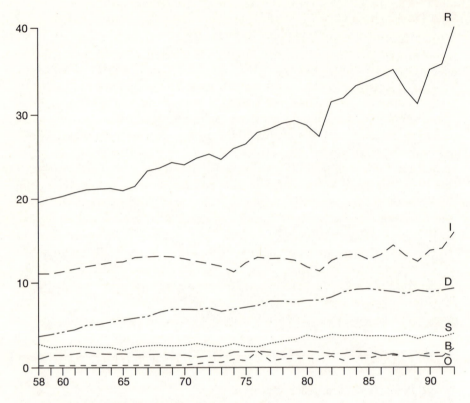

FIG 4.3 **Revenue of shares (per cent of** GDP**)**

The year 1981 not only saw the accession of Greece to full membership of the EU, but also the ascent to power of the Socialist Party. As has been noted, the latter event signalled a more pronounced and enlarged role for the State in economic activity, including the introduction of wage indexation and the takeover of large numbers of enterprises, mainly through the state-controlled banks. Public expenditure on consumption, investment and transfer payments escalated dramatically, so that by 1985 (together with interest payments) it exceeded 51 per cent of GDP. However, these increases were not matched by a comparable rise in tax revenue. Proceeds from income taxes stagnated to 5 per cent of GDP, while those from indirect taxes became the fastest growing source from 13 per cent of GDP in 1981 to 15 per cent in 1985 (mainly as a result of increasing private consumption). The deteriorating fiscal position led the (re-elected) Socialist Government to adopt a strict stabilisation programme in 1985–87, which succeeded in bringing down the share of the total of public spending and the deficit by 2 and 3 percentage units respectively in 1988. Such modest gains, however, were dissipated in the following two years of indecisive election outcomes and unstable coalition Governments, so that in 1990 the share of government spending reached an all-time high of 55 per cent of GDP and the deficit climbed to one fifth of GDP, with consumption, transfers and interest payments accounting once more for the largest rises.

The Conservative Government that came to office in 1990 announced first an adjustment programme for the period 1991–93 and then, in view of the Maastricht Treaty requirements, a convergence programme for the period 1993–98 aimed at reversing the trends perceived to be at the heart of the economic ills of the country. Not surprisingly, these programmes raised a number of general questions about the appropriate role of the public sector. By 1992 some progress had been achieved towards the objective of reducing the size of the public sector deficit, but the actual cuts were smaller than planned. In particular, a large part of the 1992 decrease in the deficit came from re-scheduling the public sector debt, which implied heavier interest payments in the future. Moreover, proceeds from the privatisation programme, which accounted for the modest increase in the contribution of 'other sources' of revenue recorded in 1992, were one-off measures which could not be relied upon as a continuous source of income.

The electoral contest of 1993 saw fiscal policy being eased up again, resulting in another hike of the deficit to 13 per cent of GDP. However, the new Socialist Government appears to have accepted the need for continuing consolidation. It has kept several of the deficit-reducing policies of its predecessor and added new ones too.

By way of comparison to other European economies, Figure 4.4 plots the paths of government expenditure, revenue and budget deficit for Greece and the EU average as proportions of GDP (denoted by GE, GR & GD and EE, ER & ED respectively) for the period 1979–93. The most prominent feature of the graph is the extremely rapid growth of government expenditure in Greece which, starting from 11 percentage units below the EU average in 1979, climbed to above the average in a span of half-a-dozen years. Sadly the Greek Government has not shown the same zeal to match revenue to the European average, resulting in an ever widening difference between its budget deficit and that of the EU average.

Table 4.3 shows the average per capita GDP and the average percentage ratios of government expenditure, revenue and financial balance for the period 1981–90. The striking feature of the Table is that Greece, with a per capita income of half the European Union mean, displays by far the largest percentage of deficit (a period average of 12.3 per cent) – almost three times the European mean. The data confirms that it is the massive shortfall of revenue (Greece is at the bottom of the league at three quarters of the mean) which has generated this marked difference.

The public sector

This section reviews the main problem areas of the Greek public sector, notably the budget deficit, the imbalance in the composition of public expenditure, the low tax yield, the inefficiency in the operation of the public sector, and their underlying causes.

Table 4.3 International comparisons

	Y	E	R	X
Belgium	104·7	59·9	50·7	−9·2
Denmark	109·9	57·9	55·4	−2·5
Germany (West)	117·5	47·1	45·1	−2·0
GREECE	50·2	45·7	33·3	−12·3
Spain	70·2	40·1	35·5	−4·6
France	112·3	51·2	49·0	−2·3
Ireland	65·2	48·4	40·0	−8·5
Italy	102·7	49·8	38·6	−11·2
Luxembourg	120·8	52·8	56·0	+3·2
Netherlands	103·2	58·2	52·8	−5·4
Portugal	53·3	43·9	36·0	−7·9
United Kingdom	101·1	42·2	40·4	−1·8
EUR (12)	100·0	48·3	43·9	−4·4
USA	145·3	36·2	33·5	−2·7
Japan	105·9	32·7	32·0	−0·8

Y: Per capita GDP at market prices at Purchasing Power
E: Gen. Government Total Expenditure per cent of GDP
R: Gen. Government Total Revenue per cent of GDP; X=E–R.

Source: European Economy

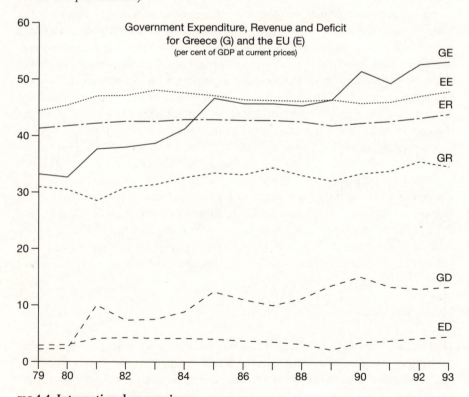

FIG 4.4 **International comparisons**

Deficit and debt

Concerns about budgetary deficits arise for two reasons, notably:

a   Their inflationary consequences, which are caused by the effect of the deficit on the growth of the money supply, and the expansionary effect of public expenditure on aggregate demand (which bids up prices).

b   The crowding out of private expenditure, which is caused by the increase in interest rates and limiting credit to the private sector.[2]

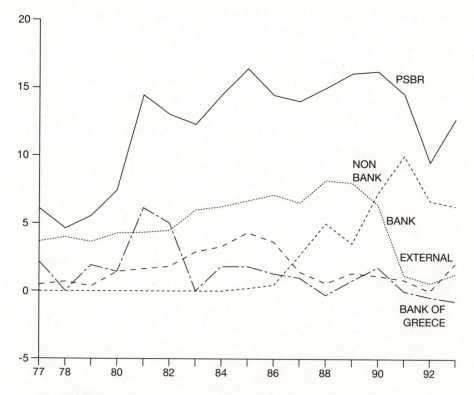

FIG **4.5a Public Sector Borrowing Requirements by source of finance** (**per cent of** GDP)

Figure 4.5a shows that during the 1980s the banking sector financed between two-thirds and three-quarters of the Public Sector Borrowing Requirements (PSBR). Credit policy arrangements, which provided for the compulsory purchase of treasury bills and other government debt by financial institutions, had secured low cost finance of the deficit and may have distorted the opportunity cost of spending decisions.[3] Credit institutions were required to invest more than half of their assets in treasury bills or bonds issued by public enterprises. The interest rate on these was set at levels below inflation, implying a negative real interest cost on the public debt. Until 1986, treasury borrowing from foreign sources covered between a quarter and a third of the deficit, while borrowing from non-bank or market sources (both resident and non-resident investors) was negligible. Since 1986, prompted by financial liberalisation, the share of the market sources of borrowing has increased steeply to approximately 40 per cent of the total, stimulated by high interest rates and a better debt term-structure.

Although expansionary fiscal policies stimulated demand, the growing public sector deficit tended to crowd out private investment. Preferential access of the public sector to credit deprived the private sector of funds needed for its own expansion. By the mid-1980s, bank claims on the public sector had risen to some 70 per cent of GDP compared with 40 per cent in 1980, while at the same time credit to the private sector had declined relative to GDP.

Figure 4.5b shows that, by 1993, central Government accounted for more than 90 per cent of the total borrowing requirements of the public sector. In the 1980s, public corporations also added to the deficit for the reasons mentioned above. The figure also shows that public entities, social insurance funds and local authorities were turning out a small surplus up to the early 1980s (partly reflecting the rapid growth of economic activity and a domestic labour force near full employment), a situation which has reversed with the generous pensions schemes enacted since then.

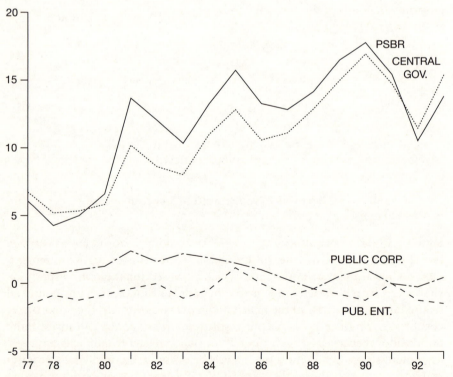

FIG 4.5b **Public Sector Borrowing Requirements by fiscal authority (per cent of GDP)**

Cumulative government deficits have contributed to the dramatic expansion of the debt of the public sector, which has more than quadrupled as a proportion of GDP in the last fifteen years. It has risen from 28 per cent of GDP in 1979 to 118 per cent in 1992, making it one of the highest in the EU. The external part of the debt accounts for more than a quarter of the total. Perhaps more striking than the relative size of the debt is the speed by which it has increased. Unless this upward trend is slowed down, Greece will face a 'debt trap' in which the expanding debt leads to mounting interest service obligations, further swelling the borrowing requirements and thus ever increasing the ratio of debt to GDP.

The spending profligacy of governments and unsustainable borrowing contrasts only too starkly with the convergence conditions for fiscal policy for joining the third stage of the EMU.[4] Under these conditions the ratio of deficit to GDP must not exceed 3 per cent and the ratio of public debt to GDP must not exceed 60 per cent. In view of the trends and developments described above, it is difficult to see how these conditions can be met by Greece in the remaining period (up to the end of 1998), even if ever achieving them were to be judged desirable.

Growth and composition

To a large extent the recent increase in consumption expenditure has been due to the rapid growth in employment by the state sector. Between 1975 and 1985 government employment increased by 50 per cent. In 1990 employment in the public sector (including utilities, banks and firms under state control) amounted to 30 per cent of total dependent employment. Although not necessarily an adverse development in some circumstances, in the case of Greece it was associated with the overstaffing of the public sector and with wage levels and pay rises above the economy-wide average. This unfavourable picture was not improved by the general impression of continued low quality of the services and products of public utilities and state-controlled enterprises.

The principal factors behind the recent escalation of transfer expenditures have been the provision of subsidies and financial assistance to the 'problematic' enterprises and the dramatic rise of pension expenditure. In the case of the former, the combined deficit of firms in the wider public sector (but excluding power and telecommunications) amounted to more than 5 per cent of GDP, of which the ten largest manufacturing loss-making firms (all state-controlled) alone produced losses amounting to 1 per cent of GDP (OECD Report 1990/91). With respect to the generosity of publicly provided pensions, the pension/GDP ratio doubled to 15 per cent in the ten years to 1989 (second highest in the OECD after Italy). Specifically, the system provided for pensions to commence after 17 to 25 years of service irrespective of the age of the pensioner, it paid pensions which often exceeded the wage at retirement, and it covered large sections of the population who had never contributed to pension insurance (like farmers and immigrants from Eastern Europe). Moreover, it depended on a rather low ratio of contributors to pensioners (2.2:1 in 1990), thereby imposing a heavy burden on other parts of the economy. These trends have had obvious adverse consequences for both the public finances and the incentive effects on labour supply, problems which are now being exacerbated by the ageing of the population.

Narrow tax base

Both indirect and direct taxes in Greece have been characterised by high tax rates relative to international tax standards (OECD Report 1989/90), but the revenue yield has been smaller than one might have expected.[5] The inability of the tax base to keep pace with the expansion of public expenditure is attributed to two main factors: notably generous tax exemptions and tax evasion. As regards tax exemptions, a couple of examples serve to give the picture. Farmers have been almost completely exempt from paying income tax; interest income from bank deposits has been subject to taxation only since 1992; and generous allowances have been applied to certain company investments. In a similar vein, large scale tax evasion has allegedly been practised by the liberal professions and unincorporated employers, who take advantage of some lax aspects of the tax regulations and the low effectiveness of the tax collection authorities. Official tax returns have even portrayed a picture in which the declared income of the above average income earners is only half the declared income of wage earners. The possibility of tax evasion in some professions, but not in others (notably dependent employment), not only has obvious distortionary implications for the structure of occupational choices, but has brought arbitrary and unfair distributional consequences as well.

As already indicated, in view of the relatively small yield of income taxes, the Government has relied extensively on indirect taxes for raising revenue.[6] Since 1987 the main source of indirect taxation has been the value-added tax, which replaced a maze of *ad valorem* taxes on transactions. Some product-specific excise duties, most notably on tobacco, alcohol and petrol and its derivative products, have been retained awaiting European-wide harmonisation.

Public sector inefficiency

In the attempt to economise on public expenditure, attention has recently focused on the possible savings that can be made by improving efficiency in the operation of the public sector.[7] In practice, inefficiency in this sector takes the form of low quality of services, overmanning (problems in *how* posts are filled), and inadequacies in infrastructure (especially in transportation, tele-communications, water and sewage works and environmental protection). Moreover, the deficiencies in public services, like state education and medical care, often lead to a waste of resources manifested in the duplication of some state activities by the private sector. For example, pupils aiming to learn a foreign language or pass university entrance examinations typically attend private institutions which teach them more intensively the subject that they are already supposed to have been taught at school. In addition to the inefficiency in the delivery of public services, concerns have been expressed by bodies such as OECD about the substantial expenditure over-runs which may reflect possible laxity and defects in the system of budgetary planning and control. Although in principle budgetary procedures are quite strict, when the Greek Parliament votes for the budget of any given year it automatically approves expenditure over-runs of the previous year, a practice which may itself encourage overspending.

The OECD has identified several factors which may have contributed cumulatively over the years to such inefficiency in the public sector. In respect of management these relate to the application of staff recruitment and promotion in state administration criteria both political – the partisan affiliation of a particular official – and social – the marital status and geographic origin of an employee; others include the arbitrary management of public enterprises, the tendency to award the status of permanent civil servant to large numbers of people recruited on fixed contract for a definite period of time, and the lack of effective supervision by an independent authority. Further contributory factors are the low motivation and standards in the civil service associated with both low scales of pay for qualified personnel, and with the fact that promotion and pay are primarily related to the length of service and only remotely to responsibility and performance. In the case of public sector investment, perhaps the most unfortunate development has been its use for stabilisation policy objectives and the consequent practice of cutting public investment in order to curb demand and limit the size of the government deficit.

Public sector reforms

With the budgetary deficit persisting at dangerously high levels, legislation has been enacted in the last few years to pursue the (complementary) objectives of reforming the finances and improving the efficiency of the public sector. As previously discussed, there are signs that, the objectives and, to a large extent the means for pursuing the latter receive wide political support, in contrast to similar attempts in the past. At least, one may expect some consistency in their pursuit.

Tax revenue

On the tax revenue side, remedial policy has focused on broadening the tax base by reducing the scope for tax evasion. The measures introduced include:

a   The application of 'presumptions', that is the practice of imputing income on the evidence of external signs of wealth (like ownership of second houses, luxury cars, motor-boats and employment of house servants).

b   The obligation to disclose the origin of funds used to buy expensive consumer goods and real estate (but not those used to buy government securities and shares traded in the Athens Stock Exchange).

c   The application of objective values of real estates, residences and commercial buildings, which are set by the Government and are used to assess tax liabilities on real estate transactions and rent income.

d   The reduction in income tax rates and the partial or total abolition of tax exemptions and deductions. These had been expected to generate favourable supply-side responses and to provide further incentives against tax fraud (thereby increasing tax revenue). However, because of the forecast shortfall in revenue, the income tax decrease was followed by an extraordinary tax levy on building ownership.

e   The abolition of the confidentiality of bank accounts for inspection by the tax authorities.

In addition to the above, other measures for increasing the tax base have consisted of the introduction of new criteria for assessing farmers' incomes (which are largely exempt from income tax), the introduction of a capital gains tax on real estate, the transfer of some items from the low VAT band to the standard rate of 18 per cent, the taxation of interest income by 15 per cent and the partial indexation of personal incomes (which increases tax revenues through fiscal drag). Incentives have also been introduced for greater tax honesty and speedier collection of tax arrears.

The final comment to make on tax revenue concerns the Greek Government's privatisation programme. The sale of 'problematic' firms and public utilities, such as the Athens buses and the telecommunications corporation, was announced in 1990. It had been expected (amongst other important virtues) to relieve the pressure on state finances, not only through the sale proceeds, but also by reducing subsidies to otherwise loss-making enterprises. Furthermore, such a move held out the prospect of future tax revenue from increased private activity. In reality, however, because the privatisation programme has moved very slowly, this source of revenue has not assumed its expected significance.

Expenditure

Economies on the expenditure side include the following measures:

a   The planned reduction in public sector employment by 10 per cent. The declared intention is to recruit one person for two officials retiring and to reduce the number of employees on fixed-term contracts.

b   The reduction in the size of the subsidisation of the social insurance organisations following the reform of the generous pension system. In particular, the age limit at which a pension can be drawn and the contribution rates have been raised. Nevertheless, savings will be realised only over the medium term because of the gradual phasing-in of these measures.

In addition, higher tax revenues and more spending economies are expected to be realised through a variety of institutional reforms aimed at increasing the efficiency of the public administration and motivating public sector employees. For example, the computerisation of tax files and information systems are viewed as essential for cross-checking tax liabilities and curbing tax evasion.

Financing the deficit

Finally, with regard to the budgetary deficit financing, the recent drive for financial liberalisation has comprised significant steps towards eliminating the distortions created by the practice of privileged credit to the State. These steps included the gradual reduction of the compulsory ratio of the increment of bank deposit into non-marketable government debt (from 40 per cent in 1990), culminating in its complete abolition in May 1993, and the conversion of banks' obligatory holdings of treasury bills into negotiable medium and long-term bonds. Such measures are in accordance with the EU Directives on capital market liberalisation and the prohibition of implicit subsidies and other privileges on public sector debt.[8]

Conclusion

The period of Greece's membership of the European Union has coincided with a marked deterioration of its fiscal position and weakening overall economic performance. Greece has experienced a surge in the size of the public sector, an acceleration of its financial deficit and a worsening of its position relative to the remainder of its European partners. There have been obvious mitigating circumstances in the emergence of these adverse developments. The fiscal imbalances began appearing before entry into the EU and, at the time of entry itself, the world economy was plunging into a severe recession with unfavourable implications for the public finances of every economy. However, given the freedom of national authorities in policy-making, there appears to be little doubt that the unsound policies followed since entry have contributed decisively to the worsening economic situation. Transfer payments have expanded in an almost unlimited fashion and government consumption has risen inexorably with income. However, tax revenue, with its heavy reliance on indirect taxes and the constraints implied by tax evasion, has responded sluggishly. As a result, the government sector has incurred massive budget deficits, mortgaging the future prospects of the economy. In addition, the quality of public sector services leaves much to be desired. Only the segments of government investment that take advantage of EU Structural Funds appear to be in reasonable shape. All in all, EU membership has so far made little contribution to bringing discipline to the fiscal position of Greece; if anything the situation seems to have worsened.

In all probability neither Greece nor the EU considered fiscal discipline as a primary objective of Greece's entry. However, the fact that the deterioration has occurred at a time when Greece has been a net beneficiary of the EU budget puts a question mark both on the efficiency of the transfer mechanism of the EU and the ability and commitment of Greece to adjust to the economic circumstances implied by EU membership. The former may partly be blamed on the budgetary policy-making process of the Union, however the latter is directly related to the unsuitability of the policies pursued by the Greek authorities themselves. It appears inescapable that inappropriate fiscal policies have both wasted national resources by delaying essential structural adjustments, and squandered the international goodwill that the country had once enjoyed.

Adjustments are long overdue as the current state of fiscal laxity cannot be maintained for prolonged periods. Perhaps the moves towards the establishment of EMU may act as the catalyst for necessary structural adjustment, and for managing public finances and the economy in general more successfully. Nevertheless, the fulfilment of the convergence conditions for full participation in the EMU requires contractionary policies with increasing tax burdens and decreasing public expenditure – policies which are likely to result in job losses and a drop in living standards. It is therefore important that due consideration is given to the relief of the adjustment pain, so that the EMU objective does not become unbearable. Such considerations make it rather difficult to predict when exactly Greece will be able to meet the fiscal policy criteria for convergence.

Notes

1 In a recent study of the pattern of public expenditures in Greece, Courakis, Moura-Roque and Tridimas (1993) identify permanent income, relative prices, stabilisation policy responses and socio-political factors as the main determinants of the various components of public expenditure.

2 *See* Price and Chouraqui (1983) for a detailed survey of this and related issues.

3 A detailed analysis of the financial arrangements that prevailed in Greece after World War II, their features, implications and deficiencies is found in Courakis (1981).

4 For an informative discussion of the issues involved in the sustainability of persistent government budget deficits and the constraints that they impose on national fiscal policy *see*, for example, De Grauwe (1992) and the bibliography cited therein.

5 *See* Georgakopoulos and Loizides (1989) for a recent description of the income tax system in Greece.

6 For an examination of the indirect taxes prevailing in Greece before the adoption of VAT *see*, for example, Georgakopoulos (1989).

7 Concern about efficiency in the public sector relates to the behaviour of bureaucrats (who may be pursuing their own sectoral interest), the absence of the profit motive in the operation of the departments of administration and the consequent imperfect financial accountability. For reviews of the issues encountered in public sector management, *see*, for example, Heald (1983) and Flynn (1990).

8 For details on the issue of seigniorage and government borrowing on preferential terms, see *European Economy* (1994).

References

Bank of Greece, Annual Report of the Governor. Various issues.

Courakis, A. S. (1981), 'Financial Structure and Policy in Greece: Retrospect and Prospect', *Greek Economic Review*, 3, 205–244.

Courakis, A. S., F. Moura-Roque and G. Tridimas (1993), 'Public expenditure growth in Greece and Portugal: Wagner's Law and Beyond', *Applied Economics*, 25, 125–134.

De Grauwe, P., (1992), 'The economics of monetary integration:', Oxford, Oxford University Press.

European Economy (1992), 'Stable money – sound finances', 53, 1–119.

European Economy, Reports and Studies, 'Applying market principles to government borrowing', 1994 1.

Flynn, N., (1990), 'Public Sector Management', London, Harvester Wheatsheaf.

Georgakopoulos, T. (1989), 'Indirect taxation: structure, consequences and Reform' in G. Provopoulos (ed.) 'Fiscal Policy Priorities' (in Greek), Institute for Economic and Industrial Research, Athens.

Georgakopoulos, T. and Loizides, I. (1989), 'Income tax' in G. Provopoulos (ed.) 'Fiscal Policy Priorities' (in Greek), Institute for Economic and Industrial Research, Athens.

Heald, D. (1983), 'Public Expenditure; Its Defence and Reform', Oxford, Basil Blackwell.

OECD Survey, *Greece*. Various issues.

Price, R. W. R. and Chouraqui, J-C. (1983), 'Public Sector Deficits: Problems and Implications', OECD, *Economic Outlook, Occasional Studies*, 13–44.

Provopoulos, G., (1989), 'Indirect taxation: structure, consequences and Reform' in G. Provopoulos (ed.) 'Fiscal Policy Priorities' (in Greek), Institute for Economic and Industrial Research, Athens.

GEORGE MICHALOPOULOS

5

Greece and EMU: inflation convergence and monetary policy

Introduction

This chapter analyses the problem of Greece meeting the monetary convergence requirements set by the EU programme for Economic and Monetary Union (EMU) in the Maastricht Treaty of December 1991. More specifically, it examines the reasons underlying the persistence of inflation in Greece and the limited effectiveness of recent disinflation policies. It argues that the lowering of inflation should be the priority of economic policy, since disinflation is a prerequisite for both nominal and real convergence. Finally, the chapter examines the possibilities of increasing the effectiveness of disinflation policies. It concludes that the Greek authorities should aim at improving the credibility of disinflation policies by demonstrating a clear commitment to low inflation in the design and implementation of fiscal and monetary policies. An important step in this direction can be made by institutionalising and implementing the political and economic independence of the Bank of Greece.

The beginning of the second stage of EMU in 1994 found the Greek economy struggling in a prolonged period of stagnation. In addition, the existence of serious macroeconomic imbalances does not allow the adoption of flexible economic policies designed to promote economic growth. The main sources of macroeconomic instability are first, the large public deficits and the accumulating public debt and second, the persistent inflation which remains at a level three times the EU average, despite the anti-inflation policies of the first half of the 1990s. High real interest rates necessary for disinflation have accelerated public debt accumulation and have exacerbated the fiscal imbalances. Moreover, high interest rates have reduced aggregate investment and total spending and therefore have hindered economic growth and the restructuring of the economy.

The combination of high inflation and considerable fiscal imbalances does not leave much room for manoeuvre in economic policy. Priority should be given to price stabilisation and reduction of fiscal imbalances for mainly two reasons: first, and more important, because sustainable economic growth can only be achieved in an environment of monetary and fiscal stability and secondly, Greece's commitment to economic convergence in the transitional phase towards EMU requires such action.

The Maastricht Treaty has committed the Greek Government to the adoption of macroeconomic policies capable of delivering economic convergence by 1997 or at least by 1999. Convergence is defined by a set of strict criteria related to inflation, excessive fiscal deficits and exchange rates. According to the Treaty, a country is qualified for entering the third stage of EMU if:

- its inflation and the nominal long-term interest rate do not exceed by more than 1.5 and 2 per cent respectively the average inflation and interest rate of the three best performing members (in terms of inflation);
- its public debt and deficit do not exceed (or alternatively they converge sufficiently towards) the reference value of 60 and 3 per cent of GDP respectively,
- and its exchange rate has remained within the normal EMS bands for at least two years before the examination.

As mentioned earlier, this chapter focuses on the problem of convergence of inflation in Greece. The next section draws the picture of the present state of macroeconomic convergence in Greece. Section 3 analyses the factors underlying the persistence of inflation, while Section 4 explains why disinflation should be the immediate priority of economic policy in Greece. Section 5 discusses issues related to the conduct of monetary policy after financial liberalisation and suggests that Central Bank independence can considerably increase the effectiveness of monetary policy. Finally, Section 6 summarises the main conclusions stemming from our analysis.

Economic convergence in Greece

Table 5.1 summarises the main macroeconomic indicators since 1980. The Greek economy underwent a period characterised by low growth and persistent macroeconomic imbalances. Real GDP grew by less than 1 per cent in total in the 1992–93 period, while only a moderate growth rate (0.7 per cent) was projected for 1994; industrial production has fallen by more than 7 per cent in total between 1989 and 1994; real fixed capital formation remained stagnant between 1991 and 1994, while unemployment reached the record level of 10 per cent in 1994. On the inflation front, the improvement is moderate when compared to targets set by previous stabilisation programmes. Inflation jumped to 20 per cent in 1990–91 from the level of 13.5 per cent in 1988–89 and since then the disinflation process was remarkably slow (*see* Fig. 5.1). Thus, for 1994, inflation averaged at the 11 per cent level, 4 points above the 1992 convergence programme target.

Table 5.1 Economic indicators, Greece (1980–94)

	GDP	IND	FCF	U	P	TB	CA
1980–84	1·1	0·9	−4·5	5·4	22·2	−13·4	−5·8
1985	3·1	3·4	5·2	7·8	19·3	−15·3	−9·8
1986	1·6	−0·2	−6·2	7·4	23·0	−11·2	−4·2
1987	−0·5	−1·7	−5·1	7·4	16·4	−11·9	−2·6
1988	4·5	5·7	8·9	7·6	13·5	−11·5	−1·8
1989	3·5	1·5	10·2	7·4	13·7	−13·7	−4·7
1990	−1·1	−1·9	9·3	7·0	20·4	−15·3	−5·3
1991	3·3	−1·5	−4·4	7·7	19·5	−14·4	−2·2
1992	0·9	−1·0	1·2	8·7	15·9	−15·0	−2·8
1993	−0·1	−3·1	−0·7	9·8	14·4	−14·7	−1·0
1994*	0·7	1·0	−0·2**	11·0	n.a.	−0·4	

*Forecasts, Economist Intelligence Unit, Report on Greece, 3rd quarter 1994.
** Projection, *OECD Economic Outlook*, no 55, June 1994.

Sources and Definitions. GDP: real GDP growth rate; IND: industrial production, annual percentage change; FCF: real total gross fixed capital formation, annual percentage change; U: unemployment rate; P: consumer prices inflation rate; TB, CA: trade balance and the current account as percentage of nominal GDP (– denotes deficit). GDP, FCF, U and CA from *OECD Economic Outlook*, no 55, June 1994. IND and P from *European Economy* no 55. TB is calculated using data from *IMF International Financial Statistics.*

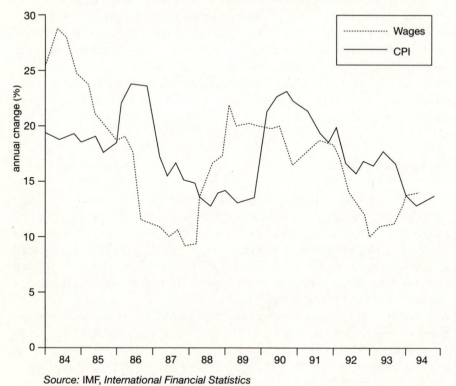

Source: IMF, *International Financial Statistics*

FIG 5.1 CPI **and wage inflation in Greece (1984–94)**

Disinflation achievements since 1990 cannot be regarded as satisfactory given the relative strictness of wage policies since 1991, the considerable slow-down of aggregate demand in the 1992–94 period, the strong anti-inflationary character of exchange rate policy and the favourable movement of the international prices, namely the falling commodity and oil prices and the depreciating US dollar.[1] Moreover, the achieved disinflation is not regarded as permanent since it was partially based on price controls (delays in adjusting the rates of public enterprises, administrative setting of price ceilings in goods and services, etc). Hence, inflationary pressures are still considerable (Bank of Greece 1994).

According to the Bank of Greece, the persistence of inflation in recent years is mainly because of the resistance of inflationary expectations caused by the lack of credibility of economic policy. The latter is explained by the continuous overshooting of fiscal deficit targeting in recent years (Bank of Greece 1994). The continuation of fiscal imbalances fosters expectations for future monetary instability and currency depreciation and considerably curtails the effectiveness of disinflation policies.

Table 5.2 shows the evolution of public finance in Greece since 1986. Although the fiscal deficit has declined since 1990, it is still the highest in the EU; the general government deficit in 1993 was at 12.8 per cent of GDP, down from 18.1 per cent for 1990, but well above the 8.6 per cent target of the con-vergence programme of 1992. This moderate reduction of the deficit was mainly due to a shortfall in revenues caused by failure to reduce tax evasion. The lowering of the tax thresholds and rates in 1991–92 did not produce the outcome that the authorities expected, i.e. a considerable increase in the declared income, while the attempted improvement in tax administration and data cross-checking was very slow. In addition, an increase in spending in 1993, together with the suspension of the privatisation programme by the new Government, further exacerbated the deficit problem.

Public debt has also increased considerably. Latest reports (Bank of Greece 1994) put total public debt (including public enterprises and defence related debt) at the level of 130 per cent of GDP.[2] While public debt as a percentage of GDP is lower compared to the debt of other countries, like Belgium and Italy for example, the dynamics of debt accumulation are more dramatic in the Greek case. Table 5.2 shows that the increase in the public debt is mainly due to an exploding debt interest payment account. Although the primary balance has converged to zero, debt interest payments as a percentage of GDP more than doubled since 1986 to exceed the 13 per cent level in 1993.[3]

The increased interest payment burden, especially after 1991, is partly because of the high real interest rates caused by a combination of tight money and high public sector borrowing requirements (PSBR). The evolution of the nominal and real interest rates in recent years is shown in the last two columns of Table 5.2: the nominal interest rates did not follow the recent fall of inflation since 1991, and thus they resulted in high real interest rates.

On the external sector, imbalances are less severe. The current account has improved considerably since the mid-1980s: the current account deficit was restricted to 1 per cent of GDP in 1993, the lowest level since the early 1970s (Table 5.1). However, this picture conceals an important structural problem in the trade balance. The trade deficit has significantly increased in recent years and reached the level of 15 per cent of GDP. This sizeable deficit was covered by increased invisible transfers, mainly from tourism and net EU transfers. The widening trade deficit reflects the structural problems of the Greek economy, namely low productivity and competitiveness of traditional sectors. Exports are concentrated in labour intensive, low technology industries and therefore face strong competition from low labour cost countries. An increasing cost of capital, caused by the crowding out effect of persistent public deficits, has also been a considerable barrier to investment, which is necessary to improve productivity and competitiveness. In addition, the exchange rate policy of recent years (the so-called 'hard drachma' policy), designed to moderate imported inflation rather than to promote competitiveness, accentuated further the trade deficit problem.

Table 5.2   Public finance in Greece (1986–93)

	GDT	GGB	GPB	GIP	R	RI
1986	58·6	−12·5	−6·7	5·8	19·0	−3·12
1987	64·5	−11·7	−4·5	7·2	19·5	3·8
1988	71·1	−13·7	−5·9	7·8	19·0	4·7
1989	76·0	−16·6	−8·3	8·3	20·0	4·8
1990	89·0	−18·1	−6·1	11·9	24·0	4·4
1991	96·8	−14·5	−2·8	11·6	22·5	4·1
1992	104·7	−11·0	−0·6	10·4	22·5	7·4
1993	107·0	−12·8	0·3	13·2	20·3	6·6

Sources and Definitions. GDT: gross public debt; GGB: general government balance; GPB: government primary balance; GIP: debt interest payments; all measured as percentages of GDP. R, RI: nominal and real interest rate on treasury bills (12 month rate, in December of each year). Data from *OECD Economic Outlook*, no 55, June 1994, except data for R which are taken from Bank of Greece, *Monthly Statistical Bulletin*.

To summarise, the Greek economy faces a combination of problems related to internal and external imbalances: large fiscal deficits and stagflation do not leave room for a flexible economic policy, while a widening trade deficit calls for structural adjustments in the Greek economy. Where does this situation leave Greece in terms of convergence? Table 5.3 summarises developments towards convergence in selected EU countries since 1990. It shows the evolution of various convergence indicators (inflation, public debt and deficit, unemployment and the current account) as well as a combined convergence indicator similar to that in Gros and Thygesen (1993). According to Table 5.3, Greece is the most divergent country, although some convergence has been achieved since 1990 mainly in the form of reduced inflation, lower current account deficit and lower public deficit.

Table 5.3 Convergence indicators for selected EU countries

	DF	DT	P	U	CA	IND
1990						
Greece	18·1	89	1·3	9	5·3	58·6
Italy	10·9	100	6·2	11·5	1·4	40
Spain	3·9	49	6·5	16·3	3·4	35
Belgium	5·9	134	3·6	8·7	−1·9	29·7
EC 12*	4·0	40	4·5	8·3	0·4	21·2
1993						
Greece	12·8	107	14	9·8	1	48·3
Italy	9·5	113	4·8	10·4	−1·3	34·7
Spain	7·2	59	5·1	22·7	0·8	41·7
Belgium	7·2	145	2·8	11·9	−4·9	31·5
EC 12	6·6	64	3·7	10·4	0·2	27·3
1994****						
Greece	13·8	110	10·8	10·7	1·3	47·6
Italy	9·7	118	3·9	11·7	−2	35·1
Spain	7·1	64	4·5	24·5	0·5	43
Belgium	5·8	146	2·4	12·8	−5·1	30·5
EC 12*	5·9	70	3·4	11·0	0·0	27·3

*Data from *European Economy* no 55. **Forecasts.
Definitions and Sources. DF: general government deficit as percentage of GDP; DT: general government debt as percentage of GDP; P: consumer inflation; UL unemployment rate; CA: current account deficit as percentage of GDP. IND: convergence indicator equal to the sum of the above indicators, with DT divided by 10. Data from *OECD Economic Outlook*, no 55, June 1994.

   · As explained above, the achieved convergence in the inflation and fiscal stance fell short of the expectations of the Greek policy-makers. However, the overall improvement since 1990 cannot be characterised as insignificant, given the fact that it occurred in a period of a considerable slow-down of economic activity in Europe. Economic recession during 1990–93 has made convergence efforts difficult for all member-states. The European economy as a whole actually moved away from the convergence criteria set in the Maastricht Treaty. As Table 5.3 shows, the convergence indicator for the EU deteriorated considerably in the 1990–93 period. Countries like Spain and Belgium worsened their position in terms of convergence, mainly because of a considerable increase of unemployment and the widening of their fiscal deficits.

    In the case of Greece, the most negative aspect of the convergence performance in this period is that fiscal convergence has been poor both in terms of significantly reducing the public deficit and stabilising the total debt. Given the economic situation in the mid-1990s, it is highly unlikely that Greece will be able to meet the fiscal requirements of the third stage of EMU by 1997 or 1999, unless a loose interpretation of the fiscal criteria prevails in the end.[4] While meeting the fiscal criteria of Maastricht – in the narrow definition – is out of the question, Greece could pursue policies that aim, first, at achieving sufficient inflation convergence and secondly, at reducing public deficits and stabilising debt.[5] Greece desperately needs to show significant achievements in these fields in the near future, in order to increase its bargaining power in the process of constructing the EMU. Both the projects of disinflation and fiscal consolidation are of equal importance for Greece in this respect. This study however focuses on the problem of disinflation (on fiscal consolidation, see Ch. 4).

The persistence of inflation

Since the early 1970s, inflation in Greece has been at the two-digit level. This persistence of inflation mainly reflects the inability, or the lack of willingness on behalf of the Greek authorities, to pursue a consistent anti-inflationary economic policy for a sufficient period of time. Political or electoral considerations, the adoption of inadequate, badly co-ordinated or even conflicting policies have limited the effectiveness of past stabilisation programmes. The disinflation policy has traditionally been based mainly on income and exchange rate policies and on direct market intervention while, in many instances, monetary and particularly fiscal policies have been counter-productive.[6]

During the 1980s, direct intervention in markets was widely employed to restrict consumer price index inflation. Measures included delays in the adjustment of administratively controlled prices of goods and services and limited increases in the rates of public enterprises. Such policies, however, were unable to produce a permanent reduction in inflation, since they resulted in a deterioration of deficits of public enterprises and subsequently created pressure for necessary price adjustments. The 1989–90 inflation episode was largely because of the necessary adjustment to prices that had been administratively restricted since the launch of the 1986–87 stabilisation programme (OECD 1991).

Government intervention in markets has been a significant factor generating widespread distortion and damaging competition with detrimental consequences in inflation performance. Severe labour market rigidities were also responsible for the limited effectiveness of past stabilisation efforts. During the 1980s, government intervention in wage bargaining and the operation of the automatic wage indexation scheme (ATA) significantly limited labour market flexibility and produced an inflationary bias in the wage setting process. The protection of real wages was sought by practices which triggered a wage-price spiral, and not by promoting rules that produce monetary stability.

This philosophy, however, has gradually changed after the dramatic demonstration of the fact that wage increases above productivity levels can only lead to inflation and economic stagnation and subsequently to declining real wages. Since 1990, institutional changes were introduced to increase labour market flexibility: the wage indexation scheme was abolished and wages are now agreed after free collective bargaining in which the government abstains from intervention. In addition, direct intervention on prices has been reduced under an ambitious programme of market liberalisation. These structural changes were aimed at improving competition and reducing market distortions caused by state intervention.

How do these structural improvements square with the poor disinflation achievements in the first half of the 1990s? The answer is that the structural changes are far from complete. Although government intervention in prices has been reduced, administratively-controlled prices still represent a significant portion of the consumer price index. In 1992 for example, the weight of price-controlled goods and services was about 15 per cent of the total goods and services included in the index (OECD 1992). Similarly, labour market flexibility, although improving, is not yet at the level sufficient to allow quick disinflation. Wage bargaining remains largely centralised at the national level. Even in cases where wages are negotiated at industry or firm level, the negotiations use wage settlements at the national level as a basis (OECD 1993). In addition, in many markets (especially of non-tradable goods and services) the level of competition remains low. As a result, prices in these markets increase much faster, keeping general inflation high. In 1993, for example, the prices of services rose by 15.2 per cent on average, while the prices of other goods included in the consumer price index increased by 10.2 per cent.[7]

The low level of competition in such markets is a result of the power wielded by organised trades and professional bodies and the dominant position of a few large firms. It also reflects the inability of Greek governments to monitor market structures and to design and implement an effective competition policy (OECD 1992). Moreover, the existence of a large and growing underground economy (*para economia*), impedes attempts to promote the restructuring of the economy and limits the effectiveness of disinflation policies to a considerable degree. The underground economy, which is relatively more extensive than in other EU States, is considerably less affected by restrictive economic policies compared to the open economy.

Turning to the role of other macroeconomic policies in the disinflation process, it can be noted that past disinflation attempts were largely based on restrictive income policies. Figure 6 shows the evolution of inflation in consumer prices and wages (hourly wages in manufacturing) since 1984. Clearly, periods of falling inflation (such as 1986–87 and 1991–93) followed periods of tight income policies characterised by a sharp decline in the rate of growth of nominal wages. Similarly, periods of rising inflation were preceded by large wage increases (especially in pre-election periods such as 1984–85 and 1988–89). Since 1991, wage inflation has been lower than consumer price index inflation, resulting in significant accumulated losses in real wages (*see* Table 5.5). Despite falling real wages, inflation remained sticky. Government policy in the 1990s has been the realisation of tight income policies. However, unless a significant reduction in inflation is achieved in the near future, the Government's ability to maintain low wage inflation could be undermined by increasing social discontent.

Exchange rate policy has also been used to support disinflation policies. It is not an exaggeration to say that exchange rate policy since the late 1980s primarily had an anti-inflationary character. In periods of high inflation a policy of limited depreciation was adopted, while in periods of falling inflation the policy was relaxed to accommodate some adjustment in the real exchange rate. Table 5.5 shows that, during the 1990–91 resurgence of inflation, effective depreciation of the drachma was kept at a low rate and thus imported inflation was below consumer price index inflation. The policy of limited depreciation and non-accommodation of the inflation differential *vis-à-vis* the rest of the world was pursued in subsequent years, although to a lesser extent. The result has been a real appreciation of the drachma and consequently a reduction in price competitiveness of the economy and widening of the trade deficit (*see* Table 5.1).

Table 5.4 Real effective exchange rate, various definitions

	1980–82	1983–85	1986–89	1990	1991	1992	1993
Real effective exchange rate calculated on the basis of:							
inflation rates[1]	111·5	103·4	97·0	105·3	106·6	109·9	109·0
unit labour costs in business sector[2]	99·2	101·1	85·0	94·1	90·2	90·4	89·5
unit labour costs in manufacturing a)[3]	86·8	98·4	91·5	106·5	100·5	98·3	102·1
b)[4]	89·9	101·6	86·3	96·9	90·6	87·5	90·7

Sources and Definitions.
[1] Relative to a group of industrialised countries, *IMF International Financial Statistics*, line rec.
[2] Relative to OECD, calculated using data from *OECD Economic Outlook*, no 56, July 1994.
[3] Relative to a group of industrialised countries, calculated using data from *IMF World Economic Outlook*, 1994.
[4] Relative to EC countries, calculated using data from *IMF World Economic Outlook*, 1994.

There is disagreement among academics and commentators on whether the exchange rate is overvalued or not. Some estimate that the drachma was, in 1993–4, overvalued by 20–30 per cent.[8] Others, including government officials, argue that the exchange rate accords to the economic fundamentals and therefore there is no need for faster depreciation.[9] Table 5.4 shows the evolution of the real effective exchange rate calculated on the basis of four different definitions of relative prices. All four indices show that the real exchange rate in the 1990s was higher relative to the late 1980s level. This supports the view that the exchange rate of the drachma is overvalued. However, the extent of overvaluation seems to be less than that suggested by other studies. Although it is difficult to determine the equilibrium level of the exchange rate, we could take as a reference value the level of the exchange rate that prevailed in the 1986–89 period, after the 1985 corrective drachma devaluation. Thus, the size of overvaluation appears to be between 5 and 12 per cent depending on the method of derivation of the real exchange rate.

Table 5.5 Prices and monetary indicators in Greece (1988–93)

	1988	1989	1990	1991	1992	1993
Prices (annual percentage change)						
Consumer Prices[1]	13·5	13·7	20·4	19·5	15·8	14·4
Prices of imports[2]	9·3	12·5	12·5	14·6	12·6	12·2
Wages[3]	21·4	20·5	20·8	14·5	12·6	12·2
Exchange rate[1]	−4·5	−7·1	−9·1	−11·2	−8·3	−9·2
Monetary indicators (annual percentage change)*						
M3[4]	22·5	24·2	15·3	12·3	14·4	15·2
	(n/a)	(18–20)	19–21)	(14–16)	(9–12)	(9–12)
Credit Expansion[4]	20·3	23·6	15·0	11·2	11·6	13·1
	(n/a)	(13–14)	(n/a)	(12–13)	(7–9)	(5–7)
of which:						
private sector	14·8	19·8	16·5	16·4	17·5	12·0
	(n/a)	(13–15)	(15–16)	(14)	(14–16)	(13–15)
public sector	27·2	21·6	14·3	8·5	8·5	13·5
	(n/a)	(13.3)	(n/a)	(12–13)	(n/a)	(n/a)
Real interest rate[5]	2·4	5·1	−0·5	3·2	7·7	10·5

*Target annual growth rates appear in the parentheses.

Sources and Definitions. 1 Bank of Greece, *Monthly Statistical Bulletin.* 2 Price of imported finished goods; Bank of Greece, *Monthly Statistical Bulletin.* 3 Wages refer to non-farm economy; Bank of Greece, *Annual report of the Governor,* 1994. 4 *EIU, Country Reports: Greece,* various issues. 5 Equals nominal short-term interest rates minus consumer inflation; nominal interest rates are the one-month interbank deposit rates from *European Economy,* 1993, no 55.

In short, exchange rate policy since the late 1980s has been used largely as counter-inflation policy, providing effective control on imported inflation and resulting in an exchange rate overvaluation. On the other hand, the contribution of monetary policy in the disinflation process was limited. Monetary targeting has been ineffective mainly because of the impact of uncontrolled PSBRs. Table 5.5 summarises monetary aggregates (targets and outcomes) since 1988. Overshooting of targets for domestic credit expansion in 1988–89 (caused mainly by an excess credit expansion to the public sector) contributed to the building up of inflationary pressures during 1990–91. On the contrary, the limited credit expansion to the public sector during 1991–92 improved the effectiveness of overall monetary control, thereby promoting disinflation. Since 1991, monetary policy has been restrictive. Real short term interest rates were increasing in the whole period (*see* Table 5.5), while they peaked as a result of the central bank's intervention in an attempt to stabilise the drachma during the recent exchange rate crises (September 1993 and May 1994). In spite of the tight monetary policy, credit expansion in 1993 was well above the target, mainly because of an unexpected rise in PSBR financed by external borrowing and an increasing instability in the relationship between means and targets of monetary policy caused by financial liberalisation.[10] Unsuccessful monetary targeting damages the credibility of anti-inflation policies, since it implies that authorities are not strongly committed to disinflation. A (tight) monetary policy which lacks credibility fails to restrict agents' inflation expectations and therefore produces only a limited reduction in inflation. Thus, the disinflation process becomes slow, generating considerable transitional costs (in terms of output and employment losses).

To summarise, the preceding discussion has shown that the main reasons for the resistance of inflation can be found in the structural weaknesses of the Greek economy, namely the low level of competition in markets and government intervention in them, the centralised wage bargaining process and in the inability of monetary and fiscal policies to increase policy credibility and effectively reduce inflation expectations.

The necessity of disinflation

There is a growing concern in Greece that giving such a high priority to disinflation and nominal convergence will lead to divergence in real terms from the rest of EU. However, there is no evidence that monetary discipline and low inflation deteriorate (real) economic performance (Alesina and Summers 1993; Grilli, Masciandaro and Tabellini, 1991). On the contrary, high inflation has adverse effects on economic performance, either by creating distortions in economic transactions or by generating price uncertainty, thereby decelerating capital accumulation.

Table 5.6 gives some evidence on the relationship between inflation and economic performance in Greece and the EU. During the 1960s and 1970s, average inflation in Greece was close to the EU average while the average growth of real GDP and real fixed capital formation were well above the EU levels. This picture was reversed during the 1980s: average inflation in Greece was 12 per cent above the EU average, while average annual GDP growth fell to 1.5 per cent, well below the EU level; during the same period the (average) growth rate of fixed capital formation was zero in Greece and 2.5 per cent in EU. This experience suggests that the high inflation of the 1980s exerted a negative impact on economic growth and thus hindered, rather than promoted, real convergence. Recent studies on the inflation experience in OECD countries suggest that a 10 per cent reduction of inflation (in the OECD area) would lead to up to one percentage point additional income or productivity growth.[11] In this case, the negative growth differential of Greece *vis-à-vis* the EU in the 1980s can be largely explained by the inflation differential of the same period.

Table 5.6 Inflation and economic growth in Greece and the EU

	1961–70		1971–80		1981–90	
	Greece	*EC*	*Greece*	*EC*	*Greece*	*EC*
Inflation	2·5	3·8	13·0	10·7	18·4	6·5
GDP growth	7·6	4·8	4·7	3·0	1·5	2·6
Fixed capital formation	9·3	6·0	2·8	1·6	0·0	2·5

Source: EC Commission, *European Economy, 1993, no 54.*

This evidence implies significant long term gains from reduced inflation. Given that inflation in Greece is close to 10 per cent level in 1995, there is no alternative to giving priority to disinflation. The potential long-term benefits from low inflation in terms of economic growth outweigh the transitional costs associated with the disinflation process. The short run costs of disinflation (in terms of output and employment losses) can be minimised by enhancing the effectiveness of anti-inflationary policies and therefore shortening the disinflation period. The key elements of a successful anti-inflationary policy in this domain are policy credibility and commitment to low inflation. The issue of improving the effectiveness of disinflation policies is discussed in the next section.

The second reason for prioritising disinflation is related to Greece's EMU membership. According to the Treaty, member-states should undergo a two-year period of exchange rate fixity before the entry to the final stage of EMU. Hence, if Greece is to enter the final stage of EMU by, say, 1999, she must be prepared to fix the exchange rate of the drachma (or to participate in the then prevailing ERM agreements) well before 1997. In this event, inflation and inflationary expectations in the financial and labour markets should converge to the EU level before 1997 to allow a smooth transition to fixed exchange rates. If inflation expectations do not sufficiently converge in advance, the entry into irrevocably fixed exchange rates would increase inflationary pressures; as a result, tighter disinflation policy would be necessary and the overall cost of disinflation would considerably increase (Smaghi and Del Giovane 1992).[12]

The third, but not the least important, reason for immediate disinflation stems from the fact that the success of the Greek Government's convergence programme critically depends on the success of the anti-inflationary policies.[13] The programme aims at reducing inflation to 3.9 per cent by 1997 from the 1994 level of 11 per cent (*see* Table 5.7). At the same time, average wage inflation is expected to fall to 4.6 per cent and short-term interest rates to 7.9 per cent from the 12.3 and 18.5 per cent respectively. The combination of falling real interest rates and increasing primary fiscal surpluses is expected to stabilise the debt to GDP ratio by 1996. However, the fall of interest rates, and hence the reduction of debt interest payments as a percentage of GDP, depends on the success of monetary policy in the battle against inflation. If inflationary pressures persist and/or the drachma undergoes depreciating tendencies, tight monetary policy and higher real interest rates will be inevitable. At that point, a tighter fiscal policy will be necessary to avoid the overshooting of the fiscal deficit targets set in the programme. Such an outcome will be costly both in social and political terms.

Table 5.7 Convergence programme (1994–99)*

	1994	1995	1996	1997	1998	1999
GDP growth	1·1	1·2	1·7	2·6	3·0	2·2
Inflation	10·8	7·9	6·1	3·9	3·5	3·3
Wages	12·3	8·4	6·5	4·6	4·3	4·2
Interest rates	18·5	14·1	10·6	7·9	6·8	6·2
Government borrowing (as % of GDP)[1]	13·2	10·7	7·6	4·2	2·4	0·9
Primary surplus[2]	1·3	3·5	4·9	5·1	5·4	6·1
Debt interest payments (as % of GDP)	13·9	13·6	11·9	9·3	7·8	7·0
Government Debt (as % of GDP)[1]	112·1	115·2	115·3	113·4	109·3	103·4

*   Revised programme of 1994.
[1]   General government, i.e. Central government plus entities but not public enterprises.
[2]   Includes share sales revenue.

Source: Economist Intelligence Unit, *Country Report: Greece*, 1994, 3rd quarter.

Recently, some authors have argued that rapid disinflation will involve considerable costs for countries with high public debt. In other words, rapid disinflation could deteriorate debt accumulation because it leads to loss of seigniorage revenue, i.e. the revenue from the implicit inflation tax on cash balances and bank reserves (Dornbusch 1988, Grilli 1989).[14] Consequently, it could be 'optimal' for such states to target relatively moderate inflation and not to converge to the EU average inflation. However, the importance of seigniorage as fiscal revenue has been significantly reduced since the mid-1980s. Recent experience shows that for many states with high or unstable public debt (like Belgium, Ireland, Italy, Austria and New Zealand) seigniorage revenue is quite small.[15] Liberalisation and increasing integration of financial markets leads to lower banks' reserve requirements and hence reduces seigniorage (Gros and Thygesen 1992). In the case of Greece, implementation of the Second Banking Directive is estimated to reduce seigniorage by an amount equal to future seigniorage losses from the convergence of inflation to EU levels (Alogoskoufis 1993).[16] Hence the argument of seigniorage losses associated with disinflation cannot provide a justification for maintaining a high level of inflation.

The preceding discussion leads to the conclusion that inflation reduction should be the priority of economic policy in Greece, since it is the main pre-requisite for convergence in both nominal and real terms. The pressure of con-vergence falls mainly on disinflation policies which have to provide low inflation as soon as possible, while keeping transitional costs to a minimum. However, disinflation policies, especially monetary policy, face the challenge of a dramatically changing operational environment. The source of change is pro-vided by the innovation and liberalisation of the financial markets.

Financial liberalisation and Central Bank independence

The Greek economy faces an increasing degree of integration of domestic finan-cial markets into European markets, as a result of the financial liberalisation stemming from the implementation of the Single European Act and the Maas-tricht Treaty. The liberalisation of capital movements and the elimination of direct controls on credit have generated unprecedented changes in the financial sector which has traditionally been highly regulated. These changes have deprived monetary policy of the use of instruments of direct control. Instead, the Bank of Greece has to rely increasingly on indirect instruments, like interest rate changes, for the implementation of monetary and exchange rate policies.

The process of financial liberalisation that started in the second half of the 1980s was intensified in the early 1990s and almost reached completion with the passage to the second stage of EMU at the beginning of 1994. Under the pressure of the Maastricht Treaty, 1993 and 1994 witnessed the gradual abolition of the monetary financing of fiscal deficits and the public sectors' privileged access to financial institutions: that is, the obligation of financial institutions to invest a portion of the increment of their deposits in government paper was abolished in 1993[17] and, since the beginning of 1994, banks are no longer obliged to finance public enterprises by a fixed portion of their deposits.

Moreover, the abolition of a number of other direct controls on credit was aimed at improving competition and efficiency in the financial sector. In this framework, the banks' obligation to earmark a proportion of their funds for loans to small and medium-sized enterprises in the manufacturing sector was abolished in 1993, the lifting of administrative controls on interest rates was completed with the abolition of the administrative setting of minimum interest rates on savings account deposits (March 1993) and finally restrictions on consumer credit were effectively reduced from the beginning of 1994.

In parallel to the abolition of credit controls, the Greek Government has gradually lifted barriers to free capital movements, in accordance with the letter of the Single European Act. In 1992, forward foreign exchange operations like futures and swaps, and capital movements for acquisition of real estate and long-term financial assets abroad were liberalised. Subsequently, restrictions on medium- and long-term capital movements with the rest of the EU were lifted (March 1993) and finally, in May 1994, short-term capital movements were freed.[18] With the removal of exchange rate controls, the Bank of Greece was deprived of the use of an exchange rate policy instrument that has traditionally been very effective, especially during periods of intense downward pressure on the exchange rate.[19]

Given the persistence of macroeconomic imbalances, the liberalisation of capital movements and the deregulation of financial markets make the conduct of monetary policy more demanding. The ability of the authorities to implement a successful monetary policy has been significantly affected by the new developments. On the one hand, the abolition of the monetary financing of deficits and the public sectors' privileged access to financial institutions enhanced the 'economic' independence of the Bank of Greece and hence its ability to use effectively policy instruments to control monetary expansion. On the other hand, however, financial liberalisation limits the Central Bank's ability to conduct an autonomous monetary policy, independently from external monetary and financial conditions. Interest rate policy can no longer be used exclusively in meeting domestic needs, but it has to consider interest rate changes abroad and (current or expected) movements of the exchange rate. In addition, monetary policy has to be adapted to systemic changes generated by the deregulation of financial markets. It has to rely solely on the use of indirect instruments, namely on interest rate policy, as a means of liquidity control. Similarly, exchange rate policy after the abolition of capital controls has to be based on interest rate changes or on foreign exchange market intervention. Finally, these financial developments change the relationship between the intermediate targets and the final objectives of monetary policy, questioning the appropriateness of the use of traditional monetary indicators (like various monetary aggregates) in the conduct of monetary policy. As a result, monetary targeting has become a more complicated exercise, since it has to consider a wider set of domestic and international monetary parameters.

The response of the Bank of Greece to this challenge was to create the institutional framework necessary for securing the effectiveness of indirect monetary policy instruments. In this respect, the Bank introduced some market-orientated instruments, i.e. a discount facility for commercial paper and a facility aimed at providing liquidity to banks using government paper as collateral.[20] In parallel, measures were taken that promote the development and the deepening of primary and secondary markets of government paper. The development of wide and deep markets of government paper is not only necessary because it allows effective intervention for the purpose of monetary control, but also because it facilitates the management of public debt.[21]

However, further changes in the institutional framework of monetary policy are necessary to promote its efficiency. In particular, the institutionalisation and implementation of the independence of the Bank of Greece could effectively enhance monetary policy credibility. A credible monetary policy is more effective in curbing inflation expectations and therefore it could accelerate the disinflation process and minimise the transitional costs involved. A central bank which is independent from governmental influence can enhance monetary policy credibility mainly because first, it could give a solution to the problem of 'time inconsistency' of monetary policy and second, it could isolate monetary policy from the influence of the 'political business cycle' or 'partisan' type policies.[22] Strong empirical evidence suggests that Central Bank independence is associated with better inflation performance and stronger monetary discipline. Moreover, it is argued that Central Bank independence has no negative effects on economic performance (in terms of output or employment).[23]

As mentioned earlier, the economic independence of the Bank of Greece has been increased with the abolition of monetary financing of fiscal deficits. However, economic independence is still restricted; the ability of the Bank to set its policy instruments is constrained by the fact that the interest rate on government paper is administratively set by the Government (although in consultation with the Bank).[24] In addition, the Statute of the Bank is inadequate in providing the appropriate legal framework for complete independence. In order to create such a framework, the Statute would need to be changed to provide institutional support for independence in the design and the implementation of monetary policy. According to the Maastricht Treaty, the Greek Government has to proceed to the institutionalisation of Central Bank independence before the end of the second stage of EMU. The necessary changes in the Statute would need to include first, a clear definition of the objectives of monetary policy in that monetary policy should aim at price stability primarily (though it can support general economic policy provided that this function does not endanger price stability); and second, a provision which guarantees that the Bank will be able to design and implement its policy without seeking or taking instructions from government or other political institutions.[25]

Although legislative changes are necessary to create the appropriate institutional framework for Central Bank independence, in practice consolidation of independence requires a consensus among economic policy-makers on the advantages of price stability and Central Bank independence. Moreover, the effectiveness of monetary policy in delivering low inflation depends largely on the extent to which other policies (fiscal or supply-side policies) are supportive. In Greece, the ability of the Central Bank to practise its independence could possibly be undermined by the existence of large fiscal imbalances and the need for successful debt management. Monetary policy independence can be effectively practised only when policy conflicts between monetary and fiscal authorities are avoided. This can be achieved if, first, all policy-makers agree on the necessity of price stability and, secondly, if the fiscal situation is improved sufficiently in the near future.

Concluding remarks

This paper has been concerned with the problem of inflation convergence in Greece. It has been argued that disinflation should be the priority of economic policy since it is the main prerequisite for both nominal and real convergence. In assessing the nature of the inflation problem, the preceding discussion has identified two main reasons for inflation stickiness: first, structural inefficiencies such as the low level of competition, and significant state intervention in markets and labour market rigidities; and secondly, the low level of credibility of monetary and fiscal policies. Therefore, a policy capable of delivering lasting disinflation should aim at increasing market efficiency and improving policy credibility. Priority should be given to improving market competition by deregulating markets and, in parallel, by enhancing the effectiveness of competition policy. In addition, a serious attempt to reduce the importance of the underground economy should be made.

The institutionalisation of the independence of the Bank of Greece would be a decisive step towards enhancing monetary policy credibility. This is necessary both for the moderation of agents' inflation expectations and for harmonisation with the Maastricht Treaty. It has been noted, however, that enhancing monetary policy credibility requires more than the legislative changes associated with Central Bank independence. The implementation of independence in practice requires the sharing of the price stability objective by all economic policy-making centres; not by the Central Bank alone. Fiscal policy, in particular, should be successful in achieving its targets in order to allow significant improvement in the credibility of the disinflation policy. Experience shows, as for example in the British disinflation of 1979–81, that the credibility of the disinflation policy cannot be restored unless both monetary and fiscal policies demonstrate a clear commitment to disinflation.[26]

Finally, the paper has argued that the emphasis that has been given to wage and exchange rate policies in the disinflation process was too strong. In particular, the policy of limited depreciation of the drachma has resulted in a loss of competitiveness and a deteriorating trade performance. The policy is based on the misleading assumptions that a faster rate of depreciation would necessarily result in a significant increase in inflation and that changes of nominal exchange rates do not affect trade and output. However, these assumptions are not justified by the evidence. The Italian and the British experience, since the abandonment of the ERM in September 1992, has demonstrated that the depre-

ciation of the exchange rate (even as large as in the Italian case) would not necessarily lead to a worsening of inflation performance.[27] The level of inflation is
determined by a wide set of current and expected factors at home or abroad.
Greek authorities could have exploited the opportunity given by the fall in
international prices (e.g. the fall in the price of oil and the weakening dollar),
during the first half of the 1990s and the low level of domestic demand to lower
the exchange rate of the drachma to a level compatible to economic fundamentals. The inflationary consequences of such policy would have been minimal.
Instead, they preferred to maintain the hard drachma policy.

Such a policy results in maintaining market expectations of a drachma
depreciation in the future and thus renders the reduction of inflation expectations a more difficult exercise. It also requires higher interest rates and thus
exacerbates the debt problem and depresses economic activity. In particular,
during periods characterised by strong depreciating tendencies in the foreign
exchange market, much higher interest rates are required to support an overvalued currency. The recent exchange rate crisis (May 1994), was a powerful
demonstration of this fact. It is therefore necessary to correct the exchange rate
before similar market pressures occur in the future, especially when Greece is
moving towards larger exchange rate fixity for the purpose of joining the EMS.
But more importantly, correction of the hard drachma policy is necessary
because of its negative effects on trade and economic activity. Contrary to what
is often believed, keeping the nominal exchange at a high level can create real
currency overvaluation and thus change the relative price of imports and
exports. According to the 'hysteresis' hypothesis, long-lived currency overvaluation can have persistent or permanent effects on trade because it changes the
industrial landscape by forcing domestic exporting firms to leave particular
markets and helping others (mainly foreign firms) to establish themselves.[28] In
this case, an even greater and longer lasting exchange rate undervaluation
might be necessary to reverse these effects.

To summarise, the emphasis of disinflation policy should be shifted
towards policies that aim at eliminating the factors underlying inflation resistance. Such policies should include an effective competition policy to improve
market structure and successful implementation of (tight) fiscal and monetary
regimes to create market confidence in the commitment to low inflation. The
credibility of disinflation policy can be enhanced further with the institutionalisation of Central Bank independence. The latter is of major importance for the
conduct of a successful monetary policy, given today's challenge of financial
market integration, in the progress towards EMU.

The employment of an effective disinflation policy is of crucial importance,
since it is necessary for Greece to win the battle against inflation as soon as possible. Undoubtedly, many of the weaknesses of the Greek economy have their
origins in the high inflation levels of the last twenty years. Therefore, achieving
sustainable economic growth requires the breaking of the vicious circle of monetary instability and economic stagnation. Furthermore, achieving low infla-

tion in the near future is very important for the success of the project of eco-nomic convergence that Greece has undertaken. A substantial reduction in inflation would increase the credibility of the economic convergence pro-gramme, resulting in a favourable change of economic agents's expectations and hence into a considerable improvement of the economic climate. In paral-lel, it would improve Greece's credibility in the EU, increasing its bargaining power in the future EMU negotiations. Given that a multiple-speed transition to the third stage of EMU is a probable option, improved macroeconomic perfor-mance would (at least) enable Greece to actively participate in the design of such a transition.

Notes

1 The price of oil and the average price of primary commodities fell by 25 and 10 per cent respectively in the period 1990–93, while the effective exchange rate of the dollar has fallen significantly since 1991.

2 GDP is measured according to the new system, in line with the European System of Accounts (ESA).

3 Debt interest payments currently amount at 47 per cent of total government revenue (*see* Bank of Greece, 1994).

4 According to the Treaty on EMU (Article 104c), a country with a public deficit to GDP ratio higher than the reference value (3 per cent) can be qualified for the final stage of EMU if the ratio '... has declined substantially and continuously and reached a level that comes close to the reference value.' Similarly a country with a debt to GDP ratio higher than the reference value (60 per cent) can be qualified if the ratio is '... sufficiently diminishing and approaching the reference value at a satisfactory pace.'

5 According to the 1994 convergence programme, the public debt is expected to be sta-bilised in 1996–97 at a level around 115 per cent of GDP and to fall at the 103 per cent level by 1999 (*see* Table 5.7).

6 An example of such a situation was the 1985–87 stabilisation programme, discussed in detail in Papademos, 1990.

7 *See* Bank of Greece, *Annual Report 1994*, p. 24.

8 *See* for example, *EIU Country Report 1994* and Alogoskoufis, 1993.

9 For example *see* Eudoridis, 1994.

10 *See* Bank of Greece *Annual Report 1994*, p.36.

11 For a summary of empirical evidence on the costs of inflation, *see OECD Economic Out-look* (June 1994), 55, 31–36.

12 Papademos (1993:148) suggests that the ERM participation for Greece, without prior adjustment of fiscal policy and labour market expectations to the ERM constraint, is likely to have pronounced negative effects on growth and external stability.

13 For a more detailed discussion on the 1994 convergence programme *see* Negrepondi and Delivani, 1994.

14 Dornbusch (1988) estimates seigniorage revenues in Greece at 2–3 per cent of GDP.

15 For empirical evidence on the relationship between the State of Public financing and the importance of seigniorage as a source of revenue, *see* Grilli, Masciandaro and Tabellini (1991).

16 Alogoskoufis (1993) argues that the seigniorage revenue in Greece will fall by 1 per cent of GDP because of the implementation of Second Banking Directive and by 1 per cent of

GDP because of inflation reduction due to participation in EMS or EMU.

17 The reduction of the banks' obligatory investment ratio (as per cent of the increment on deposits) on government paper was gradual; the ratio was reduced from 40 per cent in 1990 to 1 per cent in 1992 and to zero since May 1993. (*See* Bank of Greece, *Annual Report 1993*, p. 41).

18 For a detailed account of the process of financial liberalisation in Greece *see* Bank of Greece, *Annual Report of the Governor 1993*, and *1994*.

19 On the effectiveness of capital controls as an exchange rate policy instrument in Greece, *see* Cristodoulakis and Karamouzis, (1993).

20 *See* Bank of Greece, *Annual Report of the Governor 1993*, and OECD, *Economic Surveys: Greece 1993*.

21 *See* Bank of Greece, *Annual Report of the Governor, 1994*.

22 For a survey on policy credibility and Central Bank independence *see* Alesina (1988), and Gastello-Branco (1991).

23 For empirical evidence on this issue *see* Alesina (1989), Alesina and Summers (1993), Grilli (1991), and Wood, Mills and Capie (1993).

24 *See* Committee of Governors of the Central Banks of EU, *Annual Report 1993*, p. 76.

25 The Bank of Greece has already proposed to the Government legislative changes concerning its statutory objectives, organisational structure, and monetary functions, which aim at making its Statute compatible with Maastricht Treaty. *See* Bank of Greece, *Annual Report of the Governor 1994*.

26 During this period of disinflation in Britain initial monetary tightness was ineffective in reducing inflation expectations. Market confidence in the durability of disinflation policies was finally created by switching policy emphasis towards fiscal, rather than monetary, tightness (Minford 1990).

27 For example, the effective nominal exchange rate of the Italian lira depreciated almost by 25 per cent in the period between the third quarter of 1992 and the third quarter of 1994; during the same period consumer inflation in Italy fell from 5.1 to 3.7 per cent. The limited inflationary effect of the devaluation of the lira was due to the fact that devaluation occurred in a period characterised by falling commodity prices, low growth of domestic demand and intense competition among domestic (Italian) and foreign producers resulting in a considerable squeeze of profit margins.

28 On exchange rate overvaluation and its 'hysteresis' effects on trade, see Baldwin and Krugman (1986), and Krugman and Baldwin (1987).

References

Alesina, A. (1988), 'Macroeconomics and Politics' in S. Fischer, (ed.), *NBER Macroeconomics Annual*, Cambridge, Massachusetts, MIT Press.

—— (1989), 'Politics and Business Cycles in Industrial Democracies', *Economic Policy*, 8.

—— and L. H. Summers (1993), Central Bank Independence and Macroeconomic Performance: Some Comparative Evidence, *Journal of Money, Credit and Banking*, 25:2.

Alogoskoufis, G. S. (1993), 'Greece and European Monetary Unification', in H. J. Psomiades, and S. B. Thomadakis (eds.), *Greece, the New Europe, and the Changing International Order*, New York, Pella.

Baldwin, R. E. and P. R. Krugman (1986), 'Persistent Trade Effects of Large Exchange Rate Shocks', *National Bureau of Economic Research Working Paper*, 2017.

Bank of Greece (1993, 1994), *Annual Report of the Governor*, Athens.

Bini Smaghi, L. and P. Del Giovane (1992), 'Convergence of Inflation, Prerequisite for EMU', *Banca d'Italia, Temi di Disussione*, 186.

Christodoulakis, N. and N. Karamouzis (1993), 'Financial Openness and the Effectiveness of Capital Controls in Greece', *Centre for Economic Policy Research, Discussion Paper*, 804.

Dornbusch, R. (1988), 'The EMS, the Dollar and the Yen', in F. Giavazzi, S. Micossi, and M. H. Miller (eds.), *The European Monetary System*, Cambridge, Cambridge University Press.

Economist Intelligence Unit. *Country Reports: Greece*, various issues.

Evdoridis, G. I. (1994), 'The Drachma is not Overvalued', *O Economicos*, 11 August 1994, 27–29.

Grilli, V. (1989), 'Seigniorage in Europe', in M. De Cecco, and A. Giovannini, *A European Central Bank?*, Cambridge, Cambridge University Press.

——, D. Masciandaro, and G. Tabellini (1991), Institutions and Policies, *Economic Policy*, October 1991, 342–391.

Gros, D. and N. Thygesen, (1992), *European Monetary Integration*, London, Longman.

IMF (1994), *World Economic Outlook*, May 1994.

Krugman, P. R. and R. E. Baldwin (1987), 'The Persistence of the US Trade Deficit', *Brookings Papers on Economic Activity*, 1, 1–55.

Minford, P. (1990), 'Inflation and Monetary Policy', *Oxford Review of Economic Policy*, 6:4.

Negreponti-Delivani, M. (1994), 'Is convergence programme feasible?', *0 Economicos*, 15 September 1994, 27–29.

OECD (1991, 1992, 1993) *Countries Surveys: Greece*, various issues.

OECD (1994), *OECD Economic Outlook*, July 1994, Paris.

Papademos, L. (1990), 'Greece and the EMS: Issues, Prospects and a Framework for Analysis', in De Grauwe, P. and L. Papademos, *The European Monetary System in the 1990s*, New York, Longman.

—— (1992), 'Monetary Policy and Financial Markets in the 1990s', in T. S. Skouras, (ed.), *The Greek Economy: Economic Policy for the 1990s, Issues in Contemporary Economics* 5, London, Macmillan Press.

—— (1993), 'European Monetary Union and Greek Economic Policy', in H. J. Psomiades, and S. B. Thomadakis, (eds.), *Greece, the New Europe, and the Changing International Order*, New York, Pella.

Swinburne, M. and M. Gastello-Branco (1991), Central Bank Independence: Issues and Experiences, *IMF Working Paper*, 58.

Wood, G. E., T. Mills and F. H. Capie, (1993), 'Central Bank Independence. What Is It? and What Will It Do for Us?', Institute for Economic Affairs, *Current Controversies*, 4.

PART III

Greece and the minorities issue

Christos L. Rozakis

6

The international protection of minorities in Greece

Introduction

The focus of this chapter is the international protection of minorities in Greece, namely the protection of minorities as provided for by international law, either in the form of bilateral or multilateral agreements to which Greece is a party; or in the form of general customary rules of international law which apply in Greece, in accordance with the relevant requirements of its constitution.[1] The issues of municipal law protection are covered by Dr Stephanos Stavros in the following chapter and are not referred to here.

The recipients of international protection

Before embarking on the main analysis, one must be clear about the preliminary question of the nature of the recipients of international protection; in other words, the actual subjects of minority rights and obligations emanating directly from international law. It seems that, although the term 'minority' has so far escaped from a generally acceptable and righteous legal definition, and indeed remains one of the main obstacles to a successful conclusion of various agreements, there are, nevertheless, some constitutive elements of a definition which are present in all efforts made by States or other international entities to determine the exact purview of the term. The definition of a 'minority' given by the Capotorti Study,[2] pursuant to the UN Sub-Commission of Minorities Resolution,[3] seems to contain a compromise of the various positions of the members of the international community[4] and to adopt those basic elements on which agreement on the part of States now appears to exist:

[A minority is a] group numerically inferior to the rest of the population of a State, in a non-dominant position, whose members – being nationals of the State – possess ethnic, religious or linguistic characteristics differing from the rest of the population and show, if only implicitly, a sense of solidarity, directed towards preserving their culture, traditions, religion or language.

This definition, which closely resembles the latest form of the definition given by the Venice Commission for Democracy through Law (under the aegis of the Council of Europe),[5] combines the two fundamental qualifications of a minority deserving protection under international law. It encompasses the objective facts of the difference of ethnic origin, religion, from the rest of the population and the inferiority of the group, both from a numerical and a non-dominant position point of view;[6] and the subjective factor, namely the existence of the will of the group to preserve its separate identity, or, at least, some elements of its identity, intact. It should be assumed that the word 'group' does not have solely a quantitative connotation, but also a qualitative one. A minority is a collectivity which preserves a degree of internal cohesion and an evident distinctiveness in its way of life which differs from that of the majority in some of its aspects. The most obvious expression of this distinctiveness is the existence of common grounds of assembly such as places of worship, schools, or centres of cultural events. If, moreover, a group lives in a specific part, or parts, of a state – practising there its own culture, language, religion – then the element of cohesion is clearly shown and cannot easily be disputed. It should not be forgotten, after all, that one of the major driving forces – apart from purely humanitarian considerations and pressures exerted by interested states – which have led the international community to consider the internationalisation of the protection of minorities in the post-Cold War era, is precisely the territorial concentration of a number of minorities and the threat that this may represent to the territorial integrity of certain established states.

There are some basic observations which must be made to complement the otherwise generally acceptable definition given by Capotorti. The first is that the definition does not refer to the notion of 'national' minorities, but only to that of 'ethnic' minorities. This is probably the result of the compromise which had been reached at the time of the drafting of the study and which suggested that reference to the notion of 'national' minority should be avoided. Although the difference of national from ethnic is clearly a nominal one (both refer to the same elements of a common historical heritage, tradition and culture, which are holistic elements, with the sole difference that the term 'national' insinuates a kinship of a minority with a third state, already existing as an aspiration of the minority),[7] a number of states seemed totally disinclined to accept any reference to the term 'national'. Yet it seems that this obstacle has recently been overcome, given that the 1993 UN Declaration on the Rights of Persons Belonging to National or Ethnic, Religious and Linguistic Minorities,[8] which represents a text of 'soft law' binding upon the international community of states as a whole, employs the term 'national', using it as an alternative to the term 'ethnic'. Thus, it appears that, under general international law, national minorities are also protected, although, of course, the acceptance of their separate protection is not meant at all to encourage any claims for external self-determination, namely claims to secede from the state within which they live and to establish their own state or unite with a third state. In this respect international law remains unchanged, attaching an obvious priority to the principle of territorial integrity of states (and its corollary principle of the prohibition of changes of frontiers)[9] which is safeguarded through a number of constitutive texts of the international community.[10]

The second observation concerns the limitation of recipients of general international protection to those groups which have long historical ties with the country in which they live and in which they have, therefore, traditionally pursued their distinctive way of life. It seems that there is a wide consent among members of the international community to the effect that the notion of minority is limited to these categories of groups, and should not contain groups of persons who have recently settled in the territory of a State through gradual accumulation or even massive transfer of populations. The discussion on the *ratione personae* application of the international protection of minorities in the various instances of the international organisation, mainly through the debate on the exact purview of application of Article 27 of the UN Covenant on Civil and Political Rights,[11] has shown that states clearly prefer to exclude from the protection these latter groups of persons. This is certainly due to considerations regarding the heavy immigration of recent years and the massive transfer of populations which has occurred as a result of the events in Eastern and Central Europe. Still, the relevant debate is open and, in the absence of a comprehensive definition of the notion of minorities in international law, the eventuality of an inclusion of certain categories of 'newcomers' cannot be excluded.

The nature of minorities in Greece

One of the impressive characteristics of the Greek human landscape is the homogeneity of its population: more than 90 per cent of Greek citizens consider themselves ethnically Greek (Hellenes) and have a common religion, which is that of the Greek Orthodox Church.[12] This homogeneity is the result of historical events which allowed the concentration of a great number of ethnic Greeks into the territory of the modern state as well as the massive exodus of foreign elements; but it is also the fruit of a policy which aimed, as much as possible, at the integration of all aliens (usually peoples sharing common characteristics with neighbouring countries) into the mainstream of those speaking the Greek language and professing the 'official' religion of the Christian Orthodoxy.[13]

Despite the overwhelming predominance of Orthodox Greeks, minorities do exist in Greece – of the kind recognized by international law – and even provoke a number of problems which create tension in their relations with the majority. The category of minorities existing in Greece today are easily discernible, mainly through their collective activities, their distinctive presence in some parts of the country, or even the presentation of their claims before public and other competent fora. What is not easily discernible is the exact number of members belonging to each of them. This phenomenon is due to the fact that, unlike the 1951 census, more recent censuses have not addressed issues of national/ethnic origin, language and religion.[14] Hence no official data have been presented concerning these categories by the usually most reliable source, the National Service of Statistics. It is known that the Greek population numbers today more than ten million Greek citizens, but we are left uninformed about their origin, language and religion.

It may be assumed that this attitude of not including questions in recent censuses about even the linguistic and religious preferences of the population is consistent with a more general policy to discourage discussion on issues concerning ethnic, linguistic, or religious differences in Greek society. There are historical, but also current political, reasons for such a policy. On the one hand, as one of the main ideological tools for its preservation and as a response to external threats, a constant effort is being made by the modern Greek State to integrate the totality of the population living in its territory into the main linguistic and religious body.[15] On the other, one must consider the composition of Greek society: its predominantly conservative social and professional orientations and its minimal exposure (at least for a great number of its members) to alien cultures and different ways of life; a fact which is due to the limited mobility of a large part of the society and to the geographical isolation of the country.[16] There is, finally, the fact that some of the minorities – among them the most solid one, the Muslim minority – have been identified with territorial claims coming from neighbouring countries with whom Greece's political relations are tense.[17]

In any event, the basis for a numerical assessment of the existing minorities is the 1951 official census. One may consider that the data contained therein reflect, *mutatis mutandis*, the situation which prevails today, given that since 1951 no major, dramatic events have taken place in Greece so as to transform the structures of society and its actual composition. Moreover, various statistical surveys and analytical reports which have been made by other mechanisms – such as the European Union or the US Department of State – complement and, to a certain extent, update the picture given by the 1951 census results.[18]

The census of 1951, which contained questions on the religious and the linguistic customs or preferences of the population living within Greek territory, showed that at the time there were 112,665 Muslims, 24,965 Catholics, 4,954 Protestants, 6,325 Jews and a small number of other Christian or Catholic minorities. Insofar as language was concerned, there were 92,443 Turcophones, 41,017 Slavophones, 39,885 Vlachs, 22,736 Albanians, 18,671 Pomaks, 7,429 Gypsies, and a small number of other minorities speaking a variety of languages.[19] More recent surveys on minorities in Greece, conducted by the European Community, the US Department of State (in its regular yearly examination of the situation of human rights in the world) and by various non-governmental international organisations,[20] have added to the categories identified in 1951 the Gagauz (Turkish-speaking Christians),[21] the Slavo-Macedonians[22] (as an ethnic group, and not simply as a linguistic group speaking a Slavic language),[23] the old Calendarists and the Jehovah's Witnesses. The findings of these later surveys indicate that minority groups not referred to in the official census of 1951 actually consist of fairly substantial numbers of members (several thousands). Nevertheless, in the absence of official mechanisms and modes of calculation, the exact numerical strength of each of them cannot be determined.[24]

The enumeration of the minorities existing today in Greece shows clearly that the situation does not differ radically from those existing in the majority of Western (mainly) European States. One may discern two basic categories of minorities: religious and linguistic. In the case of the former, these comprise Catholics, Protestants, Old Calendarists (who are Orthodox Christians who have not recognized a number of reforms adopted by the Orthodox Church in the 20th century) and Jehovah's Witnesses. An obvious linguistic minority are the Albanians, who are Orthodox Greeks, but speak a language bearing similarities with the Albanian language. They are well-integrated within the Greek-speaking population, they live dispersed in various parts of the country (mainly in or around Athens) and use their language occasionally in conversation amongst themselves.[25] The same may be said of the Vlachs, who speak a Romanian dialect and who are similarly integrated into the main body of the population without raising any claims.[26] Also the Gypsies, with their unique way of life, may be considered as a linguistic minority, although, it must be stressed, the peculiarity of their life-style makes them a special type of minority, needing a particular kind of protection.

The situation is not so clear with regard to some other minorities: the most important of which is the Muslim minority, which happens to be also the most numerous (approximately 120,000 members). The Muslim minority is composed of three different groups: the Turcophones, the Pomaks and the Gypsies. Each group has a different origin and a different cultural background; yet, none of them may reasonably be considered as being solely a linguistic or religious minority, given that each one also has some other peculiarities of its own.

The group of the Muslim Turcophones is a coherent collectivity of a population living in Thrace in organised communities, in villages or in the neighbourhoods of a number of towns. They first inhabited the area during the Ottoman occupation. They remained in Greece after the exchange of populations which took place in the aftermath of the Greco–Turkish war, through an agreement excluding them from the transfer.[27] It is a minority which is actually protected by an international agreement (as a 'Muslim' minority),[28] speaking and learning its own language, practising its own religion, having a separate religious administration and pursuing a cultural life different from that of the rest of the population[29]. It also maintains a number of substantial connections with the neighbouring Turkish State (for example, in matters of higher education, the Muslim Turcophones prefer to go to Turkey to study instead of staying in Greece to study in the nearby universities of Thrace or Salonica). These connections have recently been reinvigorated, mainly as a result of a number of mistakes committed by the Greek State (and the Christian Orthodox society, more generally) and because of an interest shown by Turkey to infiltrate this minority and to attempt to influence its fate.[30] These complex elements of origin, religion and linguistic options, as well as of cultural and political ties, make this minority an ethnic minority, and not solely a religious or linguistic one.[31]

The situation with the Pomaks and the Gypsies, who are the other Muslim groups also protected by the Treaty of Lausanne,[32] is somewhat confused. Neither of them can really be considered only as a religious minority. The Gypsies have a way of life and culture peculiar to themselves; while the Pomaks live mainly in the mountains of Thrace, are Muslim in religion, but have a Slavic origin and language. They, too, have their own distinct way of life. However, it is difficult for one to assert that they are conscious of having a different identity and that they claim separate protection. On the contrary, one might say that, due to their common religion with the Turcophones and to a policy of the implementation of the Treaty of Lausanne followed by the Greek authorities, the Pomaks tend to be identified with the Muslim Turcophones.[33] It seems, therefore, that, for the time being at least, this trend determines the nature of these groups, and places them in the category of religious minorities.

Another complex minority in the country are the Slavophones. This is a minority which, according to the Department of State survey, accounts 'from well under 10,000 to 50,000' members.[34] The difference between these two figures in the survey may be attributed to the lax character of the ties among the members of this minority. In sharp contrast with the homogeneous Turcophones of Thrace, the Slavophones, who mainly live in various villages and towns of Western Macedonia, are ideologically and culturally dispersed. The main element that unites them today is the language (a Bulgarian dialect) that is spoken by the members of this minority, together with Greek, amongst themselves. The Slavophones share a common ethnic origin with neighbouring populations beyond the northern boundaries of Greece, but they do not maintain – with few exceptions – any strong ties with them. It seems that a great number of Slavophones have gradually been integrated, culturally and otherwise, into the national mainstream; but there are certain islands of resistance to this integration in the form of militant groups to be found in mixed towns or remote villages professing the ethnic character of the minority. This phenomenon has been particularly reinforced after the collapse of Yugoslavia and the emergence of a new State, the Former Yugoslav Republic of Macedonia. A number of militants of the minority have fomented the debate on their distinct Macedonian origin, and claim a minority status for the Macedonian ethnic group. These claims seem to be supported by the Government of FYROM through statements by high ranking personalities of the new entity.[35]

This initial summary of the minorities existing today in Greece has revealed two main categories: first, those bearing one major distinctive feature (religion, language, cultural ties) and second, those which are more complex in character, namely presenting more than one major difference with regard to the rest of the population (the majority). In the first category we may clearly include Catholics, Protestants, Jehovah's Witnesses (all religious minorities) and the Arvanites (a linguistic minority). In the second category we may include all those who are traditionally linked with ethnic origins other than the predominant Hellenic origin: Muslim Turcophones, Pomaks, Gypsies, Slavophones and Jews.[36] Because of the latter group's distinct ethnic origin, some of them have retained elements of difference from the rest of society which are more complex than simple religious or linguistic differences. Yet, for reasons outside the confines of this study, the majority of them have not retained their ethnic characteristics as such, but have projected them into some of the constitutive elements of their distinctiveness, such as religious, linguistic, or, to a certain extent, cultural differences. Furthermore, they are adapted to the way of life of the majority, being dispersed in low numerical concentrations in various towns and villages. In the case of the Muslim Turcophones, life is more homogeneously concentrated and sedentary; and the degree of relationships with kin outside Greek borders is considerable. In this case, one may clearly speak of an ethnic minority, which is willing (and able) to retain a number of composite characteristics which go clearly beyond religious and linguistic differences of the majority.

The international protection of minorities in Greece

The opening section of this chapter hinted that the minorities existing in Greece are subject to a number of rights and obligations which emanate directly from international law. The rules of positive international law, binding upon Greece, have as their source either international conventions, to which Greece is a party, or customary rules, namely rules which have, through the lapse of time and the establishment of a general *opinio juris*, become customs of the international community. In so far as law emanating from conventions is concerned, we must further distinguish between particular conventions dealing specifically with a concrete case of minority, and conventions which, directly or indirectly, protect minorities on the basis of general rules: namely rules of a general application at a regional or universal level. In the first category, there is only one convention still in force, binding upon Greece, which refers to the Muslim minority; while in the second category, there are some conventional arrangements which are intended to protect minorities, attributing to them a number of rights and imposing sometimes certain obligations.

The particular regime of protection of minorities in Greece

The combination of the nature of the modern Greek State, born out of the gradual secession from the multi-ethnic entity that was the Ottoman Empire – with the time of its gradual emergence, namely in the period of nationalism in Europe (which itself was coupled with the philosophy of the protection of minorities enclaved in the new international entities), soon led to the creation of particular international regimes for the protection of minorities within Greek borders. The London Protocol of 1830 and the Convention of Constantinople of 1881 expressed the will of the Great Powers to protect the Muslim minority living in the newly emerging independent State.[37] However, comprehensive provisions on protection came only after the end of the First World War with the signing of the Treaty of Sèvres (1920) and the Treaty of Lausanne (1923).[38]

The Treaty of Sèvres was signed on the 10th of August 1920 between Greece, the British Empire, Italy, Japan and France.[39] Because of the tense and unstable relations in the region that followed the end of the war, the treaty was ratified only in 1924 and came into force, for Greece, concurrently with the Treaty of Lausanne.[40] It produced legal results throughout the inter-war period, but was abolished after the end of the Second World War at the time when treaties concluded within the system of the League of Nations were being re-examined. A memorandum from the Secretary-General of the United Nations (the successor organisation to the League of Nations) seemed to imply that Greece, which was a victorious power of the Second World War, could not be bound by a treaty to which defeated powers were also party while neighbouring states in which Greek minorities were living, did not feel themselves to be bound by similar principles of protection. The Secretary-General considered that, in this case, a drastic change of circumstances had occurred:

> Si dans tel ou tel pays voisin auquel se rattachent par leur caractère les minorités nationales en Grèce, le régime de protection des minorités n'est plus considéré comme en vigueur, ce fait constitue un changement de circonstances qui justifie l'abolition du régime de protection à l'égard des Minorités en question se trouvant en Grèce.[41]

This statement of the Secretary-General (which was not incidentally supported by the following conclusions in the same memorandum),[42] was basically aimed at facilitating the position of Greece at a crucial political moment: right after the end of the Civil War, when the question of minorities in the lower Balkan Peninsula had become one major stake in the game of territorial claims of the northern neighbours against Greece. In any event, the statement of the Secretary-General was used by Greece as the legal basis of its understanding that the Treaty of Sèvres was no longer in force.[43] It should be mentioned, however, that the protection provided by that treaty also encompassed minorities other than those linked with its northern neighbours. In the absence of any real protest on the part of the parties to the treaty, one may conclude that the statement of the memorandum and the position taken by Greece hold good.

The Treaty of Sèvres was founded on the principle of non- discrimination of all the inhabitants of Greece, regardless of citizenship, ethnic, religious or linguistic characteristics.[44] It particularly referred to the religious freedom of Muslims and Jews and to the rights of minorities concerning their languages. With regard to languages, the Greek State undertook a number of passive and positive obligations, namely the obligation to accept the free use of minority languages in private, in commerce, in the press and in public gatherings. In matters of education, the Greek State undertook the obligation to establish primary schools teaching in a minority language in areas where minorities lived in considerable numbers and used their mother tongue as a language.[45] A particular clause provided for the autonomy of the Vlachs of the Pindos mountain – under a governmental control – in educational and religious matters.[46]

The Treaty of Peace of Lausanne between Turkey, Greece, the British Empire, France and Italy was signed on 24th of July 1924 and put a final end to the Greco–Turkish war, in which the Greek armed forces had been defeated on the battlefields of Asia Minor.[47] The treaty, which is still in force,[48] provides, *inter alia,* for the protection of non-Muslim minorities in Turkey and, reciprocally, for the protection of the Muslim minority living in Greece.[49]

Although the treaty refers generally to non-Muslims and Muslims as its protected subjects, it seems that the legislators aimed at the protection of, respectively, the Greeks living at the time in Turkey (mainly Constantinople) and the Turks living in Western Thrace, who both were excluded from the exchange of populations provided for by the relevant Convention of Lausanne.[50] Reference to the religious elements of these minorities did not automatically reduce them to religious minorities which deserved protection of their religion and only that. Given the peculiarities of these minorities, namely the heavy reliance of Greeks and Turks upon their religion and the all-embracing, cultural and social significance of the latter upon these ethnic groups, the religious element was used to denote a distinct group of population with complex differences from the majority living respectively in Greece or Turkey.

The Treaty of Lausanne contains a particular section[51] entitled 'Protection of Minorities', which is composed of nine articles, one providing for a general protection of the minority and the rest protecting its religious and linguistic freedom. More particularly:

a) **The General Clause:** Article 37 provides for the general obligation of Turkey and, respectively, of Greece[52] to recognise the higher legal force of the provisions contained in Section III of the Treaty of Lausanne and to consider them as fundamental laws of the State, not to be contradicted, opposed or superseded by laws, regulations, or official acts in the respective legal order of the two countries.[53]

b) **The Particular Clauses of Protection:** The protection of the Muslim/non-Muslim minorities provided for by Articles 38 to 43 – the substantive clauses – is a comprehensive protection, clearly showing the understanding of the parties to the treaty that their respective minorities are complex minorities, bearing a considerable number of differences from the prevailing majorities in the territories of the two States. The obligations of the two States have both a passive aspect (obligations to tolerate the distinctive natures of the minorities and the exercise of their rights) and a positive aspect (to assist the minorities in the exercise of their rights by contributing, financially or otherwise, to the maintenance of their distinctive features). More specifically:

> The two States have the obligation not to discriminate against the inhabitants living in their territories on the basis of birth, nationality, language, race or religion (Article 38).
>
> The two States have the obligation to protect fully the life and liberty of their respective inhabitants (Article 38).
>
> The two States have the obligation to allow to all their inhabitants the free exercise of their religion and beliefs, in public and in private, under the condition that this is not incompatible with public order or morals (Article 38).
>
> The respective minorities (non-Muslims/Muslims) have the right of free movement and immigration, under the reservation of measures which may apply, in the totality or in parts of their territory, to all the citizens of the one or the other country for the protection of the national or public order (Article 38).
>
> The members of the respective minorities, having the citizenship of the country in which they live, must enjoy the same civil and political rights with the rest of the population, be equal before the law, enjoy the same possibilities of employment, functions and honours with the rest of the population, and use freely their language in their private relations, commercial activities, press, publications, etc (Article 39).
>
> The members of the respective minorities have an equal right (together with the rest of the population) to create, direct and control, through their own expenses, charitable, religious or social institutions, schools and other institutions of education, together with the right to use their language and exercise their religion therein (Article 40).
>
> In matters of public education, the respective governments undertake the obligation to assure that in geographical areas (towns and districts) where a considerable proportion of the members of the minorities live, appropriate facilities are established allowing the instruction of their respective languages in the primary education (Article 41).[54] The respective Governments are also obliged to grant public funds in the same areas to promote education, religion and charity concerning the minorities (Article 42). These are, of course, positive obligations of the respective countries.
>
> In matters of personal or family status of members of the minorities, the respective Governments undertake to facilitate the regulation of these questions on the basis of the customs of the minorities. Protection must also be ensured for churches, cemeteries and other religious establishments (Article 42).[55]
>
> The citizens of the two countries, members of the respective minorities, cannot be bound to accomplish any act violating their faith or their religious practices and cannot be sanctioned in the case that they refuse to be present before courts or to perform a legal act on the day of their weekly holiday (Article 43).[56]

The Treaty of Lausanne provided also for some procedural guarantees concerning the implementation of the substantive clauses on the respective minorities. Article 44 stipulates that:

a) Turkey and Greece agree that every member of the Council of the League of Nations has the right to refer to the Council any violation or danger of a violation of any of the obligations of the two countries contained in the substantive provisions of the treaty and that the Council may proceed to issuing instructions, which may be considered appropriate and efficient in the circumstances of a given case;
b) The two countries agree that in case of a dispute (or divergence of opinion) on law or facts concerning the relevant articles on minorities between the two Governments and any other power, or member of the League of Nations, the dispute will be considered as an international dispute, in accordance with Article 14 of the Covenant of the League of Nations. Such disputes will be settled, if the other party so requests, by their reference to the Permanent Court of International Justice, which shall give a binding decision (judgement) on the matter.

The latter clause of Article 44, which gives competence to the International Court in The Hague to deal with a dispute without the need of the *ad hoc* agreement of the disputing parties, is a serious guarantee offered by the treaty which, of course, still applies for the determination of any inter-state dispute on the relevant section of minorities contained in it. It goes without saying that, in accordance with the clauses of the United Nations Charter, the members of the League of Nations have been replaced by the members of the UN Organisation and the competent court is the International Court of Justice, the successor judicial mechanism of the post-war international order.[57]

The application of the Treaty of Lausanne on minority rights has had a turbulent life both in Turkey[58] and, to a lesser extent, in Greece, tending to follow the highs and lows in the state of relations between the two countries. In Greece, one of the main problems of implementing the clauses has been variations on the part of the State in the interpretation of its obligations in regard to the minority: two schools of thought have emerged on the semantics of the words 'Muslim minority' (or minorities, in accordance with the Greek translation). The one, which is enunciated mainly during periods of crisis in relations between the two States, attempts to limit the nature of the minority to its religious constitutive aspect and, hence, to also limit the protection to the religious (and linguistic) rights provided in the relevant clauses. The other looks at the minority as an ethnic group, considering its members as being of Turkish origin and giving them a leverage – in the application of the treaty – which goes well beyond the religious and linguistic elements of protection.[59] It is not surprising that the latter school flourishes in the rare periods of *rapprochement* between the two countries and when enlightened Greek governments understand that the interests of the country are really best served by a full-fledged protection of its minorities and a well-balanced policy towards them.[60]

On the other hand, in order for one to have a complete picture of the situation, it must be pointed out that the frequent difficulties in Greco–Turkish relations have not prevented Greece from honouring its basic obligations contained in the treaty. The religious prerogatives of the minority have, by most measures, been adequately safeguarded. There are 258 mosques and 78 religious institutions fully functional in the area; the administration of the Church is left to the Muftis, the Muslim religious leaders, who, it should be stressed, not only exercise their religious duties but also have competence to adjudicate personal and family matters such as marriages, divorces, pensions, emancipation of minors, inheritance, etc.[61] The only control on their decisions is a court control on the limits of their competence and not on the merits of the cases examined by them.

Education in the Turkish language, provided for by the treaty, has also been secured. Domestic laws, in compliance with the treaty, together with some additional inter-state arrangements,[62] stipulate specific regulations on the exercise of this right. There are, today, in Thrace 234 minority schools of primary education, two colleges, two lyceums, and two religious schools with over 10,000 pupils. In 1968, a Pedagogical Academy was created, which included university level courses, to educate Muslims to become minority teachers. Yet the minority is not always satisfied with the education offered by the Greek State, and a number of complaints have been aired by the local press and by its representatives. Today, an ongoing debate on the appropriateness of the school books written in Turkish seems to be a central issue which calls for a more general consideration of the education offered by the minority public schools.[63]

Freedom of expression is also safeguarded by the publication of a number of Turkish language newspapers and periodicals. Yet complaints have been raised recently on the question of freedom of speech by representatives of the minority, mainly in connection with the criminal prosecution of members of the minority (some of them political personalities) and their eventual conviction for statements and declarations in which the words 'Turk' or 'Turkish' have been used in reference to the Muslim minority. Greek courts have found guilty members of the minority because, by using these words, they threatened public peace and contributed to the arousal of public opinion against the minority.[64]

Finally, it should be stressed that the Muslim minority is represented in the Greek Parliament through its elected representatives. Indeed, a new draft law will give it a wider margin of regional representation, far beyond the one it enjoys now, allowing it to elect representatives in local authorities.

The implementation of the Treaty of Lausanne on minority issues has shown that, with a varying degree of willingness and with a number of manipulative efforts, Greece has respected her basic obligations. On the other hand, it is common knowledge that problems between the minority and the Greek State are not infrequent. Some of them may be attributed to the drawbacks of the treaty itself. For instance, the extremely general terms in which some of the rights are delimited in the text of the treaty, combined with an overtly too narrow protection of some other rights, give rise to arbitrary interpretations and applications of the relevant clause.

The problems are not solely institutional. It seems that the two crucial factors which have contributed to the sometimes strained relations between the minority and the Greek State are, first, its particularity as a social group within the wider context of the Greek society and, secondly, the influence of Greco-Turkish disputes. Insofar as the first factor is concerned, it is an indisputable fact that the Muslim minority is a predominantly agricultural community, attached to old Muslim traditions, living in specific areas of Thrace and exposed only in an elementary manner to the rest of the world. Unfortunately, the Greek State has never made any concerted effort to change the social and economic posture of the minority by affirmative action beyond the confines of the Treaty of Lausanne, so as to allow its integration into the wider society and its positive participation in all aspects of the social and economic life of the country. The second factor is also a serious one: since the early 1950s Greece and Turkey have co-existed, more or less, in a state of crisis. Turkey has been perceived as the main threat to Greek security. Unfortunately, the former has done much to reinforce such a perception, including, of course, allowing the maltreatment of the Orthodox minority in Istanbul and the Turkish islands in violation of the relevant obligations of the Treaty of Lausanne. Under such circumstances, the muslim minority became the recipient of suspicion, reservation, and, sometimes, anger of the Greek State and society at large. It should, however, be stressed that in recent years – the late 1980s and early 1990s – Greece has started a meaningful campaign for the improvement of the life of the minority and some positive results have already been accomplished through the implementation of this new policy.

The general conventional regime of protection
The Treaty of Peace of Lausanne is the only international instrument which directly protects a specific minority in Greece with regard to at least some of its differences from the majority of the population. All other minorities living in the country do not enjoy any international protection other than the one provided by general agreements in force, to which Greece is a party, that protect certain aspects of their distinct character.

The most prominent and effective international instrument of protection is the European Convention of Human Rights.[65] This instrument is, of course, a general human rights convention protecting civil and political rights of all peoples under the jurisdiction of States party to it, without any distinction (discrimination) on any ground 'such as sex, race, colour, language, religion, political or other opinion, national or social origin, association with a national minority, property, birth or other status.'[66] However, the interplay of the protected substantive rights with the clause on non-discrimination, which may directly or indirectly apply in cases of minorities, allows members of the latter to present their complaints to the judicial organs of the Convention on matters of protection of their civil and political rights, such as freedom of religion, association, expression. Since the early 1990s in particular, the organs of the Convention (the European Commission and the Court of Human Rights) have received a great number of applications of complaint from the Muslim-Turcophone minority, the Slavophones and the Jehovah's Witnesses, referring to their treatment as regards certain aspects of their minority status (such as freedom of religion, expression or political equality). In those cases where complaints have been declared admissible, some have clearly established the existence of a violation, while others have been rejected on substantive or technical grounds.

Apart from the European Convention of Human Rights, minorities may be partly protected by a number of other instruments to which Greece is a party, such as the Convention on the Elimination of all Forms of Racial Discrimination,[67] the Convention on the Prevention and Repression of Crime and Genocide[68] and the European Convention on Torture and Inhuman and Degrading Treatment.[69] Useful as these treaties may be in cases of extreme malpractice by the State, they cannot offer any solutions to the everyday problems of a minority. Furthermore, not all of them have effective machineries for the monitoring and sanctioning of violations.

The protection of minorities under customary international law

One of the controversial aspects of the international protection of minorities is the extent of this protection in the absence of a particular agreement binding a state to that effect. In other words, the problem is, first, whether there are positive rules of general customary law which protect minorities and are, hence, binding upon all states of the international community and, second, the definition of the exact content of these protecting rules.

The question is not easy to answer. It is true that the interest of the international community with regard to the protection of minorities increased considerably immediately after the dramatic events which led to the collapse of communist regimes in Central and Eastern Europe. It is also true that major international organisations such as the United Nations, the Conference on Security and Co-operation in Europe and the Council of Europe have shown a strong interest in producing resolutions, recommendations and draft conventions dealing with the international protection of minorities. However, it could not be easily maintained that any concrete rules of customary international law binding upon all states of the international community have yet emerged from these evolving processes. The difficulties involved in this mode of 'norm-creation', combined with the absence of a universal (or even regional) agreement on the protection of minorities[70] and the wide divergence in the approaches of states to certain aspects of international protection, blurs the picture of the customary protection and the exact purview of the obligations of individual States in this respect.

However, some *minima* standards of protection have been admitted in the realm of customary rules. These *minima* standards can be found today in the text of the UN Declaration on the Rights of Persons belonging to National or

Ethnic, Religious and Linguistic Minorities.[71] While protecting the states from any mis-construction of its text, which could affect their territorial integrity, political independence and sovereign equality, the Declaration nevertheless refers to a number of minority rights.

Its main text, which may be considered as containing clauses of 'soft law', provides that minority members must exercise:

a) All their human rights and fundamental freedoms without any discrimination and in full equality before the law:
b) All the rights which may secure their identity as a minority within a State's society.

If one reads the Declaration carefully, one may conclude that the rights, which are indisputably admitted, are the rights of non-discrimination, equality before the law and application of human rights to the minorities on a footing of equality. Insofar as the specific rights of minorities are concerned, the Declaration provides for a number of passive obligations (tolerance of the State towards the exercise of the manifesting elements of a minority's identity), phrased in a general and, sometimes, ambiguous manner.[72]

Under such circumstances, it may be asserted that, whilst the international community has helped to set new norms and has thus 'internalised' the concern over minorities, its customary rules of protection remain ambivalent. It requires the international community to reconcile this discrepancy.

Concluding remarks
The preceding analysis has indicated the rudimentary character of the protection of minorities in Greece, with the exception, of course, of the Muslim Turcophones. However, Greece alone cannot be held responsible for this situation. It is the result of a longstanding antipathy in the international community, including European States, which has neglected to develop particular legal regimes of protection and which has only recently accepted that international law, in the absence of an agreement to the contrary, compels states to protect their minorities by special rules.

The situation is, however, changing dramatically today. The question which therefore arises is whether Greece will be prepared to adapt to the new realities of protection. It may be assumed that the Greek State will have a number of difficulties in assimilating all these novelties – if they ever become positive law. The degree of homogeneity of its society, the composition of the latter and its rather limited exposure to alien elements, as already mentioned,[73] have contributed to the creation of a low degree of tolerance and of a high degree of fear of external threats. The fact that a number of minorities living in Greece are ethnically (or otherwise) linked with foreign countries in the turbulent area of the Balkans maximises the fear that they may be used as Trojan horses for the territorial claims for these countries. Only a comprehensive regional agreement dealing with all aspects relevant to minorities – territorial integrity, boundaries, co-operation, settlement of disputes, and so on – may eventually dissipate suspicion and enhance the possibility of the effective protection of minorities in this area of the world.

Notes

1 Article 28 of the Greek Constitution of 1975, as amended in 1986, provides, *inter alia*, that the rules of customary international law are part and parcel of the rules applicable in the Greek legal order: '1. *Les règles du droit international généralement acceptées ainsi que les traités internationaux après leur ratification par voie législative et leur entrée en vigueur conformément aux dispositions de chacun d'eux, font partie intégrante du droit héllénique interne et ont une valeur supérieure à toute disposition contraire de la loi ...*' (French text: Chambre des Députés, *Constitution de la Grèce*, Athenes, 1975).

2 Capotorti, F., *Study on the Rights of Persons Belonging to Ethnic, Religious and Linguistic Minorities*, UN Document E/CN.4/Sub. 2/384//Revision 1 (1979).

3 Resolution 9 (XX) of the UN Sub-Commission (of the UN Commission on Human Rights) on the Prevention of Discrimination and Protection of Minorities. *See* Shaw, M. N., 'The Definition of Minorities in International Law', in Y. Dinstein and M. Tabory, (eds.), *The Protection of Minorities and Human Rights* (Dordrecht: Kluwer, 1992), 1–11.

4 Attempts at defining the notion of minority under international law are abundant. For many years the most authoritative definition was that of the Permanent Court of International Justice, given in its judgment on the *Greco–Bulgarian Communities Case* (1930, Ser. B, No 17, at p. 19) where it declared that '[b]y tradition ... the "community" is a group of persons living in a given country or locality, having a race, religion, language and traditions of their own and united by this identity of race, religion, language and traditions in a sentiment of solidarity, with a view to preserving their traditions, maintaining their form of worship, ensuring the instruction and upbringing of their children in accordance with the spirit and traditions of their race and rendering mutual assistance to each other.' Also in the *Minority Schools in Albania Case* (1935, PCIJ, Ser. A/B, No 63, at p. 17), the same Court referred to minorities as 'certain elements in a State, the population of which differs from them in race, language or religion' and to whom the State must secure 'the possibility of living peaceably'. For other initiatives see Shaw, M., pp. 8 *et seq.*

5 *See* Malinverni, G., '*Le project de la Convention pour la protection des minorités élaboré par la Commission européenne pour la démocracie par le droit*', 3 *Revue Universelle des Droits de l'Homme* (1991), pp. 157 *et seq.*

6 Capotorti, in his study (Note 2) deals with the question of the numerical factor and he concludes, after having referred to a number of observations submitted to him by States-members of the United Nations, that 'States should not be required to adopt special measures of protection [for minorities] beyond a reasonable proportionality between the effort involved and the benefit to be derived from it' (on the question of when a minority is worthy of protection in accordance with its size). On the non-dominant factor, it should be stressed that the element of weakness of a social group, in other words its inability to impose its own will on a given State, is precisely the paramount factor which makes that group worthy of international protection. As it is correctly pointed out by Shaw (Note 2), '([t]here is little need in protecting a minority in such a position of power that it dominates the State in question' (such as, e.g., the white elements in South Africa, during the period of racial segregation).

7 *See, inter alia*, Shaw, M., at pp. 20 *et seq.*; Gjidara, M., '*Cadres juridiques et règles applicables aux problèmes européenes des minorités*', 37 *Annuaire Français de Droit International* (1991), pp. 348 *et seq.*, at pp. 375 *et seq.*

8 UN General Assembly, Resolution A/RES/47/135, 3/2/93, in 32 *International Legal Materials* (1993), pp. 912 *et seq.*

9 It is an undisputed fact that the principle of territorial integrity weighs more heavily than the principle of self-determination of peoples (in its 'external' form, i.e. in cases of claims of secession from an already existing State), provided, of course, that the already existing State conforms with the requirements of international law, and that the totality of its population is duly represented in the structures of the State. See, *inter alia*, Gjidara, M., at pp. 362 *et seq.*

10 *See*, in particular, paragraph the [UN] Declaration on Principles of International Law Concerning Friendly Relations and Co-operation among States in accordance with the Charter of the United Nations (2625(XXV), 1970). Aranzo-Ruiz, G., *The Declaration on Friendly Relations and the System of the Sources of International Law* (Leiden:. Sijthoff, 1979), at pp. 140 *et seq.*

11 Article 27 of the UN Convention on Civil and Political Rights contains one of the basic positive rules of international law on minorities which seems to transcend the barriers of conventional law – which is binding only on the parties to the convention – and to apply generally to all members of the international community (*see infra*). The wording of the article was intentionally drafted (through the inclusion of the words '[i]n these States in which ... minorities exist ..') so as to cover only these categories of minorities existing in a State over a certain period of time. The *travaux préparatoires* of the Covenant support such an interpretation, which, moreover, has been supported by a number of States in the application of the Covenant. Yet, one cannot exclude altogether a dynamic reversal of such a trend, and the acceptance of a new meaning of the word 'existing'. Nowak in his article on 'The Rights of Self-determination and Protection of Minorities in Central and Eastern Europe in Light of the Case-law of the Human Rights Committee' (Nowak, M., 1 *International Journal of Group Rights*, 1993, pp. 7 *et seq.*) writes in this context: 'This formulation ["exist"] was introduced by immigration countries with the explicit purpose of preventing immigrants, migrant workers and other groups of so-called "new minorities" from enjoying special rights of minority protection. The traditional view that only citizens have a right to minority protection can, however, no longer be upheld in light of both a historical, grammatical and contextual interpretation of Article 27 and the practice of the [Human Rights] Committee. Consequently, second generation immigrants or migrant workers which have established themselves in the host country for a longer period without changing their nationality have the same right to enjoy their own culture, to profess and practise their own religion, or to use their own language, as members of long-existing "old minorities" ' (p. 2) It should be noted that so far legislative efforts for the drafting of a definition of minorities insist on connecting the characteristic features of a minority with the nationality of the State in which they live.

12 *See* Dimitras, F., 'Minorités linguistiques en Grèce,' in Giordan, H. (ed.), *Les Minorités en Europe, droits linguistiques et droits de l'homme* (Paris, Kime, 1992), pp. 301 *et seq*; and Pazartzis, P., 'Le statut des minorités en Grèce', 38 *Annuaire Français de Droit International* (1992), pp. 378 *et seq.*

13 A number of studies deal, directly or indirectly, with the crucial problem of the ethnic composition of Greece and the efforts made by the modern Greek State to 'hellenize' foreign populations living in its territory. *See* particularly, Kitromilides, P., ' "Imagined Communities" and the Origins of the National Question in the Balkans', in Blinkhorn, M., Veremis, T. (eds.), *Modern Greece: Nationalism and Nationality* (Athens, Sage ELIAMEP, 1990), pp. 23 *et seq*; Mavrogordatos, G., *Stillborn Republic: Social Coalition and Party Strategies in Greece. 1922–1936* (Berkeley, University of California Press, 1983), Pentzopoulos, D., *The Balkan Exchange of Population and its Impact upon Greece* (Paris, Mouton, 1962).

14 *See* Pazartzis, P., p. 381.

14 *See* Dimitras, F., p. 178; Pazartzis, *ibid*.

16 Despite impressive social and economic development in the post-war era, Greece remains attached to a number of conservative patterns, mainly in the field of human relations. The influence of the Orthodox religion, which has shown few signs of adapting to modern realities, the traditional social values of the agricultural regions of the country (which have been transposed to the urban areas through the relatively recent internal migration), the basic categories of the professional occupation (mainly first and third sector, namely agriculture and services) and lack of immediate exposure to the outside world (and more particularly to Western European countries) have all contributed to the creation of intolerance *vis-à-vis* the alien element. With regard to the latter, it should not be forgotten that contrary to what has happened in most Western European countries, which have had ample opportunities to communicate (e.g. colonialism, immigration, etc) with different cultures and civilizations, Greece, after its overall integration as a nation-state, has remained outside the exposure to different ways of life, with a low degree of everyday communication with different cultures and mentalities. Furthermore, Greece is surrounded by countries with whom it has usually experienced tense relations. As a result, the development of normal, constructive, everyday exchanges is seriously disrupted. This mentality of seclusion and defensiveness has thus prevailed over that of openness and tolerance.

17 Greece and Turkey have a long history of tense relations, punctuated by waves of crisis. The most recent one - which is an ongoing crisis - began with the invasion of Cyprus by Turkish armed forces in 1974 and the occupation of 36 per cent of the island. Turkey has also raised a number of claims over the air and sea regimes in the Aegean and, quite recently, over the Muslim minority in Thrace (*See, inter alia*, Constas, D. (ed.) *The Greek–Turkish Conflict in the 1990s* (London, Macmillan, 1991)). After the fall of the communist regimes in the Balkan peninsula, some problems between Greece and her other neighbours, which had remained latent during the Cold War era, have come to surface and created tensions which are well known to the international community (in particular, the dispute between Greece and the Former Yugoslav Republic of Macedonia (as a result of the latter's adoption of a name supporting irredentist claims on a wider geographical area in the region, including parts of the northern territory of Greece) and the question of the Greek-Orthodox minority in Albania and its maltreatment by the new regime).

18 *See* Commission de la Communauté Européenne, *Les Minorités linguistiques dans la CEE: Espagne, Portugal, Grèce* (1990)and US Department of State, *Country Reports on Human Rights Practices for 1993*. Also reports of private (non-governmental) organisations, such as the Helsinki Watch, the Minority Rights Group, Amnesty International, the Minority Rights Society, etc.

19 Data referred to by Pazartzis, P., p. 381, and Dimitras, P., 'Minority Problems in a "Homogeneous" Country: The Case of Greece' (written together with Kalogeropoulou, T.).

20 *Ibid.*

21 *Ibid.*

22 *Ibid.*

23 *Ibid.*

24 *Ibid.*

25 The Orthodox Greek-Albanians are called 'Arvanites'. Before the end of the Second World War another category of Albanians lived in Greece, and particularly in Epirus, the so-called Cams. Cams were of Muslim religion and fled Greece after the end of the war, fearing reprisals because of their close collaboration with the Axis powers during the war. (*See*, Pazartzis, P., p. 382 (n. 26)).

26 The Vlachs maintained a number of ties with the state of their origin (Rumania) before the Second World War. Rumania made a number of efforts, in the pre-war period, to cultivate these ties, by subsidising private schools and cultural events and by fomenting the distinct identity of the minority. Yet the collaboration of segments of the minority with the occupying forces during the war and efforts to create an independent territorial entity (the principality of Pindos) had a number of repercussions upon the post-war protection of the minority by the State (dissolution of the minority schools). The only remaining element connecting the Vlachs today – who are otherwise integrated into the mainstream – is their Latin idiom which resembles the Rumanian language.

27 *See* below.

28 *See* below.

29 *See* below.

30 *See* below.

31 *See* below.

32 *See* below.

33 Gypsies are Muslims and use an idiom of Romany, together with the Greek and Turkish language. Their number is estimated to be around 14,000. They maintain their distinctive ethnic features, but they have recently allied with the Turcophones and the Pomaks in the areas in which they live. The Pomaks constitute the one-sixth of the Muslim population and they mainly live in the mountainous areas of Xanthi and Rodopi (Thrace). They use, together with the Turkish language, a Bulgarian dialect and maintain a number of ethnic characteristics (cultural features of their way of life). Due to the uniform way in which Greek authorities and local communities have treated Gypsies and Pomaks, the latter tend to identify with the stronger elements of the minorities in Thrace, who are, of course, the Muslim Turcophones (data from the doctoral thesis – under preparation – of Mr Tsitselikis on minorities in Greece).

34 US Department of State, *Country Reports on Human Rights Practices for 1992: Greece*, p. 1129: 'Northern Greece is home to a small number of Greek citizens who are descended from speakers of a Slavic dialect and who have the same rights and responsibilities as other citizens. Some of them still speak that dialect (along with the predominant Greek) and a small number of them identify themselves as "Macedonians". The exact number of all citizens of Slavic descent is difficult to determine, but unofficial estimates range from well under 10,000 to about 50,000.' (in Pazartzis, P., p. 383, n. 32).

35 *See, inter alia,* Lafazani, D., 'Appartenance culturelle et différenciation sociale dans le Bassin du Bas Strymon: l'intégration nationale d'une région de la Macédoine,' 17 *Cahiers d'etudes sur la Mediterranée Orientale et le monde Turco–Iranien* (1994), pp. 123 *et seq.* On recent claims about a Macedonian minority, see statements of the CSCD Commissioner on Human Rights (Mr Van der Stoel) concerning allegations of FYROM's President, Mr Gligorov, on the existence of a Macedonian minority in Greece.

36 Having suffered severe persecution by the Axis powers during the Second World War, the Jews constitute today 'communities' in the main Greek towns and are well integrated into Greek society. They retain their own religion and cultural identity and, in the eyes of international law, are a religious minority worthy of protection.

37 *See* Pazartzis, P., p. 386.

38 In the period before the Treaty of Sèvres, a major event for the protection of minorities was the conclusion of the Treaty of Athens (1/14 November 1913) between Greece and Turkey and particularly its Protocol No 3, through which an arrangement was made for the regime of private Muslim schools already existing, or to be created, in the territory of the Greek State. It should also be stressed that in the same year, the Greek Prime Minister, E. Venizelos, wrote a letter, which was appended to the Treaty of Bucharest (in answering a letter of the Minister of Foreign Affairs of Rumania), through which Greece undertook the obligation to grant special autonomy to schools and churches of the

Vlachs, and to allow the creation of an independent diocese for the Kutsovlachs. (*See Greek Official Journal,* 229/1913 for the Treaty of Athens, and de Martens. *Receuil* 3 VIII p. 61 *et seq.*). The Treaty of Neuilly (27 November 1919) is also of relevance, providing for the exchange of population between Bulgaria and Greece (*Greek Official Journal,* 1522/1922).

39 *Receuil des Traités de la Société des Nations,* vol. XXVIII, p. 243 *et seq.*

40 'Legislative Decree of 29 September 1923' (*Greek Official Journal,* 311 (30 October 1923).

41 UN document E/CN 4/367 (Française) pp. 76–77. The text also refers to two other general circumstances 'pouvant affecter tous les engagements': '1) La disposition de la Société des Nations, 2; La reconnaisance des droits de l'homme et du principe de la non-discrimination par la Chartre des Nations Unies.'

42 In the conclusions concerning the validity of the Treaty of Sèvres, the Secretary-General contents himself with saying that: 'En ce qui concerne les causes ordinaires d'extinction des obligations on n'en voit pas qui auraient eu pour effet d'éteindre les engagements de la Grèce concernant la protection des minorités' (p. 77), while he passes into silence the effects of the change of circumstances referred to in his previous paragraph of the memorandum. It should be noted that in other cases of minority conventions, where the Secretary-General also referred to change of circumstances, a definite stance was taken by him concerning the validity of agreements, in his conclusions. (*See,* for example, the case of Yugoslavia, where the Secretary-General concluded that: '... 2. En ce qui concerne le changement des circonstances, celui-ci est important et permet de considérer que tout au moins à l'égard des minorités qui ont prêté leur concours aux enemis de la Yougoslavie, le régime établi par le Traité de 1919 n'est plus applicable.' (p. 76)).

43 Pazartzis (p. 387) refers also to the general conclusion of the Secretary-General of the UN, who states that 'l'ensemble des circonstances a changé dans une telle mesure que le système, d'une façon générale, doit être considéré comme ayant céssé d'être en vigeur,' and draws the inference that this general conclusion attacks the validity, *inter alia,* of the Treaty of Sèvres.

44 Article 2 paragraph 1 and Article 7 paragraph 1.

45 Article 7 paragraph 5 and Article 9.

46 Article 12.

47 The Treaty of Peace of Lausanne replaces the Treaty of Peace of Sèvres (not to be confused with the already mentioned treaty on minorities), and it was the fruit of long negotiations in the Lausanne Peace Conference. It is a general peace treaty settling a considerable number of territorial problems of Greece and Turkey, which, incidentally, contains matters of protection of minorities. (For the text of the Treaty *see, Receuil des traités de la Société des Nations,* vol. XXVIII, p. 12 *et seq.*)

48 It must be noted that in the memorandum on the continuing validity of conventional arrangements of the inter-war period, the Secretary-General of the UN specifically excluded the regime of minorities established by the Treaty of Lausanne from extinction due to changes of circumstances or other reasons. Contrary to the rather nebulous position on the continuous validity of the Treaty of Sèvres, the Secretary-General was quite clear with regard to the former treaty: 'La situation respective de la Grèce et de la Turquie est restée ce qu'elle était. On ne note donc aucune cause ordinaire d'extinction des obligations ni de changement particulier des circonstances.'

49 Articles 38 onwards determine the rights which are conferred by the treaty to the non-Muslim minorities of Turkey, while Article 45 of the treaty binds Greece to recognize the same kind of protection to the Muslim minority of Greece. It is worth noting that while the text of the treaty refers – both in English and in French – to non-Muslim minorities (minorités non-musulmanes) concerning Turkish obligations, it refers only to protection of one Muslim minority (minorité musulmane) when it comes to the Greek oblig-

ations of protection. The Greek translation transposes the word minority to its plural form (minorities), a thing which has resulted, eventually, in creating a number of confusions in the application of the treaty.

50 *See*, above, note 49. An exchange of populations took place between Greece and Turkey, in the application of the Convention of Lausanne on Exchange of Greek and Turkish Populations (30 January 1921). Muslims living in the Greek Thrace and Greeks living in Constantinople were specifically excluded from the exchange. See Pentzopoulos, D., *The Balkan Exchange of Minorities and its Impact upon Greece* (The Hague: Mouton, 1962); Koufa, K., Svolopoulos, E., 'The Compulsory Exchange of Populations between Greece and Turkey', in Smith, P. (ed.), *Comparative Studies on Governments and Non-Dominant Groups in Europe 1850–1940* (Dartmouth, New York University Press, 1992), pp. 275 *et seq.*

51 Section III, *Protection des minorités* (Articles 37 and 45).

52 It should be stressed that all provisions of Section III refer to the obligations of Turkey to respect the non-Muslim minorities in its territory; but the same obligations also apply with regard to Greece, as it is provided for by Article 45: 'Les droits reconnus par les stipulations de la présente Section aux minorités non-musulmanes de la Turquie, sont également reconnus par la Grèce à la minorité musulmane se trouvant sur son térritoire.'

53 The character of a general clause may also be attributed to the provisions of Article 44 which determines the extent of the international commitment of the two countries: 'La Turquie [La Grèce] convient que, dans la mesure ou les articles précédents de la présente Section affectent les ressortissants non-musulmanes de la Turquie, ces stipulations constituent des obligations d'intérêt international et soient placées sous la garantie de la Société des Nations. Elles ne pourront être modifiés sans l'assentiment de la majorité du Conseil de la Société des Nations …'.

54 The Article also stipulates: 'Cette stipulation n'empechera par le Gouvernement turc [grec] de rendre obligatoire l'enseignement de la langue turque [grecque] dans lesdites écoles.'

55 The second paragraph of Article 42, which completes the clause on the personal and family status of the members of the respective minorities provides that: 'Ces dispositions seront élaborées par des commissions spéciales composées en nombre égal de representants du Gouvernement turc et de representants de chacune des minorités interessées. En cas de divergence, le Gouvernement turc et le Conseil de la Société des Nations nommeront d'un commun accord un surarbitre choisi parmi les jurisconsultes européenes.' Also, concerning protection of churches etc, the third paragraph of the same article provides that '…[t]outes facilités et autorisations seront données aux fondations pieuses et aux établissements religieux et charitables des mêmes minorités actuellement existant en Turquie [en Grèce], et la Gouvernement turc [grec] ne refusera pas, pour la création de nouveaux établissements religieux et charitables, aucune des facilités nécessaire qui sont garanties aux autres établissements privés de cette nature.'

56 The second paragraph of Article 43 stipulates: 'Toutefois, cette disposition ne dispensera pas ces ressortissants turcs [grecs] des obligations imposées à tous autres ressortissants turcs [grecs] en vue du maintien de l'ordre public.'

57 Article 37 of the Statute of the International Court of Justice provides that: 'Whenever a treaty or convention in force provides for reference of a matter to a tribunal to have been instituted by the League of Nations, or to the Permanent Court of International Justice, the matters shall, as between the parties to the present Statute, be referred to the International Court of Justice.'

58 Turkey has grossly violated the Treaty of Lausanne with regard to her minority obligations. (*See*, Alexandris, A., *The Greek Minority of Istanbul and the Greek–Turkish Relations* (Athens, Centre for Asia Minor Studies, 1983)).

59 The reference to the religious element of the minorities in the Treaty of Lausanne came as the result of the insistence of Turkey not to accept ethnic or racial elements in the Greek minority living in Istanbul. During periods of good relations between Greece and Turkey, the ethnic character of the minority in Thrace was accepted and, also, furthered by legal stipulations. In the early thirties, the Greek Prime Minister, Venizelos, had accepted that the minority was a secular, and not only a religious one. In the fifties, the local authorities in Thrace received the order to replace the word 'Muslim' by the word 'Turc' in all references to the minority (Turkish schools, Turkish community, etc.). The Turkish language became obligatory in all minority schools through the bilateral cultural agreements of 1951 and 1958. On the other hand, the position of the Greek authorities has changed, basically after 1974, and the use of the word 'Turc' has been prohibited. (*See* Pazartzis, P., pp. 388 *et seq.*)

60 *See* below.

61 Pazartzis, P., p. 390.

62 *See* note 59, and *ibid.*, p. 390 *et seq.*

63 The school books in Turkish are supplied by Turkey, in accordance with a protocol signed by the two States. The minority has made a number of complaints because the Greek authorities have delayed the examination of the new books supplied by Turkey in 1991 (an examination concerning their conformity with the relevant protocol). These delays oblige the minority to rely for educational needs on old school books, originating from a supply which had been made in the 1970s. (*See* Pazartzis, P., p. 391.)

64 *See, inter alia*, the case of Sadik, a leader of the minority, who was sentenced to eighteen months of imprisonment for using such words in his pre-electoral campaign. (*See* Decision on Admissibility, *Sadik against Greece*, European Commission of Human Rights).

65 *Convention for the Protection of Human Rights and Fundamental Freedoms* (Rome, 1950).

66 Article 14 of the Convention.

67 Law 494/1970, in *Greek Official Journal* 77/1970.

68 Ratified by Greece on 8 December 1954.

69 Ratified by Greece in 1993.

70 Yet, it must be stressed that after the firm position taken by the member-states of the Council of Europe (in the summit meeting which took place in Vienna, in 1993), on the need for a regional arrangement on minority protection, the Council is preparing a draft convention on the protection of minorities in Europe.

71 UN A/RES/47/135, 3 February 1993, 32 *International Legal Materials (1993)*, pp. 912 *et seq.*

72 The way in which the Resolution of the UN is phrased shows that States do not consider that the Declaration annexed to it contains customary rules of international law. On the contrary, references to already existing instruments (such as the UN Charter, or the International Covenant on Civil and Political Rights), to the work of international bodies (Commission of Human Rights) and to the need of protection and of future action, indicate the limits of the present protection. Furthermore, the too general wording of the Declaration does not promote the cause of protection, particularly when it is not accompanied by other general clauses safeguarding, in essence, the laxity of the implementation of the obligations by States.

73 *See*, above.

Stephanos Stavros

7

Citizenship and the protection of minorities

Introduction

The official ideology of the Greek State has been built almost exclusively around the concept of a single nation, with a common creed and language.[1] This incontrovertible fact is reflected in, amongst other things, all the constitutions by which the country has been governed in its 160-year history, including the one currently in force. This constitution, adopted in 1975 when Greece emerged from military rule, aimed to prepare the country institutionally for participation in the European family of democratic states.

Further and even more convincing evidence of Greece's self-perception as one of the most homogeneous countries in ethnic, religious and linguistic terms may be found in a series of laws concerning the acquisition and loss of Greek citizenship[2] and the position of minorities.[3] It is, however, the policies of the Greek State in precisely these two areas which have recently come under attack.

The Greek reaction to international criticism has been, as usual, rather defensive and can be summarized in the following two statements. In the first place, exclusion on the basis of ethnic origin, religion or language is practised to varying degrees, directly or indirectly, in most parts of the world. Assimilation is merely a more sophisticated version of it. Secondly, the policies towards citizenship and minorities of Greece's immediate neighbours are a great deal worse.

The first argument is granted. It must be stressed, nevertheless, that Greece is not alone in being singled out for criticism. Most states are increasingly coming under international scrutiny in respect of the manner in which they treat those who are in some way different from the majority.

However, claiming the supposed moral high ground of the second argument does a great injustice to the country. Greece forms part of a privileged

group of European States which have elevated non-discrimination to a fundamental principle of the new legal order they are striving to create[4] and which, in
addition to setting up quasi-federal political structures, are beginning to
encourage diversity at sub-state level.[5]

The aim of this chapter is to contribute a lawyer's point of view to the ongoing debate about the uneasy relationship between Greece and those, albeit few,
inhabitants who are not ethnic Greeks, Greek Orthodox or Greek-speaking. A
legal analysis is proposed not because it purportedly offers a more objective
means of measuring a problem which has been allegedly exaggerated by anthro-
pologists and sociologists. A dry legal analysis, if anything, will only tell part of
the story. However, the laws of a country, if interpreted correctly, could provide
useful insights into official policy in particular areas. Moreover, although an
appropriate legal framework might not suffice, it is a necessary condition for
the achievement of justice for those who may suffer exclusion on the basis of
their ethnic origin, religion or language.

In the light of all the above, it would appear necessary to assess in some
detail the extent to which ethnic origin, religion and language affect the enjoyment of certain key constitutional rights. Having done that, it is proposed to
examine whether a different approach to some of these issues is possible or necessary under the Constitution of 1975 to ensure a constructive response to the
current expectations of the international community.[6]

Ethnic origin and constitutional rights

The Greek Constitution does not directly create distinctions on the basis of
ethnic origin. Yet the concepts of Greek people (*laos*) and the Greek nation
(*ethnos*), which figure in the first article of the Constitution, are not necessarily
coextensive.[7] The nation appears to be both wider and narrower than the
people. It includes some persons who do not have the Greek citizenship and
excludes some who do. In order to understand the criteria by which one is considered to be part of the nation and the legal significance of such inclusion, one
must examine the application of certain rules in the Code of Citizenship which
facilitate the acquisition of Greek citizenship by those who belong to the nation
(*omogeneis*) and its loss by those who do not (*allogeneis*). At the outset, it should
be noted that both kinds of rule are fully in accordance with the 1975 Constitution. Article 4 paragraph 3 of the same allows Parliament complete freedom
to determine the criteria for the acquisition of citizenship.[8] Article 111 paragraph 6, however, preserves section 19 of the Code of Citizenship until it is
repealed by Parliament. Section 19 allows for the withdrawal of Greek citizenship from persons who do not belong to the nation and who have left the country with no intention of returning. Insofar as the provision distinguishes
between Greek citizens on the basis of ethnic origin, it would have violated the
Constitution[9] had it not been expressly saved.

However, by what criteria is one considered part of the nation? In 1981 the Council of State, being the highest administrative court in Greece, issued a noteworthy decision on the appeal of a person of Jewish origin against the application of section 19 in his case.[10] In this decision, the Council of State considered that an *allogenis* is a person who is born of non-ethnic Greek parents and has demonstrated a lack of Greek national conscience, not having been assimilated to the Greek nation, which is composed of all those who are tied together by common historical traditions, aspirations and ideals. The decision clarified two issues. In the first place, participation in the Greek nation is not determined on the basis of ethnic origin alone, in the sense that non-ethnic Greeks may participate, provided they assimilate. Secondly, a Greek national conscience and a non-Greek ethnic identity are mutually exclusive.

The thinking of the court raises some very interesting issues when applied to minorities. Article 16 of the Constitution, for example, considers the development of the national conscience of pupils to be one of the principle aims of education.[11] Could it be argued, on the basis of the above position of the Council of State, that the Constitution requires the education system to aim at the creation of *omogeneis*, namely the elimination of ethnic diversity? A 1978 ministerial decision concerning the manner in which Greek national days must be celebrated in the minority schools in Thrace takes the contrary view.[12] While the aim of the celebrations must be the strengthening of the national conscience of pupils, the 1968 Protocol between Greece and Turkey[13] (which enjoins respect for their separate ethnic identity) must be observed.[14] National allegiance, being loyalty to the Greek State, and ethnic identity are clearly distinguished.

On closer inspection, however, the case of the minority schools in Thrace may be the exception that verifies the rule. While it is commonly known that the Muslim minority in Thrace is composed of three separate ethnic groups, those of Turkish ethnic origin (*tourkogeneis*), the Pomaks and the Gypsies, the only non-Greek ethnic identity referred to in the 1968 Protocol is Turkish. Foreign policy considerations, rather than respect for the separate ethnic identity of the minorities, appear to have caused the only significant question mark over the self-perception of the Greek State as the embodiment of the Greek nation. Moreover, the very same considerations appear to have recently led 'Areios Pagos', the supreme civil and criminal court of Greece, to issue two decisions casting significant doubt on the continued validity of the above-mentioned exception.

In the first judgment, Areios Pagos upheld the disbandment of the Union of the Turkish Youth of Komotini in 1984 on the grounds that the use of the word 'Turkish' created the impression that a youth association of foreign nationals operated on Greek soil.[15] In the second, Areios Pagos upheld the conviction of two minority candidates who had campaigned for the parliamentary elections of November 1989 on a 'we are Turkish' platform, considering that, by using the word 'Turkish', the accused had intended to create dissension and hatred among the Muslim population of Thrace and make them enemies with the Christian population.[16] Both decisions of the supreme civil and criminal court of Greece rest on the premise that one cannot be a Greek citizen and an ethnic Turk at the same time.[17]

In summary, with one extremely dubious exception, Greek laws appear to encourage the assimilation of persons of non-Greek ethnic background. Section 19 of the Code of Citizenship facilitates the severing of the links between the Greek State and those who do not assimilate.

Religion and constitutional rights

Freedom of religion is enshrined in Article 13 of the Greek Constitution which, in addition, stipulates that the enjoyment of civil and political rights cannot be made dependent on a person's religious beliefs. Article 3 of the same instrument, however, refers to the Eastern Orthodox religion as the prevalent religion in Greece. Most constitutional experts[18] argue that this provision merely describes a factual situation, namely that the vast majority of Greek citizens adhere to the Orthodox faith. It cannot be relied upon to limit the rights of non-Orthodox Greeks.

However, this argument does not appear to have been taken on board by parts of the administration. In 1986, for example, a Muslim woman from Western Thrace who, having lost her Greek citizenship under section 19 of the Code of Citizenship, applied for naturalisation. Her application was refused by the Ministry of Interior Affairs on the basis that she had not adapted to 'Greek reality'. This was deduced from the fact that she had remained a Muslim. Therefore, according to the Ministry of Interior Affairs, assimilation presupposes adherence to the prevalent religion. The citizenship policy of the Greek State cannot undermine the privileged links between Church and nation.

The woman appealed to the Council of State. The supreme administrative court of Greece does not normally require that decisions concerning the naturalisation of aliens be adequately reasoned, on the basis of the broad discretion that the Minister of Interior Affairs enjoys in the area.[19] In the case of the Muslim woman, however, reasons had been given. Since these demonstrated religious discrimination, the Council of State annulled the decision.[20] The case illustrates, if anything, the lengths to which the Council of State is prepared to go in protecting members of religious minorities from direct discrimination.

The Council of State, however, cannot always be relied upon to solve all the problems that religious minorities face in Greece. Some of these problems are of an institutional character, having a firm statutory basis. Moreover, constitutional provisions are frequently invoked to justify the preservation of these unequal laws.

Article 3 of the Constitution, for example, in addition to referring to the Eastern Orthodox faith, contains a set of rules concerning the organisation of the Greek Orthodox Church. On this basis the Church is treated as a legal person incorporated under public law (*nomiko prosopo dimosiou dikaiou*). Broadly speaking, this means that the Church enjoys all the privileges of the state, being at the same time a distinct legal entity. Its legal status must be contrasted with the absence of any provision regarding the legal personality of other Churches in Greece. This legal vacuum has forced some Churches, such as the Old Calendarists and the Jehovah's Witnesses, to operate as ordinary voluntary associations (*somateia*). However, this has not proved to be an entirely satisfactory solution.

In accordance with Article 12 paragraph 1 of the Constitution, Greek citizens must respect the law when exercising the constitutional right to associate. Interpreting this provision rather broadly, a civil court in Crete in 1987 refused to approve the constitution of a Jehovah's Witnesses Church, on the basis that the aims of the association were illegal, since they encouraged its members not to serve in the armed forces and not to authorise blood transfusions for their children.[21] The weakness of the reasoning[22] of the court becomes clear when the decision is compared with other judgments rendered by Greek courts in two cases where the religious beliefs of the Jehovah's Witnesses were at issue. In the first such judgment, the Council of State considered that the refusal of Jehovah's Witnesses to bear arms could not be relied on by the administration to deny them permission to operate a place of worship.[23] In the second, another civil court awarded custody to the mother in a divorce case, despite the fact that she was a Jehovah's Witness, considering that any dangers which her religious beliefs could present for the health of the children were eliminated by section 1534 of the Civil Code. This section authorises the intervention of the public prosecutor in cases where parents refuse to give their consent to the medical treatment of their children.[24]

Other Churches which claim historical privileges have refused to become voluntary associations. The Roman Catholic Archdiocese of Athens, for example, prefers to leave the issue of its legal personality open, with all the inconvenience that this entails.[25]

Another constitutional provision, Article 13 paragraph 2, prohibits proselytism. To enforce the prohibition, Greek courts continue to apply Act 1363/38, introduced by the Metaxas regime, which criminalises proselytism. The intention of the Metaxas regime was to prohibit all promotional activities of non-Orthodox groups. Since 1975, some Greek criminal courts have begun to interpret the act rather restrictively to make it more compatible with religious freedom.[26] However, others continue to interpret it broadly. As a result, non-Orthodox groups find it difficult to foresee what is and is not punishable and operate amid great legal uncertainty. It is not clear whether the prohibition of proselytism also applies against members of the Orthodox Church, because two different chambers of Areios Pagos have issued conflicting decisions.[27]

In addition to criminalising proselytism, the Metaxas regime made the functioning of all non-Orthodox places of worship subject to prior ministerial approval. According to the relevant laws, which survive to this day,[28] the minister must be satisfied that there is an actual need for the functioning of such places. The connection with the law on proselytism becomes apparent when one examines what is understood by 'actual need'. The law requires proof that a sufficient number of followers already exist. The creation of a place of worship, to cater for any future needs of an expanding non-Greek Orthodox Church, appears to be excluded, the assumption being that such expansion will be the result of proselytism.

Article 13 paragraph 4, the third constitutional provision which will be discussed in this respect, does not, from a strictly legal point of view, introduce any discrimination against religious minorities when it prescribes that 'no person may, by reason of his religious beliefs, refuse to discharge his obligations towards the State or refuse to obey the laws.' However, this provision inevitably creates a number of problems for minorities. The drafters of the Constitution obviously had in mind the problem of Jehovah's Witnesses and their claim to exemption from military service. However, the provision has been applied in other circumstances as well: to deny, for example, the right of Seventh Day Adventist pupils not to attend school on Saturday.[29] The courts appear to be arguing that any kind of law, however trivial, prevails over claims to religious freedom.[30]

It must be emphasised, of course, that Article 13 paragraph 4 of the Constitution does not in any way prevent Parliament from enacting, or the administration from enforcing, laws which exempt members of particular religious minorities from the scope of generally applicable rules. A series of such laws was enacted after the territorial expansion of Greece pursuant to the Balkan wars. Persons of Jewish faith, for example, enjoy the right not to work on Saturday,[31] as opposed to Sunday, which is a day of rest for all other Greeks. Muslims have their own religious courts which hear disputes concerning family, and to some extent, inheritance matters and pass judgment on the basis of Islamic law,[32] as opposed to the Civil Code which applies in the case of all other Greeks.[33] However, some of these exceptions are currently being questioned. A new law, for example, stipulates that the decisions of the Muslim courts are not to be enforced if they are based on rules which violate the Constitution[34] including, presumably, the principle of equality between men and women.

In summary, although direct religious discrimination is not easily tolerated by the majority of the Greek courts, most notably the Council of State, there exists a number of laws which fail to take into account religious diversity and, as a result, some old problems persist.

Language and constitutional rights

In the case of the Muslim woman who applied for naturalisation mentioned above, the Council of State did not appear to consider that lack of knowledge of the official language of the Greek State constituted, in itself, a sufficient reason for the rejection of her application. However, the case involved a member of a linguistic minority and thus, arguably, this decision can be distinguished. As a matter of fact there are a number of minority languages spoken on Greek soil. Of these, the only language which is currently protected by law is Turkish and, together with Greek, is the language used in the minority schools in Thrace.

As already seen, Article 16 of the Constitution considers that education is one of the principle concerns of the State. Greece, however, has delegated part of its responsibilities in the field of minority education to Turkey. It has concluded a number of bilateral agreements giving Turkey the right to provide school books and a number of teachers for the minority schools.[35] These agreements are based on reciprocity and the aim of the Greek Governments which concluded them was to obtain an equivalent set of rights for the Greek minority in Istanbul.

However, adhering to the logic of bilateralism, Greece conveniently forgot the linguistic diversity of the other Muslim minority in Thrace. As a result, the Pomaks (who constitute a separate linguistic minority within the larger religious minority and thus who do not speak Turkish, but rather a Slavic idiom close to Bulgarian) ended up having to attend schools where many courses are taught in Turkish, using books provided by the Turkish Ministry of Education and where teachers from Turkey exchanged under the bilateral agreements are occasionally employed.

The situation in Thrace constitutes in itself sufficient proof of the lack of a true linguistic minority policy in Greece. The only exception to the policy of linguistic uniformity has again been dictated by foreign policy considerations. However, reciprocity has not produced the desired results for the Greek minority in Istanbul.

Recapitulation

It emerges clearly from the first part of this study that the enjoyment of several constitutional rights can vary depending on ethnic origin, religion and language. This trend appears to be related, in the first place, to a citizenship policy the principal aim of which is to protect ethnic homogeneity, in the second to a minority policy built exclusively around the sacred concept of reciprocity with Turkey[36] and finally to the privileged links between the Orthodox Church and the Greek State which derive from the historical links between the Church and nation.

Is a different approach possible or necessary?
Insofar as citizenship is concerned, it is submitted that the 1975 Constitution incorporates a clear understanding as to what should be the relationship between the Greek State and nation. Article 1 paragraph 3 solemnly declares that all powers deriving from the Constitution must be exercised in favour of

both the Greek people and the Greek nation. As already argued, the reference to the nation must be seen as including the Greek diaspora and the ethnic Greek minorities abroad. Naturally, Greece is a peace-loving country which must pursue, in accordance with Article 2 of the Constitution, friendly relations with the rest of the world on the basis of international law.

Although it is clear that the Constitution does not leave any room for the encouragement of irredentism, it is equally clear that the Greek State is entitled, if not obliged, to pursue a policy which will preserve and strengthen its links with the wider Greek nation. A naturalisation policy which favours ethnic Greeks appears a perfectly acceptable way of reinforcing these links. On the other hand, the withdrawal of citizenship on the basis of ethnic origin appears rather questionable, in that it introduces distinctions between members of the Greek people. In the light of the foregoing, Parliament should consider exercising the option given to it by the Constitution and abolish section 19 of the Code of Citizenship which has the potential to cause so much embarrassment.

Insofar as minorities are concerned, it is submitted that many of the shortcomings described above derive from the failure of successive Greek Governments to take into account, when formulating minority policies, the requirements of Article 2 of the Constitution. This Article provides that 'the main obligation of the State is to respect and protect the value of the human being'. The thesis of this study is that this key constitutional provision, read in the light of current developments in international law, creates an obligation for Parliament to recognise and protect the distinct identity of the members of all the ethnic, religious and linguistic groups which can demonstrate a stable presence in Greece. Parliament should not only abolish all forms of direct or indirect discrimination, but should bring in special measures designed to give each of these separate identities an equal chance of surviving.

Minority schools in Thrace, for example, should make pupils aware not only of their religious distinctiveness but also their different ethnic identity, be it Turkish, Pomak or Gypsy. This ethnic identity should be, in turn, distinguished from the minority pupils' Greek national conscience, the development of which is one of the principle aims of education, in accordance with Article 16 of the Constitution. It is submitted that, under Article 2 of the Constitution, the development of the Greek national conscience of ethnic minorities cannot mean encouragement of assimilation but rather respect for the Greek Republic and the Constitution,[37] which is after all the fundamental obligation of all Greek citizens in accordance with Article 120 paragraph 2 of the latter.

Similar measures are required in favour of religious minorities as well. In its well-known Kokkinakis[38] judgment, the European Court of Human Rights has given a new interpretation to the concept of proselytism, considering that Greece may criminalise only the use by one of improper means to change the religious beliefs of another. This interpretation is binding for the Greek judiciary under Article 28 of the Constitution. As the full implication of this judgment filters through, the Metaxas laws mentioned above (*see* page 121)[39] will lose all their remaining teeth. They could even be abolished without violating the Constitution. It is submitted, in this regard, that the constitutional prohibition of proselytism is already enforced by general criminal laws which punish coercion or fraud.

However, will this provide a final solution to the problem? It has been suggested that the Church and the State should be completely separated before one can even begin talking about freedom of religion in Greece.[40] It cannot be disputed that existing Church–State relations have several questionable aspects, including increased intervention of the State in the affairs of the Church. It must be stressed, however, that a state which legislates without taking into consideration the religious beliefs of its citizens is neither a fair nor a peaceful one.

From many points of view, Article 2 of the Constitution commands Parliament to take into account as much as possible the demands that religion makes on the life of Greek citizens. Certain aspects of the existing Church–State relationship in Greece today must be seen as examples of a global deal struck between the State with the major Church in the country. It is proposed here that the State should negotiate similar deals with all the major religious groups with a view to ensuring peaceful coexistence. A variety of issues, such as legal personality, holidays, family law and exemption from military service will be then regulated in accordance with the needs of each group. This can happen without sacrificing individual rights and certain basic principles of the Constitution.

It has been shown in this connection that the recognition of the right to perform an alternative to military service would not be incompatible with Article 4 paragraph 6 of the Constitution, which prescribes that every Greek who can bear arms must contribute to the defence of the Country.[41] Conscientious objectors could be involved in those sectors of state activity which are closely connected to the defence of the country, without necessarily coming under the responsibility of the armed forces. The separate Muslim jurisdictions can be made compatible with the Constitution as well. The Muslim courts could become, for example, courts of arbitration, the verdicts of which will be enforced only if it can be shown that both parties have submitted their disputes to them voluntarily. In such cases it will have to be assumed that the right to equality of the sexes has been freely waived.

Finally, in the case of linguistic minorities, respect for the value of the human being, in accordance with Article 2 of the Constitution, can only mean recognition and protection of all minority languages spoken by groups with a sufficiently stable presence in Greece. This protection could take the form of state sponsored instruction of the minority language. The formulation of a coherent minority linguistic policy will, by necessity, involve some rethinking of the viability of some of the bilateral agreements concluded with Turkey in the field of education. Moreover, one should not lose sight of the fact that protection of the language of the Pomaks in Thrace will be a measure of questionable validity, if it is not followed by the protection of other minority languages spoken outside the Thracian area.

Conclusions

In conclusion, it could be said that the interpretation of Article 2 of the Constitution proposed in this chapter will only entail some minor adjustments to a few laws of peripheral importance which regulate the situation of just a tiny fraction of the Greek people. A. Pollis, in her pioneering work,[42] argues that this would involve nothing less than a total reconstruction of the Greek identity. Whichever of the two is true, it has been shown that the 1975 Constitution can be interpreted in a manner which will continue to guarantee Greece's position in the changing European order.

Notes

1   *See* A. Pollis, 'The State, the Law and Human Rights in Modern Greece', *Human Rights Quarterly*, 9 (1987) and 'Greek National Identity: Religious Minorities, Rights and European Norms', *Journal of Modern Greek Studies*, 10 (1992) 171–195.

2   The concepts of nationality and citizenship in English and *ithageneia* and *ipikootita* in Greek are considered to be co-terminous under both domestic and traditional international law.

3   The definition given to the concept of minority by F. Capotorti will be used for the purposes of this study. In a study on the *Rights of Persons belonging to Ethnic, Religious and Linguistic Minorities* submitted to the United Nations in 1977 in his capacity as Special Rapporteur of the Sub-Commission on Prevention of Discrimination and Protection of Minorities, Capotorti defined minority as 'a group numerically inferior to the rest of the population of a State, in a non-dominant position, whose members – being nationals of the State – possess ethnic, religious or linguistic characteristics differing from those of the rest of the population and show, if only implicitly, a sense of solidarity, directed towards preserving their culture, traditions, religion or language.' Although Capotorti's definition is not in any way binding, it is widely accepted as the most authoritative one by most international lawyers. It must be noted that Capotorti considered in his study that some stability of presence in a particular state is required before a group can qualify as a minority.

4   *See* Article 14 of the European Convention on Human Rights and Title I Article F paragraph 2 of the Treaty on European Union.

5   *See, inter alia*, the 1991 proposal of the European Commission for Democracy through Law for a European Convention for the Protection of Minorities, the 1992 European Charter for Regional or Minority Languages, the 1993 recommendation of the Parliamentary Assembly of the Council of Europe for an additional protocol on the rights of minorities to the European Human Rights Convention and the 1994 Declaration of the European Parliament concerning the Linguistic and Cultural Minorities in the European Union.

6   *See* C. L. Rozakis's contribution to this volume.

7   The third paragraph of the first Article of the Constitution solemnly proclaims that all the powers deriving from the Constitution must be exercised in favour of both the Greek people and the Greek nation.

8   'Greek citizens are all those which fulfil the criteria prescribed by law.'

9   Article 4 paragraph 1 of the Constitution stipulates that all Greeks are equal before the law and Article 4 paragraph 3 provides that a Greek citizen may be deprived of his

nationality in two cases only, namely if he voluntarily acquires a new nationality and if he undertakes services abroad contrary to the national interest.

10 Decision No 57/1981.

11 *See* G. Sotitellis, *Religion and Education* (in Greek), (Athens, Kornotini, 1993).

12 Decision of the Minister of Education No 55369/16 May 1978.

13 Protocol adopted in Athens on 20 December 1968 by the Greek-Turkish Committee on Culture which had been established in accordance with the Greek–Turkish Cultural Agreement signed in Ankara on 20 April 1951.

14 *See* section 17 of the above-mentioned decision.

15 Decision No 1729/1987.

16 Decision No 208/1991.

17 For extensive criticism see S. Stavros, 'The Legal Status of Minorities in Greece Today : The Adequacy of their Protection in the Light of Current Human Rights Perceptions', *Journal of Modern Greek Studies*, 13 (1995) 1–32.

18 *See* Sotitellis, *Religion and Education*, pp. 69-119 with further references, above.

19 *See* decision No 2457/1982.

20 *See* decision No 169/1990.

21 Decision No 354/1987 of the Court Appeal of Crete.

22 For extensive criticism see Stavros, *The Legal Status of Minorities*, above.

23 Decision No 2484/1980.

24 Decision No 1328/1987 of the single-member first instance civil court of Patras.

25 *Cf.* Decision No 360/1994 of Areios Pagos where it was held that a Catholic church and monastery in Crete lacked legal personality and, as a result, could not sue two individuals who had interfered with their property rights. Identical reasoning had been used to reject the claims of a Protestant church in Katerini against the administration in decision No 530/1965 of the Court of Appeal of Thessaloniki.

26 *See* S. Stavros, 'Proselytism and the Right to Religious Freedom',(in Greek), 43 *Poinika Chronika* 964 (1993).

27 *See* decisions Nos. 1304/1982 and 480/1992.

28 *See* section 1 of Act No. 1363/1939 in conjunction with section 41 of Act No. 1369/1938 and section 1 of the Royal Decree of 20 May/2 June 1939.

29 *See* decision No. 4079/1976 of the Council of State.

30 The Council of State in its above-mentioned decision No. 4079/1976 referred to 'laws concerning education, national security, public health, the functioning of the public services, etc'.

31 Section 26 of Act No. 2456/1920.

32 *See* Act No. 147/1914 in conjunction with Acts Nos. 2345/1920 and 1920/1991.

33 On the rights of Muslims in Greece in general *see* S. Minaides, *The Religious Freedom of Muslims in the Greek Legal Order* (in Greek), (Athens, Komotini, 1990).

34 *See* section 5 paragraph 3 of Act No. 1920/1991.

35 *See* the above-mentioned Protocol of 1968 and the *ad hoc* agreements of 10/21 November 1952 and 27 January 1955.

36 *See* P. Pazartzis, 'Le Statut des Minorités en Grèce', 38 *Annuaire Français de Droit International*, 377 (1992).

37 It is submitted in this connection that the word 'national' has more than one meaning in the 1975 Constitution. In addition to referring to a concept wider than the Greek people, it also refers to Greek nationals in the ordinary sense of the term, ie Greek citizens. Article 51 paragraph 2, for example, which reads 'The members of Parliament represent the nation' can only mean that the MPs represent the entirety of Greek citizens.

38 Judgement of 25 May 1993 on the case of Kokkinakis v. Greece.

39 *See* above.

40 I. M. Konidaris, *Act No. 1700/1987 and the Recent Crisis in the Relations between Church*

and State (in Greek), (Athens 1988) and 'Issues of Religious Discrimination' (in Greek) *Iperaspisi*, 405 (1992).

41 *See* N. Alivizatos, *The Armed Forces under the Constitution*, (in Greek), (Athens, Komotini, 1992), 75–128.

42 *See* above.

PART IV

Greece and the new security agenda

THANOS VEREMIS

8

A Greek view of Balkan developments

Introduction

The disintegration of Yugoslavia and the carnage in Croatia and Bosnia that allowed the media to hold Western attention to ransom had a direct impact on Greece's relations with its partners and allies.[1] Greece's fear that unqualified recognition of secessionist states would destabilise the Balkan region, and its subsequent predilection for the Serbian side in the conflict, served to isolate it from mainstream Western perceptions of the war. This chapter seeks to present and evaluate Greece's own view of the conflict and the lessons to be drawn from it.[2]

Ethnic nationalism and statehood

The resurgence of ethnic nationalism in the Balkans resembles the state of affairs that prevailed in Europe after the end of the First World War. US President Wilson's well-meaning principle that every nation was entitled to its own state emanated from a liberal concept that was unacquainted with the darker aspects of ethnic exclusivity. It did not take fully into account the symbiosis of the different ethnic groups closely intermixed within the same territory, a factor that is all too present in the political geography of Eastern Europe and the Balkans in particular.

Many have argued that, once the Pandora's box of statehood based on ethnic preponderance was tampered with, misfortunes were likely to follow in rapid succession. New states with substantial ethnic minorities would view such peoples as potential threats to the new-found unity of the preponderant national culture.

Yet the climate of international opinion in the early 1990s generally favoured the creation of new states. A sympathetic attitude towards ethnic groups that had suffered loss of freedom under the communist regimes convinced many Western Europeans that the supplicant ethnicities were entitled to self-determination and indeed statehood. To date, at least, no more stark example of the consequences of such thinking exists than the chaos of the former Federation of Yugoslavia.

A Greek view of recent events

The role of History

Two forces were at work at the foundation of Yugoslavia as a modern state in the aftermath of the First World War.[3] The one championed by the Serbs, whose nationalist aspirations to unite the South Slavs under their leadership, became the consistent force behind Yugoslav unity. The other was promoted by the Croats and Slovenes, who believed that they would safeguard their independence from the Habsburg Empire within the framework of the new state.[4] The expediences and conjunctions that brought the South Slavs, with all their different religions, into a unitary state in the inter-war period, and a federation after the Second World War, did not allay the original divergence of purpose between the two incompatible motives present at the birth of Yugoslavia.

The Communist ideology expounded by the Croat partisan (Tito) who led the largest resistance movement against the 'Axis' occupation in the Second World War subscribed to the first of these motives, the principle of a unified Yugoslavia. By destroying the opposing separatist Ustasha Croats, Tito upheld in essence the cause championed by the Serbs. The federal structure which he adopted was aimed at minimising conflict between nationalities and religious groups. In reality, however, the system provided a framework for some nationalities to create embryonic nation-states.[5] The subsequent friction between the Federal Government and the Republics became a constant feature of Tito's regime and was only kept under control by his own personal authority and vigilance over republican and provincial leaders.

However incompatible the two forces of unity and independence were, they shared at least one characteristic: nationalism. Serbs that aspired to unify the community of South Slavs were no less nationalistic than their separatist Croatian and Slovenian adversaries, who looked to national independence for fulfilling their perceived destinies. Serbia clung to its own brand of Communism because of its unifying mission, while the others professed liberal credos to convince the EU of the legitimacy of their cause.

The role of the EU

The EU wielded significant influence from the outset of the Yugoslav crisis. Yet its role has been characterised by inconsistency. At first the Union committed itself to upholding the principles of the 1973 Helsinki Final Act that codified

Europe's post-war borders: a fact which affected the policy of states with historically disputed territories. Hence when an EU delegation led by Jacques Delors met with the Slovene President Milan Kucan, it was made clear to the latter that the fragments of an exploded Yugoslavia would not be considered for membership and that the unity of the state was a precondition for future application. Yet in the European Parliament resolution on Yugoslavia of 13 March 1992, the EU altered the requirements for admission from a single state to a 'single political entity'.[6]

The similar lack of consistency was the main characteristic of other European institutions, which wavered between the integrity of Yugoslavia and the self-determination of its constituent parts. The Alpe–Adria Association for regional economic co-operation between Slovenia, Croatia, Austria, Hungary and parts of Italy (as opposed to the Hexagonale which included the entire Yugoslavia) recognised the separate identities of the two Republics. Italy, the moving force behind Alpe–Adria and the Hexagonale, gave conflicting messages of its position *vis-à-vis* Yugoslavia's future. Although the Italian Foreign Minister at the time, Gianni De Michelis, stated his Government's determination to conform with the EU line, on various occasions he intimated his own preference for a break-up of the state to avoid bloodshed.[7]

It can be asserted that, in overall terms, all European States at the outbreak of the Yugoslav crisis were influenced by varied and often conflicting motives in their dealings with the former Federation, which defy neat classification. For example, at least four general motives can be identified:

a   Fear of cultural assimilation in a future federation of Europe induced some smaller members of the Community to sympathise with the secessionist cause of Slovenia (and later Croatia and Bosnia). Such member-states also championed self-determination (Holland, Denmark).
b   There were those whose preference for the status quo was influenced by their own vulnerability to secessionist demands (Spain, Czechoslovakia, Rumania).
c   The solidarity with former parts of the Germanic Habsburg Empire, and aspirations of sub-regional (Austria) and regional influence (Germany, Italy) elicited support for secession.
d   Fear of undermining the territorial status quo of the Balkans, with unforeseen consequences for the rest of Europe, constituted yet another position championed by France and to a lesser extent by Britain.

The inconsistency and fragmentation of motives bedevilled all European attempts to mediate in Yugoslavia until December 1991 when the German Foreign Minister, Hans-Dietrich Genscher, made a forceful, but in the eyes of many ill-conceived, entry into the debate. Spurred on by the need to represent the shared sentiments of the Catholics of the German south as well as vociferous claims of the large Croat community supporting independence in Germany itself, Genscher managed to convince his reluctant colleagues in the Brussels EPC meeting of 16–17 December 1991 to recognise the independence of Slovenia and Croatia by threatening a unilateral German initiative.

Germany's role, although it dispelled the previous ambiguity of the Community's policy, ignored two important principles. One was of a legal nature, the other political. The Badinter Arbitration Commission set up by the EU to advise on the applications of the Yugoslav Republics for recognition had disqualified Croatia, while suggesting that Slovenia and the Yugoslav Macedonia deserved recognition. Genscher, however, secured a deal with Greek Foreign Minister, Andonis Samaras, that he would exclude the Yugoslav Macedonia from recognition if Greece agreed to fall in line with the others on Croatia.[8] Genscher's more serious political error, which was to prove detrimental for the Community's subsequent Balkan position, was to ignore the ethnic minorities within the seceding entities.

> This meant leaving Yugoslavia in those internal borders outlined by Tito, thus taking a partly unwilling Serbian minority with it. With reference to those Serbs, does such a policy mean that the right to self-determination is subordinated to the principle of inviolable borders?[9]

Croatia's leader, Franjo Tudjman, not only failed to address this problem, but displayed incredible lack of foresight by declaring his state a unitary entity based on the national preponderance of the Croats. Once recognition was secured, Germany's interest in the Balkans dissipated.

The consequences of this hasty recognition of independence at a time when the EU could still have put pressure on Slovenes, Croats, Serbs and Muslims alike to seek alternative arrangements of cohabitation (whether on the confederal or the commonwealth model) proved to be far-reaching. If the dissolution of Yugoslavia occurred because Croats, Slovenes and Muslims refused to live in a state with an overbearing Serb element, the five resulting states have reproduced the very same problem within their own realms – exchanging one dominant ethnic group for another in each instance. What the EU has succeeded in doing by recognising the new states on the basis of ethnic prevalence, is to legitimise the ethnic basis of unitary states replacing a federal state.

The role of the US
The United States continued to play a decisive role in the region, although its post-Cold War priorities were unclear. Some of the status quo heritage of the previous era persisted initially in American moves.[10] Early support for Serb President Slobodan Milosevic was reversed after it became clear that he was promoting Serbian nationalism rather than Yugoslav unity. Albanian and Croatian lobbies in Washington, along with the decline of Milosevic's credibility, produced the Nickles Amendment according to which continuation of US aid to Yugoslavia depended on the improvement of human rights in that country. The eventual removal of US financial support to Yugoslavia as a whole appeared to prepare the way for recognition of individual Republics as independent

States, which was implicit in US Secretary of State James Baker's announcement that future assistance would be on a case to case basis.[11] In January 1992 EU recognition of Slovenia and Croatia, and Russia's peaceful dissociation with the Soviet Republics, began to change the American view of what its policy ought to be in Yugoslavia. Convinced that recognition of Bosnia-Herzegovina would safeguard it from attack, the US agreed with the EU to recognise Slovenia and Croatia if the Europeans were willing to cast in their lot with Bosnia. In the spring of 1992, Secretary of State Baker, condemned Serbia and fell in line with the members of the EU.

The role of Greece

Greece's Balkan interests are, for reasons of proximity, more vital than for any other member of the EU. As the most affluent, stable, democratic and well-allied state in the region, Greece has been ideally situated to play the role of interlocutor in the troubled Balkans. Moreover, Greek views on its interests have not been affected by irredentist claims on its neighbours nor by fear of secessionist possibilities within her own territory. For example, the Greek Government has renounced its claims on Southern Albania and the Islamic minority in Greek Thrace, even if its Turkish element has always been dominated entirely by the priorities of Turkey, constitutes just a small percentage of Greece's total population. Rather it has been a case of Greece's motives in the Balkans being driven by the possibilities of a violent disintegration of the southern part of the former Yugoslavia bringing outside powers into the conflict, or causing the flight of more refugees into Greek territory. There are, at the time of writing, half a million economic immigrants from former Eastern Europe in Greece – more than half of which come from Albania. In a period of recession and high unemployment, these illegal (many moonlighting) workers have put an extra strain on the ailing Greek economy.

Despite the advantages, and in spite of the greater risks present than for other Union members, Greece has been as ambiguous in its policies towards Yugoslavia as both the EU and the US. Initially Athens was totally committed to the territorial status quo, opposing instant recognition of secessionist Yugoslav states and counselling caution on its EU partners before any alternative state arrangements were explored. However, Foreign Minister Andonis Samaras's agreement with Genscher in 1991 to exchange Greek recognition of Slovenia and Croatia for the exclusion of Yugoslav Macedonia deprived Greece of a strong principled position and entangled the country in the 'Macedonia problem' (*see* Ch. 8).

With some German help Samaras managed to extract EU support on Athens's position *vis-à-vis* Skopje which sought to counteract territorial claims and propagandist activities. The common EU Declaration on Yugoslavia set out conditions before Yugoslav Macedonia was granted recognition as an independent state:

The Community and its Member States also require a Yugoslav republic to commit itself, prior to recognition, to adopt constitutional and political guarantees ensuring that it has no territorial claims towards a neighbouring Community State and that it will conduct no hostile propaganda activities versus a neighbouring State, including the use of a denomination which implies territorial claims.[12]

The declaration introduced into EU politics a prodigiously complex problem such that it never succeeds in attracting the undivided attention of the public or even policy-makers. Instead, Greece has been showered with simplistic abuse for denying the weak state recognition; as if weakness legitimises any demand in international politics.

Macedonia

In the Greek part of Macedonia, out of a present population of approximately 2.2 million, only 30,000 to 40,000 are also Slavonic-speakers. The exchange of populations with Bulgaria following the First World War and the flight of Communist guerrillas in 1949, who included in their ranks a considerable percentage of local Slavo-Macedonians, by and large ended internal demands for autonomy. The Slavonic speakers who remained, and who still inhabit the north-western part of Greece, are mainly loyalists who had embraced the cause of the Greek State during the 1946–49 civil struggle. Today the memories of the Civil War in this part of Greece have faded, but the surviving inhabitants of the eastern half of Greek Macedonia, annexed by the Bulgarian forces during the period of the Axis occupation (1941–44), still remember that traumatic experience.

The concept of the territorial unification of the three Macedonias into an autonomous whole was first expounded by the Bulgarian Communist Party before the Second World War. It was part of an overall plan to destabilise the bourgeois states in the region and create a new state entity that would effectively be controlled by any future Communist regime set up in Bulgaria. During the war, the unification plan was adopted by the pro-Axis forces in the region, and the Germans tolerated the annexation of both Greek and Yugoslav territory. After liberation, with his resistance credentials and high reputation among the Communists, Tito usurped the plan and replaced Bulgarian tutelage with that of his reformed Yugoslavia. The old 'Vadar Serbia' was named for the first time 'Socialist Republic of Macedonia'. The irredentist cause of this federal State was recreated and enshrined in the preamble of the current Former Yugoslav Republic of Macedonia's (FYROM)[13] constitution which refers to principles laid down in 1944, expounding the ultimate unification of the three Macedonias.[14]

A Greek view of the future

The role of Greece

Whether or not FYROM's constitution represents a real or imagined threat, the

present Greek Government must still rid itself of the fears that have undermined Greek foreign policy in the Balkans and look to the unique opportunities that are already being exploited by the private sector. Greek businessmen in
Rumania and Bulgaria are setting the cornerstones of a stability which will out-
last political rhetoric. Once Albania drafts its legislation which protects foreign
investment, it will also attract substantial Greek capital. As things stand, Albania merely survives on the remittances that Albanian immigrant workers draw
from Greece.[15]

The 'Pinheiro Package', proposed by the Portuguese Foreign Minister in
1992, allegedly included 'New Macedonia' as the name of the FYROM. A return
to the 'Pinheiro Package' would prove beneficial to all parties concerned: for
Greece it would avail the quickest land route to Western Europe and for FYROM
(as 'New Macedonia') the most vital benefits that recognition entails, namely
access to the port of Thessaloniki and Greek investments. The survival of FYROM
has been, and still is, in Greece's interest. Should it expunge its irredentist
founding doctrine from its constitution and desist from using a provocative
national symbol which preceded the appearance of the Slavs in the Balkans by
a thousand years, then the way would be clear for normal relations.

The role of the EU

The performance of the EU in Yugoslavia has suffered more invective than it
deserves. The criticism usually ignores the humanitarian work of EU States via
their UN representatives in Yugoslavia, which far outweighs their presence (or
absence) in other parts of the world where ethnic groups are also being slaugh-
tered. That the EU was not equipped for peacemaking should come as no surprise to an institution that was not originally conceived for armed intervention
and began to think in terms of a common security at a time when the most
credible threat to the West had collapsed. NATO, on the other hand, had no man-
date (until recently) for out-of-area operations which also involved co-ordination with the American *primus inter pares*.

The Common Foreign and Security Policy (CFSP) (under the Maastricht
Treaty) was based on the assumption that, if the EU was to become a fully integrated political entity, it required a military arm as well. However, enthusiasm
for a common security policy is tempered by the absence of a credible common
threat, the persistence of a recession responsible for the creeping 'renationalisation' of defence in individual member-countries, and the dilemmas posed by
'enlargement' of the EU to include states with security traditions that differ
widely from the rest.[16] The entry of Austria, Sweden and Finland will certainly
not make the task of the CFSP any easier. No doubt other threats have become
more visible with the collapse of the hitherto predominant Soviet threat; for
example, ecological catastrophes, nuclear proliferation, terrorism, fundamen-
talism and nationalism. However, these problems have not yet appeared to con-
front the EU as a whole and therefore have not had a general rallying effect.

Yugoslavia has not been perceived as a credible threat to EU security.

Although countries closer to this risk region are naturally more concerned, their interest does not appear to merit Western European involvement. At worst, Yugoslavia will isolate the rest of the Balkans from Western Europe as a backwater region and as an exporter of economic and other refugees.

The only credible source of concern that could rekindle in the West a sense of common threat is Russia. The persistent evocation of that possibility, however, could also have the effect of a self-fulfilling prophecy. The journalistic barrage both in Western Europe and the US on the emergence of a dangerous brand of Russian nationalism exemplified by Zhirinovski, is both superficial and dangerous. Western involvement in the disputes between Russia and Ukraine, or the welfare of the Baltic States, might further inflame the battered self-image and insecurity felt by the declining superpower. Even more superficial is the linkage of the Ames espionage case with current threats posed by Russia.

The United States

The whole affair, which was covered with alarmist articles by the American press, was an anachronism which looked to the remnants of a once dangerous adversary as evidence of an evolving threat.[17] Some journalists are already reconstructing Russia into a future concern of western security: 'The relief with which the Russian entry into Sarajevo was greeted in the United States was extraordinarily shortsighted. Americans were relieved of the need to carry out the threat of air strikes. But the Russians are not in Sarajevo on America's behalf. They are there on behalf of the Serbs'.[18] On the Bosnian issue, western journalists were advising Mr Izetbegovic not to rush into an agreement with the Serbs and to hope for the construction of a 'unitary state of Bosnia.[19] If the mass media have it their way, the war in Yugoslavia will drag on indefinitely.[20]

The 'unitary state' raises its head once more, although it was among the original causes of the present carnage in Bosnia. Unitary states are based on a dominant ethnic culture disseminated through all the means that a modern state possesses. The Yugoslav drama might at least have taught us a few useful lessons: that the ethnic state is a product of political imagination and cannot become a reality without considerable violence;[21] that since ethnic groups are not recognised as international actors, they feel compelled to acquire statehood to justify their existence;[22] that an inter-ethnic conflict does not have to be ancient to be destructive (the Serb–Croat conflict began only in 1941);[23] that majority decisions to secede are inoperable when large dissenting groups are involved; and finally, that self-determination is not necessarily a liberal concept if it leads to unitary states based on a overly represented ethnic group, when substantial minorities are not represented.

The questionable liberal credentials of certain states born out of struggles for self-determination and the current proliferation of states following from the disintegration of the Soviet Union and Yugoslavia are revising public attitudes towards the use, rather than the principle, of self-determination.[24] Such movements, when they aspire to ethnic statehood, could undermine the potential for democratic development in non-democratic countries and threaten the foundations of democracy in democratic ones.[25] Furthermore, should the trend of ethnic groups to statehood acquire global application, the outcome could prove explosive. There are about 3,000 recorded ethnic groups in the world and only a couple of hundred states. Should half of these ethnic groups attain statehood, international relations would change beyond recognition.

Self-determination has both internal and external dimensions. The internal dimension regulates relations between citizens and the State and aspires to democratic governance and the rule of law. The external determines relations between a community (be it ethnic or religious) and the world of nation-states and international organisations.[26] When an ethnic group demands the right to self-determination within a given territory, it can be presumed that it is in control of the majority vote within that territory and is interested in exercising the external aspects of self-determination. However there is no guarantee that ethnically-defined majorities will offer any rights to minorities that come within their sovereignty. It is logical to assume that many ethnic groups will feel insecure at the prospect of belonging to new states with new dominant ethnic groups. The minorities may, in turn, claim or assert their alleged right to self-determination as a defiance mechanism against the nationalist policies of aspiring state-builders.[27] If, however, the international community discourages the proliferation of ethnic statehood, it ought to offer a remedy for oppressed ethnic groups within existing states. International organisations should be allowed to intrude in the internal affairs of states oppressing or slaughtering their ethnic minorities.

The members of the EU have not yet agreed on a principled response to the phenomenon of ethnic self-determination. In Yugoslavia EU reactions developed from initial innocence, to submission to the interests of one state, to ultimate impotence and confusion. By insisting on the inviolability of internal borders between the republics of the former Yugoslav State, the EU made it difficult for any negotiated alteration without violence. When faced in 1991 with the question by Serbia on whether the Serbs in Croatia and Bosnia had the right to self-determination, the European Commission admitted that international law was unclear on the issue, but that anyway the right ought not to involve changes to existing frontiers at the time of independence. Thus the EU excluded the option of a negotiated alteration of boundaries between Croats, Serbs and Bosnian Muslims.[28] The Commission should have encouraged negotiations for redrawing the map of Yugoslavia before bloodshed commenced.

The embargo imposed on FYROM by Greece in February 1994 caused considerable Western criticism. Yet although Greece's allies were quick to lecture her for the harsh decision, no one admonished FYROM for refusing to shed its irredentist symbols and constitutional preamble. Any superficial solution imposed on Greece by Western policy-makers that ignores the Greek side to the argument is destined to fail and will not therefore serve the cause of stabilisation.

Notes

1 T. Veremis, 'Greece: The Dilemmas of Change', in F. S. Larrabee (ed.) *The Volatile Powder Keg. Balkan Security after the Cold War*, (Washington DC, The American University Press/RAND, 1994).

2 Y. Valinakis, 'Greece's Security in the Post-Cold War Era', *Stiftung Wissenschaft und Politik* 394 (Ebenhausen, April 1994).

3 I. Banac, *The National Question in Yugoslavia: Origins, History, Politics* (Ithaca, Cornell University Press, 1984).

4 In 1918 Croatia 'isolated, ignored by the Allies, its men on the coast repressed by the Italians, … (its) National Council was increasingly driven to seek Serbian intervention', Banac, p. 131.

5 J. Gow, 'Deconstructing Yugoslavia', *Survival*, 33:4 (July–August 1991), 292.

6 *Ibid.* p. 309.

7 A. Heraclides, 'Secessionist Minorities and External Involvement', *International Organization*, 44:3 (Summer 1990), 342–378.

8 Y. Valinakis, 'Greece's Balkan Policy and the Macedonian Issue', *Stiftung Wissenschaft und Politik* (Ebenhausen, April 1992), 21–22.

9 M. Glenny, *The Fall of Yugoslavia* (London, Penguin, 1993), 237.

10 C. Cviic, 'Yugoslavia: New Shapes from Old', *The World Today*, 47:8–9, (August/September 1991), 125–126.

11 Gow, *Survival*, p. 306.

12 Extraordinary EPC Ministerial Meeting, 'Declaration on Yugoslavia', *EPC Press Release* (Brussels, 16 December 1991), 129/91.

13 The name with which the State was recognised by the UN in 1993.

14 *See* proclamation of the Anti-Fascist Assembly of the National Liberation of Macedonia (ASNOM) Skopje, August 1944. 'Macedonians under Bulgaria & Greece , … the unification of the entire Macedonian people depends on your participation in the gigantic anti-Fascist front.'

15 T. Veremis, 'Priorities for Athens – A Greek view', *The World Today* (April 1994).

16 WEU Institute for Security Studies, Seminar for the heads of planning at foreign and defence ministries of WEU member-states and directors of the major European foreign policy research institutes discussing 'Factors Shaping the Development of a CFSP for Europe', (20–21 January 1994).

17 'Dealing with Russia will require that US officials grow up and adopt a nuanced view of Russian actions and intentions. Russia is a great power. It seeks a sphere of influence. Some of this seeking Americans do not like and will oppose. The result will be conflict. The next major flash point is Crimea, the formerly Russian province now part of Ukraine, which late last month voted overwhelmingly for a president pledged to Crimean independence (from Moscow). A major conflict is brewing, possibly now; a war that would make the Bosnian conflict look tame. US sympathies and interests lie with Ukraine. A Crimean war, if not headed off by some compromise, threatens a serious US–Russian confrontation.' C. Krauthammer, 'Honeymoon Over, the Two Powers Go their Own Way', *International Herald Tribune* (26–27 February 1994).

18 *Ibid.*

19 F. C. Curry, 'NATO Gives the Bosnians a Chance to Gain Control', *International Herald Tribune*, (26–27 February 1994).

20 R. Cohen, 'In the Sarajevo Hills, Flexibility Towards the Serbs,' *International Herald Tribune* (23 February 1994)'.

   Voicing caution, Simon Jenkins of *The Times* (5 March 1994) points out the dangers of chronic war and Western involvement. 'Bosnia could keep half a million occupied for a lifetime.' 'Mr Clinton sabotaged the recent Croat–Serb *rapprochement*, which both sides acknowledge out of sheer exhaustion.' Albert Wohlstetter, an octogenarian vision-ary of the Cold War, pushes the Washington plan to create a Croat–Muslim Federation in Bosnia that will defend itself against Serbian forces with only 'a transient use of allied ground forces....' Professor Wohlstetter is the Dr Strangelove of the new American power projection. 'Nothing would do more to boost the militancy of the Serbs than a Croat–Muslim spring offensive. Nothing would do more to tighten its moral hold on its new Russian friends.'

21 W. Pfaff, 'Invitation to War', *Foreign Affairs*, 72:3 (Summer 1993), 99.
22 J. Mayall, *Nationalism and International Society*, (Cambridge, Cambridge University Press, 1990).
23 Pfaff, *ibid.*, p. 103.
24 G. B. Helman and S. R. Ratner, 'Saving Failed States', *Foreign Policy*, (Winter 1992–93), 3–6.
25 A. Etzioni, 'The Evils of Self-Determination', *Foreign Policy* (Winter 1992–93), 21.
26 K. S. Shehadi, 'Ethnic Self-determination and the Break-up of States', *Adelphi Paper*, 283 (IISS, London, December 1993), 4–5.
27 *Ibid.*, p. 7.
28 *Ibid.*, p. 30.

COMMENT BY JONATHAN EYAL

A western view of Greece's Balkan policy

Introduction
The intention of this chapter is to pick up on some of the strands discussed by Thanos Veremis. It aims not so much to suggest a Western perspective (which would probably be summarised by many in just a few words, namely that Greece is a nuisance), but rather to identify why such a perspective exists and what Greece must do to change it.

Greece's influence in the EU
There is a tendency, mirrored in other European countries such as Britain, for Greece to handle parts of foreign policy based on the outcome of internal political struggles. But when, for example, Mr John Major formulates his policies towards the EU exclusively against the background of disputes within the British Conservative Party, he has to accept that eventually there will be a price to pay. The cacophony of noises coming from the British Government about what needs to be done in the EU has resulted in the discrediting of the British position within the Union. The same applies to the many internal disputes between PASOK and New Democracy, or indeed within New Democracy, that were conducted through foreign policy initiatives. Such externalising may have been inevitable, but a price, usually in terms of influence and the seriousness with which a country's concerns are reflected in EU policies, is almost always exacted.

More doubt is cast on the seriousness with which Greece conducts its foreign policy by the scarcity of well-trained civil servants being sent to Brussels to prop up both the image of Greece and the interests of Greece within the apparatus of the Union itself. Many Greek representatives are given posts as a result of political patronage and not because of their capabilities. It is priorities such as these that have led some West Europeans to question Greece's true commitment.

Minor, but telling, examples exist that have had serious consequences in terms of the image of the country in the West. A deeply damaging impression has been left by the issue of the citizenship of King Constantine. Irrespective of the arguments as to whether Greece should remain a republic or return to being a monarchy, the idea of removing a passport from someone that was born a Greek, of Greek parents on Greek soil, is, to say the least, controversial. At issue is not whether Constantine is the King of Greece. It is whether citizenship leg-islation, as upheld in most European countries, is to apply to Greece as well. Granted this touchy issue can be interpreted in many various ways, but the real-ity is that the negative image is the one that gets across in most of the Western press.

Yet the crucial problem for Greece is that the difficulties that it has with the geographic western half of Europe are not simply those of presentation. Essen-tially Greece has become embroiled in conflicts which, as far as the rest of West-ern Europe is concerned, are marginal to its interests. Greece is a reminder that problems which were supposedly solved in Western Europe remain unsolved in the Balkans. So, while Greece could well have played a much more responsible and positive role in the Balkans, it cannot be suggested that presentation alone would have done the trick; it takes two to tango, particularly in the deadly game currently being played out in the Balkans.

The Balkans

Thanos Veremis's chapter emphasises very clearly the dangers of simply taking a pessimistic view of Balkan developments. The three states that have collapsed since the end of the Cold War – Czechoslovakia, the Soviet Union and Yugoslavia – each have two major things in common: all of them were ruled by Communist regimes, and in all of them the very ethnic identity of the State was questioned. Yet as far as the wider Balkan scene is concerned, there appears to be little chance of the disintegration of other states in the region. It is true that most have serious minority problems from time to time, but that is a long way from asserting, as many Western politicians do, that there will be a succession of other 'Yugoslavias'. There is very little scope for further territorial changes in the Balkans. Moreover, at least in security terms, the leaders in the Balkans have been extremely responsible up to the present (June 1994).

The problem is rather different. The forces unleashed by the thaw in the Cold War are now outside the control of any one local leader. The Skopje crisis is a classic case in point. However much the Greek Prime Minister and the Pres-idents of Bulgaria and Albania (or even Mr Gligorov himself) may assert that they have absolutely no interest at all in becoming embroiled in a conflict, the truth of the matter is that the dynamics within the Former Yugoslav Republic of Macedonia have the potential to create a situation which can drag the others in. It is not an issue which can be resolved by one individual country.

Coupled with that is the paralysis of the Western institutional thinking towards most former Communist States. The same EU that claims its greatest achievement is the fact that it has prevented any possibility of war in the West expects East Europeans to solve their problems before, rather than after, joining the Union. The reason is very simple: the West is quite content to continue with an agenda of the last 40 years and not be diverted by the true agenda of Europe today. Unfortunately Greece reminds the rest of the EU that there is another agenda and a set of unpleasant choices to be made in the near future.

Furthermore there is a misunderstanding about what the membership of the Union is meant to mean for Greece. The misunderstanding is on both sides: both in Brussels and in Athens itself. It is a simplification, but it is nevertheless a fact, that for most of the Greeks who overwhelmingly support membership in the Union do so because membership appears to represent an escape from the problems of the Balkans, be they in material, political or security terms. On the part of Western Europeans, it is a fact that many accepted Greece into the EU because they wanted to believe that it was not somehow 'a Balkan country'.

The war in Yugoslavia has served to remind all concerned that Greece is indeed in the Balkans and that the EU itself cannot avoid involvement there. What is more, the Greeks cannot escape the turmoil that may occur on their frontiers. Hence the basic feeling of insecurity that can be sensed in the streets of any town in Greece has some foundation. The problem in terms of the relationship between Greece and the western part of the continent is essentially that what the Greeks need most is what the European institutions are least able to provide: a multilateral security framework which at once binds Greece into these institutions, but also involves the West seriously in the handling of the conflicts of the region.

Meeting needs such as these is not what the agenda of the West over the last four years has been about. In almost every conflict, except for the hot war in Yugoslavia, the approach from Brussels has been a bureaucratic one; whether over lengthy negotiations to bring about cease-fires or over the question of recognising the emerging states of the former Federation, apparently ignoring the fact that recognition of a state can never be a policy on its own. It is the end of a process in which a state is anchored in a local security framework. Yet recognition for recognition's sake was essentially what the EU offered at every stage.

However fashionable it is to criticise Greece for other reasons (for example to accuse them of spongeing off EU funds), on a number of issues concerning the Yugoslav conflict Greece's solitary position was completely right and has been justified by events. First, Athens made the point as long ago as October 1991 that it would be impossible to pluck out individual republics and recognise them in isolation, yet this position was ignored. Secondly, the Greeks contended that it would be foolhardy to accept the referendum in Bosnia as a justification for giving the Republic recognition. That is now accepted wisdom in almost every Western capital; it was the Greek position from January 1992, yet that, too, was ignored. Continual assertions that the Greeks have no position or are simply complicating matters only serve to heighten Greek frustration with the EU and further reinforce the feeling that Athens and Brussels are working off two totally different agendas.

Coupled to the fact that Greece has always lacked the ability to influence the political choices taken in the Union is the hard truth that the aim of the EU in handling the Yugoslav conflict is not actually to solve it, but rather to close the dossier. The EU will accept almost any settlement as long as the file can be closed and the Union can get back to its own agenda. The fundamental issue is simple, states commit themselves to indivisible security, but in reality all are very selective about applying the concept. The reason that not one Western government judges that ending the war in Yugoslavia is worth the life of a single Western soldier is precisely because all states accept that, in many circumstances, security is quite divisible. A Serbian artillery shell cannot explode in London. That is a fact. Therefore London and the other Western capitals can prevaricate and negotiate almost at their leisure. The problem for Greece is that these facts are not avoidable.

One of the consequences of differing perceptions of the crisis in Yugoslavia is that, although historically membership of the EU was not an issue that was ever seriously debated in Greece itself, Greeks will not be able to avoid the question for much longer. The fear must be that it will come in the worst possible way, with many Greeks asking themselves what is it that the Union does for them in terms of security, and conclude that their most basic needs are not being met.

The Former Yugoslav Republic of Macedonia

The Government in Skopje is engaged in a policy of nation building. It may succeed or it may not. The experiences of nation building since 1945 are not very encouraging, apart from the Bosnian experience which may suggest that the Muslims have become a nation in the traditional way by means of being prepared to fight and die for their sovereignty. Only time will tell whether the East German example of creating a nation could be somehow bettered by either the Moldavians or the so-called Macedonians. The truth of the matter is that, in the case of the latter, an essential part of the process of nation building is to goad and aggravate Greece. Moreover, as far as Skopje is concerned, Athens represents a much less risky target than Sofia. The Macedonians cannot win a dispute with Bulgaria in the long term and, in fact, will do everything possible to avoid one.

Needling Greece, however, carries a fairly low level of risk, as long as Skopje can assume that Athens continues to assess that any escalation to an armed conflict would be far more costly than any potential gains to be made from it. Moreover it is difficult to see when Skopje will tire of these tactics; it seems hard to predict any *rapprochement* between the two capitals, irrespective of any changes of leadership. The truth of the matter is that Greece faces a classic Balkan conundrum: nations that are being created are trying to reassert the identity which they either lost or which supposedly lay dormant.

Turkey

Greece's place in future European institutions will continue to depend on the subject that the Greeks usually dismiss – its relations with Turkey. Turkey remains important not only to the West, but also, one can argue, to the Greeks themselves. However, the West owes it to the Turks to say very clearly when divisions and disputes are opening up. It is not acceptable that two United Nations reports have clearly identified which party is hindering the process of peace in Cyprus and yet these are ignored in order not to provoke Ankara. Such acquiescence serves neither Greece nor Turkey: it increases frustration in Greece and lessens responsibility in Turkey. However, on their part, it is important for Greece to realise that the current Turkish Government, with all its faults, is just about as good as either the Greeks or the West will get. It is at least a government that is prepared to contribute to regional security within certain limitations.

Conclusion

Greece today is at a crossroads, which is very similar to the one it faced in the late 1940s. Either the European institutions change and become more involved in the region, or these institutions will simply shed the southern tier of the Balkans. The tragedy for Greece is that it does not have control over either of these processes.

KOSTAS IFANTIS

9

Greece and the USA after the Cold War

Introduction

In post-war Greece the notion of dependency took on a new meaning when the US took over from Britain in the role of 'protector'. However, the post-1974 transition (*metapolitefsi*) saw a radical departure from the pre-Junta status quo of Greek–US relations. The Cyprus crisis, EU membership and eight years of socialist Government in the 1980s altered fundamentally the nature of the bilateral relationship. By the early 1980s, attempts were being made to place future explanations of Greek–US relations in a more interdependent framework of analysis.[1]

The fundamental transformation of the international system in the late 1980s/early 1990s poses a new challenge. The aim of this chapter is to evaluate the impact of the systemic change on the Greek–US relationship. The main argument is that Greek–American relations can be better understood when set against a highly interdependent international system, which is free from the bipolar East–West confrontation. The focus is an analytical one. It recognises the complexity of the relationship: the variety of actors operating within (national) and around (international) the Greek–American arena. It highlights those actors, allowing for discussion of their relative power and influence. The analytical framework identifies the existence of four interlocking environments. The first is the US foreign policy-making process, within which policy towards Greece (and the region) is elaborated. The second environment is that of the bilateral interactions between Greece and the US. The third is that of Greece, which is shaped by an aggregation of different domestic and external influences. Finally, there is the wider world environment insofar as it impinges on the Greek–American relationship. It is the combination of, and the interaction between, these four environments that underpins Greek–American relations.

The foundations of the relationship

In order to understand the morphology of Greek–US relations in the 1990s, it is essential to identify their foundations as well as the ways in which these foundations were changed and reinterpreted through historical experience. Although an historical analysis is beyond the scope of this chapter, it is important to note that Greek–American relations do not operate in a vacuum. The international system exerts an enormous influence.

As a historical benchmark, the genesis of the current relationship can be found in the immediate post-war period. The year 1947 marked the beginning of an era in which Greece was greatly, if not absolutely, dependent on the US. As the commentator, Theodore Couloumbis, has pointed out: 'Greek Governments in the 1947–55 period faced a condition of structural dependency *vis-à-vis* the United States that could be referred to as a patron–client relationship.'[2]

Containing the Soviet Union on all fronts (military, political, economic, ideological) was the most durable foreign policy priority of the US. Indeed, containment became a national fixation.[3] It is in this framework that the early post-war US policy towards Greece should be interpreted. In 1947, the prevailing view within the State Department was that unless the tottering Greek Government received immediate assurances of large-scale military and financial aid, the regime would lose all authority. President Truman translated the local situation into the starkest global terms: if Greece fell to the Communists, Turkey would become highly vulnerable to Soviet power play and subversion. Inevitably, the entire eastern Mediterranean would be sealed behind the Iron Curtain.[4] Here, full blooded, were the central premises of what came to be called the Cold War: the two-way polarisation of the international system around two great powers; an unbridgeable ideological hostility between the two groupings. From these premises, it was deduced that any allowance of an (even limited) extension of Soviet control would not reduce Soviet aggressiveness, but, on the contrary, would stimulate further aggressiveness by adding to the material and political resources with which the USSR hoped to impose its will. To many the policy implications were clear: a balance of power had to be maintained, and the intention to apply this power had to be unambiguous.[5] It was, therefore, bipolarity and the American overriding geopolitical interests that led to the US being involved surreptitiously in Greek internal affairs. However, domestic factors also contributed to Greece's heavy dependency on the US: internal polarisation and civil war, economic and security needs and the emergence of the Cyprus problem have been especially important elements in the external orientation of successive governments in Athens.[6]

The 1974 Cyprus crisis and the collapse of the military dictatorship in Greece marked a very distinct period for Greek–US relations. Because of the widely-held view in Greece, and elsewhere in Europe, that American foreign policy was greatly responsible for the success and preservation of the Colonels' regime,[7] and the way in which American policies in Cyprus seemed to have consistently favoured Turkey to the detriment of Greece and the Greek Cypriot majority, successive Greek governments attempted to re-evaluate and redefine the bilateral relationship. The 1974–81 New Democracy Governments, by setting as a primary goal the accession of the country to the EU, took a strategic decision which had a most positive impact on the consolidation of Greece's democratic institutions and on its formulation of long-term political, economic and security policies.[8] Apart from the fact that EU membership served Greece both as a diplomatic lever and as a restraining mechanism, it also operated as a means to change the nature of Greek–US relations from a highly hierarchical to a more balanced one. Economic development, interdependence and geo-economics became the dominant variables of Greek strategy. Europe offered a powerful alternative to Greek foreign policy-makers and gradually led to the normalisation of Greek–US relations through Greece's participation in the European integration process, especially in a period during which Western Europe as a whole had been actively addressing the issue of rebalancing its relationship with the US.

Indeed, as the Cold War began to thaw, relations between the US and Western Europe began to take on a different hue. While bipolarity continued to characterise the overriding military layer of the international system, this was the period of the emergence of factors that began to dilute the influence of the superpowers and marked the transition to (sub)systemic multipolarity.[9] In this new environment, the extent of US hegemony greatly diminished as the EU questioned the role of the US in its security and the future of a bipolar world order, and as it slowly began to assert its own interests in international affairs.

The 1980s saw the consolidation of the nature of Greek–US relations as 'asymmetrically interdependent'. Although in opposition the Greek socialists (PASOK) appeared to reject the essence of Greece's Atlantic orientation that dated back to the Second World War and its integration into the EU,[10] in government PASOK's foreign policy decisions and actions converged with those of their New Democracy predecessors and opened up, perhaps for the first time in the post-war period, the prospect of a grand national consensus in foreign and defence policy.[11] As the New Democracy Governments had done in the 1970s, PASOK had to adjust its policies to reality. The Turkish threat was at top of the Greek foreign policy agenda and the maintenance of the regional balance of power was the ultimate priority. In this context, the US was the only actor in a position to determine and safeguard such a balance of power. When in the mid-1980s, the Greek Government formally identified the Turkish threat by redesigning the country's defence strategy, Papandreou, in effect, recognised that the vital interests of Greece continued to require that its ties to the US and its place in the Atlantic framework be given the highest priority. As Iatrides has put it:

> Even as East–West tensions diminished, the Athens Government continued to rely on the US and NATO for military assistance, which was no less vital now that the per-

ceived enemy was Turkey rather than the Warsaw Pact. Indeed, the US and NATO remained potentially important assets to Greece: they might be persuaded to bring pressure to bear on Turkey to alter its policies.... Relations with Washington and the alliance thus became hostage to the rising tension between Athens and Ankara.[12]

In effect, that meant the re-establishment of what Couloumbis has termed a 'linkage' policy *vis-à-vis* the US, which had been abandoned in the late 1970s. Thus the smooth development of Greek–US relations could only be achieved through the US becoming active in persuading Ankara to abandon its revisionist policies in the Aegean and reverse them in Cyprus. Although for the US any disturbance in its relations with Turkey was unthinkable given the role of Turkey in American geopolitical interests, the US came gradually to accept the necessity of preserving the Greco-Turkish balance of power. In policy terms, that meant sustaining the 7:10 ratio in military aid and arms sales to the two countries, and adopting a policy of conflict management and conflict maintenance at tolerable levels of tension so as to retain a maximum leverage on Greece and, to lesser extent, on Turkey.[13]

Greek–US relations in the post-Cold War era

The latest phase in the development of Greek–US relations is marked by the monumental events of the late 1980s and early 1990s. The collapse of the USSR, the disintegration of the Communist bloc and the end of the Cold War signified the most radical changes in the political map of Europe since 1945. With the end of the bipolar structure of East–West competition Europe's morphology was transformed and with it the nature of the Greek–American bargain. In order to assess the evolution of Greek–US relations in the 1990s and the likely future trends and patterns of behaviour, several questions should be addressed: how did the behaviour of the US and Greece change as a result of systemic transformation? Has the nature of issues changed and how have the actors involved reacted to the new challenges? Finally, and this is central to the purpose of this chapter, has the US-Greece–Turkey triangle been affected by the new security setting and, if so, how?

The US in the new international environment
The Gulf War and the admittedly impressive US exhibition of capacity to go to war shows that military power is not obsolete. However, the assumption that the military victory of the US in the Gulf implies that Washington has become once again hegemonic would be simplistic. The promise contained in former President Bush's concept of a New World Order should not be viewed as a new Pax Americana.[14] There can be no such US dominance. If there is 'order' it will surely not be premised on the absolute primacy of the US, save where, as in the Middle East, military power can still be a major arbiter of events with implica-

tions far beyond the region. Having said that, it should be emphasised that the US is the only state with the capacity to exercise global political leadership in the short term. However, in the long run, we need to think about the diffusion of power in the world capitalist system. This phenomenon has two major dimensions: the expansion and globalisation of interdependence and the economic decline of the US. Both dimensions have been well accounted for. What is important in the context of this paper are the implications, if any, for US foreign policy.

According to the writer, S. D. Krasner, the US has changed its policies in response to its decline in power, but has not yet found a new strategic vision.[15] However, Krasner is only partly right. There is an undercurrent of disorientation in the US resulting from difficulties in translating military power into political success. Having claimed credit for winning the Cold War, US policymakers have now confronted the equally daunting task of managing peace. Building constructive relations among all the emerging great powers is a challenge which is exacerbated by the simultaneous existence of military and economic competition. Because the issues and the hierarchy of power are different on each of these playing fields, solutions on one level are likely to pose problems on the other, and vice-versa. However, although international policy co-ordination was never more difficult, there is evidence to support the thesis that the US foreign policy-making elites are attempting to craft a coherent policy by pursuing a strategy that promotes American power, position and primacy, in order to enhance the capacity of the US to exercise influence abroad.

American action in the Gulf, Somalia, Haiti, the Korean Peninsula and Yugoslavia represent the continuation of Washington's commitment to an active internationalist agenda, even without a geopolitical and ideological rival. This American globalisation is compatible with a set of principles that have come to be associated with world order and stability, and thus vital US interests. Another case in point is the US's post-Cold War European strategy. As Nye and Keohane have commented, American influence in Europe was greater in the early 1990s than during the mid-1980s.[16] The US successfully sought to prevent a loss of influence in Europe by maintaining a complex of interests that had formed around institutions, chiefly NATO, that it had itself created. Although the Bush administration, under strong congressional pressure to reduce the defence budget in the spring of 1990, implemented a 25 per cent contraction in the American force structure which included a sharp cutback of US troops in Europe, it succeeded in maintaining the centrality of NATO in European defence (against French attempts to undermine that strategy), and was thus by and large able to keep intact its policies, preferences and interests. NATO was central to the American strategy for remaining the most influential state in the world in the post-Cold War era, and emphasis on the alliance was consistent with the US position throughout the Cold War years.

There is, therefore, a US international strategy with a very strong element of continuity: a global foreign policy inspired by *realpolitik* efforts to prevent other states from 'renationalising' their foreign and security policies. Such a policy of renationalisation would destroy the reassurance and stability upon which American interests are presumed to rest.[17] American global activism is, therefore, the prism through which Greek–US relations should be examined.

The impact of international change on Greece

In the past, the advent of multipolarity stimulated repositioning. States were expected to readjust their alignments and change the course of their national security policies to accommodate shifts in the hierarchy of world power. The challenge for Greece has been similar. What was the impact of the dramatic systemic transformation on the country's international position and foreign policy strategy?

For many the collapse of the Soviet pole meant the triumph of the Western paradigm of pluralist democracy, free market economy and their institutional safeguards (NATO, EU, GATT, IMF). However, for Greece, world transformation represented a grave need to learn and readjust. Cold War stability was replaced by post-Cold War stress and turbulence affecting the country's northern neighbourhood. Less than orderly political transitions, bankrupt economies, sharp ethnic conflicts and border disputes on Greece's northern periphery threatened and still threaten regional stability and vital national interests.

Throughout the post-1974 period, Greece's national strategy was based on containing the Turkish threat. The end of the Cold War added another problem to that of the 'danger from the east': the collapse of a stable regional environment. Greece could not remain indifferent to these developments. The disintegration of Yugoslavia clearly signalled potential dangers to the country's territorial integrity and to its social and political order. Athens had to deal with the complex issues of the region brought about by the end of the Cold War. Events are well known, as is the failure of Greek governments to formulate a coherent and effective Balkan policy and thus play a key role in the resolution of the crisis. Instead, to a certain extent, Greece became part of the problem.

Although the problems in the Balkans were not the result of Greek actions, Athens governments can be charged with failure on two grounds. The first was the inability to grasp the complexity of the situation which, apart from the problems of ethnic, political and social disorder, was being aggravated by the involvement of third regional and non-regional powers that pursued divergent policies, and whose interests were not always compatible. The complexity of actors, roles, policies and perceived interests partly explains why the crisis in Yugoslavia was bound to cascade into neighbouring countries such as Greece, who were otherwise not directly involved. Undoubtedly the FYROM quest for statehood and nationhood, as well as the incoherent Albanian attempt to create a new ideological identity in the place of a bankrupt Stalinist model, resulted in considerable security anxiety in Greece which itself led to policy-making that lacked basic direction and well-assessed goals. Although Greece was adequately equipped to deal effectively with the negative Balkan conditions, Athens was caught in a vicious cycle of reacting to individual events, rather than under-standing, evaluating and being ahead of them. The second, and perhaps more important failure was that the Greek response to the Balkan changes fell victim to the antithesis within New Democracy both at government and party levels (Mitsotakis/Samaras) as well as the government/opposition confrontation that found expression in an oral nationalist competition, the focus of which was the 'Skopje problem'.[18]

The impact of recent international change has, on balance, had a negative effect on Greece. Foreign policy in the 1990s has been in a state of Balkan 'suf-focation', while at the same time the Turkish threat, a 'political heritage' of the 20 years since 1974, has not simply remained undiminished. Rather it has taken on a different and more complex form, given the new geopolitical realities affecting both Turkey's international position and its internal development.

Greece and the US: issues and policy problems

In the context of the effects that systemic transformation had on the US and Greece, a central question is the extent to which change has been cyclical or cumulative. The general course of events is well known and has also been reviewed earlier in the chapter. That study now needs to be amplified by an assessment of the implications of the new structural changes that have occurred and the extent to which assumptions of continuity and change are valid. A cen-tral question relates to the nature of change: is there a series of cycles or fluctu-ations in an essentially continuous flow of Greek–US relations, or are there more fundamental structural and systemic differences which must be recog-nised when considering future trends and patterns of behaviour? Two areas will be briefly explored here: Greek–US–Turkish relations and the Balkan problem. To these can be added a broader problem of policy definition and implementa-tion, which reflects in part the changing nature of the substance as well as polit-ical circumstances.

Greek, US and Turkish relations

For 20 years the threat to Greece has emanated from a single adversary: Turkey. Military and diplomatic deterrence was indispensable to the concept of Greek survival. To Greek policy-makers the stakes seemed extremely high; successful deterrence generated at best an uneasy peace, whereas failure would mean the transformation of Greek islands and Cyprus into a battlefield. Ironically, although the end of the Cold War resulted in the overnight metamorphosis of the military situation in Europe, no other country experienced the change less intensely than Greece. The New World Order did not alter the basic parameters of the Greek–Turkish competition. Greece remains a 'status quo' country, yet Turkey has never stopped pursuing revisionist policies in Cyprus, the Aegean, and Thrace as well as aiming to alter the balance of power and interests in the region. Turkey's international position and its importance for the US has not changed either. Many observers in Turkey and the West anticipated that Turkey would be a leading casualty of strategic neglect after the Cold War. Although the longer-term implications of developments in Europe, Central Asia, and the Middle East for Turkey's interests and geopolitical orientation are not clear (yet), the Gulf War has returned Turkey to the strategic front rank.[19] For the US, the Middle East remains an area of vital importance. Turkey's growing significance is much more powerfully defined by its centrality to a region of major instability and conflagration.

At the same time, however, this growing significance has produced a set of uncertainties directly linked with what has been an unusually poor (for Turkish diplomacy) perception of national capabilities and post-Cold War opportunities. For the first time in Turkey's post-Ottoman history, the country's foreign policy elites attempted to revise the traditional Ataturkist precepts regarding the dangers of international activism.[20] This attempt was largely in accordance with many analysts's suggestions. According to the commentator, I. O. Lesser, for almost 40 years Ankara's geo-strategic reach was largely limited to its place within NATO's southern region. With the disintegration of the Soviet Union and turmoil in the Balkans, Ankara was poised to play a leading role across a vast region, from Eastern Europe to Western China.[21] However, this attempt to establish new spheres of influence has not been successful. As the former Turkish Foreign Minister, Mumtaz Soysal, pointed out in a speech to the French National Assembly's France–Turkey Committee in March 1994, the desired results of this 'new thinking' in Turkish foreign policy have not been forthcoming.[22] In addition, the implicit rejection by Brussels of the Turkish EU application has also contributed to the sense of disappointment and uncertainty, and has made Turkish behaviour towards Greece more unpredictable and perhaps hard to control.

In that respect, the Greek–US–Turkish entanglement becomes even more complex. At issue is the extent to which US strategy will remain the same as far as the management of the Greek–Turkish conflict is concerned. We have already identified strong elements of continuity in US foreign policy in general. In the context of Greek–US relations, the analysis was, in the past, shaped predominantly by the Greek–Turkish debate. This was appropriate, given the pre-eminence of the Turkish threat for Greece since 1974. However the rhetoric of this debate continues to shape both Greek and American thinking and strategy today. As a result, the issue of US leadership – whether the US can continue to fulfil a balancing role or whether there should be a different American approach and subsequently a different Greek response – is given continuing prominence.

A full discussion of the history and points of contention in Greek–Turkish relations is beyond the scope of this analysis. What is important here is that the overall American strategic interests in the area have almost inevitably drawn the US into the dispute. The Washington approach was always a pragmatic one, since no American initiative has succeeded in achieving the normalisation of

Greek–Turkish relations. That is why the US has not been actively involved in the search for a solution. Moreover, during the Cold War, successive US administrations felt that the Aegean issues were not as acute as many problems elsewhere and therefore were placed well down in the list of Washington's priorities.[23] Although the dispute was recognised as posing a threat to NATO's south-eastern flank, the primary objective of US foreign policy elites was to control Greek–Turkish tensions and thus their effect on the smooth-running of the alliance.

Successive governments in Athens have conceptualised the problem in a fundamentally different way. For Greece, the issue has always been one of a Turkish revisionist threat. Any attempt to normalise bilateral relations is inevitably conditioned not only by the thesis that Ankara should stop pursuing all anti-status quo policies, but also by the need to find a viable solution to the Cyprus problem, acceptable to both communities. The policy pursued by Greece has two dimensions: it has been both a policy of deterrence and a policy of political de-escalation. This twin character has been compatible with the crisis prevention policy of the US and has enabled Athens and Washington to converge on the specific issue of relaxation of tension in the Aegean.

In the 1990s, the prospects for Greek–Turkish relations remain highly uncertain. The Aegean and Cyprus will remain potential flashpoints and pose a continuing problem of crisis prevention for the US (and Europe). The Greek sense of insecurity in relation to a neighbour of continental scale and uncertain strategic orientation has already been reinforced by the Turkish threat that a Greek declaration of a 12-mile territorial sea limit would be a *causus belli*. Of course, this is not a new development. Successive Turkish governments have employed such a threat since 1974.[24] The new element is Turkey's post-Cold War domestic and foreign policy uncertainties and the extent to which US policy will prove to be successful in diffusing the new crisis.

Greece, the US and Balkan disorder

During the 1974–1990 period, Greek defence policy was relatively simple: Turkey to the East and the Warsaw Pact to the North. In reality, however, the latter had been given little attention because the country's NATO membership and bilateral co-operation with the US were guarantees of not only a relatively small economic burden but, most importantly, a high degree of deterrence.[25] Throughout this period, therefore, Greece's defence preoccupations in the Balkans were integrated in the bipolar, superpower-dominated international security system which, by its nature, guaranteed a compatibility of interests between the US and Greece.

The collapse of Communism, however, brought an end to that style of security system, with its familiar arrangements. The potential consequences of possible conflicts are now less all-encompassing than any direct East–West confrontation, but the likelihood of smaller, more complex conflicts is greater.[26] While for Greece the Balkan problem was rightly perceived as affecting vital national interests, for the US it merely represented the first serious challenge to the American attempt to come to terms with post-Cold War security threats and a complication in the process of identifying its security interests in Europe. The Yugoslav crisis and the overall tension in the region have required adjustment in security concepts and policies, as well as a rapid adjustment to events on the ground. In sharp contrast to, for example, Middle East oil and the former Soviet nuclear arsenal, where American interests are clear cut and more or less easy to deem vital, the Balkan conflict is an issue that has posed questions concerning the purposes and power of the US in the emerging system of world politics for which both the Bush and Clinton administrations had no answers. An appropriate conceptual apparatus would have to be evolved along the way.[26]

As was indicated earlier, there is evidence to suggest that Washington is committed to a global foreign policy pursuit. Proponents of this policy believe that an American hegemony in a setting of diffused global power would calm the fears of those who worry that the only alternative to US preponderance is anarchy. The starting point of the interventionist position – and the foundation of the US's world order strategy – is the conviction that American prosperity depends upon international economic interdependence and that the precondition for it is the geopolitical stability and reassurance that flow from US security commitments. The quest for world order has been the link that connects the Balkans to US national interests. This quest is what potentially makes Greek national interests compatible with American ones. However, there are several reasons why this convergence is not enough to make effective the partnership so much desired by Athens.

First, the US policy of supporting the Skopje and Tirana regimes, although in line with US perceptions of improving stability, is not helpful to Greek foreign policy objectives. Secondly, the Clinton administration has failed to articulate foreign policy objectives clearly or to employ the various foreign policy instruments effectively in order to attain these goals.[28] On Yugoslavia, US leaders vacillated, often declaring that the crisis was a European problem to be resolved under the aegis of the EU, only then to endorse reluctantly NATO's first strikes against Serb targets when public opinion condemned the Sarajevo market massacre. From outrage against the Serbs to the denunciation of the Vance–Owen partition plan, the US reacted spasmodically, especially when trying to promote the once preferred option of lifting the arms embargo against the Bosnian Government. Thirdly, the internal power struggle in the US political system serves to alarm Athens more than reassure her. Like the President and his advisers, Congress is struggling to comprehend the emerging foreign policy agenda if not to control it. The issue of the arms embargo in Bosnia is a glaring example. After intense denunciation of the President's dithering on Bosnia, Congress passed on a single day an amendment that would force the US to lift the embargo unilaterally. The latest decision of the Administration to stop enforcing the embargo came only days after the mid-term elections which produced hostile Republican majorities in Congress. Fourthly, it is doubtful that the US would help reinforce the Greek role in the Balkans, if such a role would upset its relations with Turkey. Finally, co-operation cannot be assured because Greece is, by all accounts, part of the overall problem that causes tension and instability in the region, either by default (Albania) or by design (FYROM). The failure of Greek governments to disentangle the country from issues that have negatively affected its regional and European relations has led to its inability to act as a stabiliser and to promote peace and co-operation.

Conclusions

In this chapter the focus has been primarily upon the challenges that Greek–US relations are facing in the 1990s. The challenges facing Greece today are more complex, more mercurial and less predictable than at any period during the Cold War era. They demand innovative and imaginative responses at a number of levels: domestic, regional, European and international. In that respect, good and functional relations with the US are very important, as they are with the EU. It should be noted that the 1990s have already witnessed an impressive improvement in bilateral relations. Prime Minister Mitsotakis met with President Bush in Washington, and the latter was the first US President to address the Greek Parliament. Even more important was the meeting between Andreas Papandreou and Bill Clinton in the White House on 21 April 1994. This meeting marked a new era in Greek–US relations given the fact that the former was always regarded as a black sheep by the American foreign policy establishment. The argument here has identified some underlying issues which have been dictating the conduct of the bilateral interaction: wider US geo-strategic interests, regional turmoil and national uncertainties. Unprepared for the Cold War's end, Greek as well as American leaders have been slow to devise a comprehensive strategy to cope with the plethora of social, political, economic and security problems deriving from the collapse of the old European States system.

For the US, the task is to understand that Greek security concerns regarding Turkey are valid. This truth should not be ignored in the transformed conditions of the 1990s. If American foreign policy-makers are not ready to work towards a settlement acceptable to both parties, the US should, at least, resist any pressures to disturb the vital (for Greece) balance of power. At the same time, a healthy and beneficial evolution of Greek–US relations should be among the top Greek priorities. 'De-Skopjeisation'[29] of Greek foreign policy will act as a catalyst. Full and permanent normalisation of Greece's relations with the post-Communist societies to the north, as well as effective and successful integration of its foreign, security and economic policies into the highly institutionalised European environment, have the potential to transform Greece into a facilitator of less turbulent political and economic transition in south-eastern Europe.

Notes

1 *See* especially, T. A. Couloumbis and J. O. Iatrides, *Greek American Relations. A Critical Review* (New York, Pella, 1980).

2 T. A. Couloumbis, 'Greek–US Relations in the 1990s: Back into the Future', in H. J. Psomiades and S. B. Thomadakis, *Greece, The New Europe, and The Changing International Order* (New York, Pella, 1993), 381.

3 J. L. Gaddis, *The United States and the End of the Cold War. Implications, Reconsiderations, Provocations* (New York, Oxford University Press, 1992), 18.

4 S. Brown, *The Faces of Power. United States Foreign Policy from Truman to Clinton*, 2nd ed., (New York, Columbia University Press, 1994), 26.

5 *Ibid.*, p. 28.

6 T. A. Couloumbis, 'Defining Greek Foreign Policy Objectives', in Couloumbis and Iatrides (1980), 21–48.

7 Among others, *see* L. Sterns, *The Wrong Horse: The Politics of Intervention and the Failure of American Diplomacy* (New York, Times Books, 1977); A. Papandreou, *Democracy at Gunpoint: The Greek Front* (London, Andre Deutsch, 1971); T. A. Couloumbis and S. M. Hicks, *US Foreign Policy Toward Greece: The Clash of Principle and Pragmatism* (Washington, DC, Center for Mediterranean Studies, 1975).

8 Couloumbis. (1993) 'Greek–US Relations in the 1990s', p. 383.

9 K. Ifantis, 'Europe and America: Continuity and Change in the New World', in *The Southeast European Yearbook 1993* (Athens: Hellenic Foundation for European and Foreign Policy, 1994), 266–7.

10 J. O. Iatrides, 'Papandreou's Foreign Policy', in T. C. Kariotis, *The Greek Socialist Experiment. Papandreou's Greece 1981–1989*, (New York, Pella, 1992), 127.

11 Couloumbis (1993), pp. 383–4.

12 Iatrides, (1992), p. 152–3.

13 Couloumbis (1993), p. 385. 'As long as the US foreign policy formulators considered that the basic, if not the only, motive that led Greek Governments to accept the continued functioning of US facilities on Greek soil was the Turkish threat (and the resultant need to perpetuate a sufficient Greek–Turkish military balance), the Americans had no incentive whatsoever to move in the direction of defusing and/or settling the Greek–Turkish conflict'.

14 Ifantis (1994), p. 274.

15 S. D. Krasner, 'Power, Polarity, and the Challenge of Disintegration', in H. Haftendorn and C. Tuschhoff, *America and Europe in an Era of Change* (Boulder, Westview, 1993), 21–42.

16 J. S. Nye and R. O. Keohane, 'The United States and International Institutions in Europe after the Cold War', in R. O. Keohane, J .S. Nye and S. Hoffmann, *After the Cold War. International Institutions and State Strategies in Europe, 1989–1991* (Cambridge Massachussetts, Harvard University Press 1993), 105.

17 The assumption is that if Washington cannot or would not solve other's problems for them, the world order strategy would collapse. Compelled to provide for their own security, others would have to emerge as great or regional powers and behave like independent geopolitical actors. See C. Layne and B. Schwartz, 'American Hegemony – Without an Enemy', in *Foreign Policy*, 92, (Fall 1993), 15.

18 *Kyriakatiki Eleftherotypia*, 12 July 1994.

19 I. O. Lesser, 'Bridge or Barrier? Turkey and the East After the Cold War' in G. E. Fuller and I. O. Lesser, with P. B. Henze, and J. F. Brown, *Turkey's New Geopolitics. From the Balkans to Western China* (Boulder, Westview Press/RAND Corporation, 1993), 99.

20 An 'Ataturkist' foreign policy attitude refers to a policy of non-expansion and the respect for post-Ottoman borders.

21 Lesser, (1993), p. 99.
22 According to Soysal, Ankara's policy in Central Asia has not been a success, not only because of limited economic capabilities, but also because it clashes with dominant Russian interests in the area. Also, the Turkish attempt to 'return' to the Balkans by filling the power vacuum that the disintegration of Yugoslavia created, has also been unsuccessful (so far), given the strong Serbian, Bulgarian and Greek objections to any such policy. In addition, its failure to emerge as the protector of Muslim interests in Bosnia, as well as the Kurdish problem within Turkey, has also contributed to the relative stagnation of Arab–Turkish relations. *See To Vima*, (20 March 1994).
23 C. W. McCaskill, 'US–Greek Relations and the Problems of the Aegean and Cyprus', Paper delivered in a conference on United States foreign policy regarding Greece, Turkey and Cyprus. *The Rule of Law and American Interests*, (Ohio State University, 29–30 April 1988).
24 M. Stearns, *Entangled Allies: US Policy Toward Greece, Turkey and Cyprus*, (New York, Council on Foreign Relations Press, 1992).
25 Y. Valinakis, 'Greece and the European Cosmogony', in *Yearbook on Greek Defence and Foreign Policy 1992*, (Athens, ELIAMEP, 1992), xii.
26 M. Smith and S. Woolcock, 'Learning to Co-operate: the Clinton Administration and the European Union', in *International Affairs*, 70:3 (July 1994), 462.
27 Brown, (1994), p. 591.
28 L. B. Miller, 'The Clinton Years: Reinventing US Foreign Policy', in *International Affairs*, 70:4 (1994), 628.
29 T. Veremis and T. A. Couloumbis, *Greek Foreign Policy. Perspectives and Dilemmas*, (in Greek), (Athens, ELIAMEP, 1994), 27–39.

THEADORE A. COULOUMBIS
& PRODROMOS YANNAS

10

Greek foreign policy priorities for the 1990s*

Introduction

This chapter focuses on the presentation and evaluation of Greece's security challenges and priorities in a rapidly changing domestic, regional and international setting. The analysis is designed to fit in a 'unit-environment' framework. The 'unit' is the random Greek Government and its foreign policy-making apparatus. The relevant 'environments', arrayed in an order of concentric circles, involve, in the innermost circle, Greece's domestic setting (covering political, economic, social, leadership and other variables); in the intermediate circle, the regional setting (covering the Balkans and Eastern Mediterranean) and in the outer circle, the global setting (covering the international system after the Cold War and bipolarity).

The paper is divided in two parts: the first seeks to point up the impact of environmental changes on Greek foreign policy choices. The second part, adopting a normative orientation, outlines a strategy of 'peaceful engagement' between Greece and its immediate neighbours to the North and to the East. Without entering the conceptual debate, Greece is assumed to be a 'small State'.

Seeking to assess the impact of major changes in domestic and international environments upon Greece's foreign policy profile is a difficult conceptual task. The concept of 'influence', despite its centrality in the field of international relations, has been quite elusive in having a scientific definition placed on it. Ultimately the matter has gravitated to identifying comparative perceptions of the influencer and the influencee. The task of this chapter is further complicated by the fact that the last decade has been one of drastic change

---

* This chapter is a revised and updated version of T. A. Couloumbis, 'Greece and the European Challenge in the Balkans',*The Southeast European Yearbook*, Athens, ELIAMEP, 1992, 75–88 and T. A. Couloumbis and Prodromos Yannas, 'Greek Security in a Post-Cold War Setting', *NATO's Sixteen Nations*, 38:2, 18-21.

in the structure and functions of the international system, the EU and the Balkans. Moreover, in the case of Greece's domestic setting, the period since 1974 has been one of virtual political metamorphosis.

Part I – The impact of environmental changes on choice

From praetorian zone to EU partner

The year 1974 is the gate connecting two different eras in the history of 20th century Greece. In the period 1909–1974 this small and strategically located country experienced considerable turbulence in its external and internal relations. Economically, it was classified in the category of poor, agrarian, raw material-producing, trade-dependent and externally indebted. In short, it was underdeveloped. Politically, it was polarised, functioning with personalistic and clientelistic political parties whose main purpose was to distribute the largesse controlled by a hypertrophic state sector. Deep schisms – pitting Royalists against Republicans and Communists against Nationalists – marked the years from 1915 to 1974, resulting in frequent military interventions in politics. Accordingly, dictatorial rule was imposed in 1925–26, 1936–41 and 1967–74. Between 1946–49, a bloody, destructive and socially traumatic civil war scarred deeply the body politic and the society of the country. Given the instability and fragility of its democratic institutions – constantly challenged by competing models of monarchical authoritarianism and communist totalitarianism – Greece during this long period was classified by political scientists in the 'praetorian zone' together with States such as Spain, Portugal and Turkey as well as countries in Central and South America.

Its external relations were set in the cauldron that was Europe of the two world wars, of totalitarian ideologies, competing nationalisms and the holocaust. Greece itself was actively involved in international conflicts such as the Balkan Wars (1912–13), World War I, the Greco–Turkish War (1921–22), and World War II. All these adventures, that were very much a reflection of general turbulence in Europe (and particularly in the Balkans), affected the delimitation of the boundaries of Greece which were formally defined in 1923 (the Treaty of Lausanne) and 1947 (the Treaty of Paris).

Given its strategic location in the Mediterranean and the Balkans, Greece throughout the 20th century was subject to the competing bids for Great Power penetration. Its near total exposure by sea placed the small state under the direct influence of whatever Great Power exercised naval control in the Mediterranean (Great Britain before 1947 and the United States after that time). In the area of Greek–Great Power relations, political scientists classified Greece among those states with penetrated (dependent) political systems.

The collapse of the Colonels' dictatorship, triggered by the Cyprus imbroglio in the summer of 1974, opened the gates of a new era. The infrastructure for change had already been put in position, given the high (highest in the OECD) rates of economic growth in the 1950s and 1960s, the rapid urban-isation of the population (a product of the Civil War, immigration/emigration and rapid economic development), and the consequent creation of a sizeable middle class.

In mid-1974 Constantinos Karamanlis returned from political exile and, possessing strong political instincts and considerable foresight, presided over a remarkably smooth transition process that led to the establishment and con-solidation of durable and, with the passage of time, adequately tested democra-tic institutions. The deep divisions of the past were gradually bridged, leading to the effective reintegration of Greek society. The question of the Monarchy was resolved in a free and fair plebiscite in December 1974, removing a thorny symbol that had for decades polarised a revolutionary Left against an authori-tarian Right. More importantly, the vanquished in the Greek Civil War were permitted to re-enter the political process through the legalisation (and subse-quent participation in the November 1974 elections) of the Greek Communist party(ies). Also, the handling of 'dejuntafication' in 1974–5, confined primarily to coup leaders and those responsible for the ordering and the practice of tor-ture, prevented the upsurge of a new schism between the 'ins' and the 'outs', thus putting an end to the long cycles of mutual revanchism in the Greek polit-ical arena, while reducing the opportunities (as well as removing the causes) of patron–client relationships between warring political parties (or coalitions) within Greece, and involving external Great Powers.

The Greek Government's (Karamanlis's) decision in 1974–5 to redress, in a deliberate and long-term manner, the imbalance of forces between Turkey and Greece – an imbalance so dramatically manifested by the effortless Turkish invasion of Cyprus – reflected the deep impact that the prospect of EU acces-sion exercised on post-1974 Greek foreign policy. Following the Colonels-inspired coup in Cyprus, which offered Turkey an opportunity to land its troops and partition the island Republic, the Karamanlis Government had three options, the first of which was to go immediately to war with Turkey. But the Greek dictators, paradoxically, had left Greece militarily exposed by leaving the Greek Aegean islands undefended and at the mercy of a Turkish military oper-ation. The second option was to seek a truce so as to gain time and, later, to mount a massive rearmament programme so as to force the Turks at an oppor-tune moment to withdraw their occupation army from Cyprus. Had this option been chosen, Greece and Turkey would have initiated a chain-reaction of revan-chist wars of the Arab–Israeli variety. Needless to say, a climate of high tension and protracted conflict would not have permitted Greece to secure membership of the EU. The third option was to rearm Greece to a level adequate to deter future Turkish revisionist contingencies in Cyprus, the Aegean and Thrace, and to apply in parallel a mixture of political, economic and diplomatic pressures, in other words all means short of war itself, in order to secure a viable settle-ment in Cyprus and the Aegean.

Karamanlis opted for the third strategy outlined above. He had been summoned from self-exile in Paris in late July 1974 to help rescue a sinking ship. He had become firmly convinced that Greece's destiny would have been bleak outside the greenhouse of democracies that had been carefully erected by the master builders of European integration. In order for Greece to qualify for entry into the EU, it (like France, Germany and others) had to abandon concepts and policies such as ultra-nationalism, irredentism or other forms of territorial revisionism and to accept instead the challenges of functional integration and economic interdependence which were at the heart of the grand European experiment.

Despite the spirited debate that had preceded Greece's entry into the EU between 1976–79 (PASOK, the Greek Socialist Party, had been strongly opposed to Greek membership during this period), in the years that have elapsed since formal accession in January 1981 the EU has become almost universally accepted by the full range of political parties as the centrepiece of Greece's external relationships. It is well beyond the scope of this chapter to assess the deep impact of EU membership on nearly every aspect of Greek economic, political and social expression. However, it is safe to assume that the comprehensive impact will probably prove to be of monumental proportions in nearly every walk of Greek life.

In the field of foreign policy, it is possible to advance the proposition that EU membership in the period 1981–1994 has served Greece both as a diplomatic lever and as a restraining mechanism. For example, Greece adopted a stance of 'conditionality', by using its membership in the EU as a lever designed to convince Turkey that Turkish–EU relations cannot be normalised unless the occupation of Cyprus is terminated. In the past two years the EU membership status was also employed *vis-à-vis* FYROM (the Former Yugoslav Republic of Macedonia) in order to prevent the latter from monopolising (in the Greek view expropriating) the historic name of Ancient Greek Macedonia.

Simultaneously, the EU has functioned also as a restraining instrument. Membership in an elaborate structure that is highly institutionalised required the abandonment of some of the trappings of undiluted sovereignty and national independence. Both with respect to Turkey (as suggested above) and also in its relations with its northern neighbours (especially FYROM), Greece has found itself, like Odysseus, tied to an EU mast inclining it to resist the tempting siren songs of atavistic nationalism and irredentism. Without such a mast, the Greek ship of state could have veered off course and into the rough and tumble of the Balkan vortex, thus becoming much more a part of the problem than acting as a channel for solutions.

The challenges of partnership

During the four decades of the Cold War the undisguised adversarial relations between NATO and the Warsaw Pact, always overshadowed by the threat of general nuclear war, provided a high degree of stability and focus for the world's Northern Hemisphere. At the same time, the 'South' remained unstable and conflict-prone. Scores of internal, inter-state and Great Power proxy conflicts cost the inhabitants of the Third World over 25 million deaths in the years 1950–1990. Today the post-Cold War global structures are in a state of flux. Analysts and policy-makers in small countries are attempting to identify and to predict trends as well as to recommend policies of adjustment to emerging global patterns.

Greece can safely be described today as democratic, internationalist, Western, status quo, free-trade and free-enterprise oriented. Moreover it is a sensitive strategic outpost of the EU and NATO located in the troubled regions of the Balkans and the Central-Eastern Mediterranean. The challenge for this small and dangerously placed country is to safeguard its territorial integrity and to protect its democratic system and values.

To promote its security interests most effectively, Greece has sought to aggregate its voice and to integrate its policies with those of its EU partners and NATO allies. Greek policy-makers have long believed that, in partnership, these powerful clusters of democratic and industrial states can effectively maintain regional and global stability. Accordingly, it was widely accepted that the security objectives of Greece could be best served by collective Atlantic–European policies that would facilitate a stable, conflict-free transition to political democracy and a market economy in post-Communist societies in the troubled Balkans and elsewhere. The challenge for Greece in the early 1990s, phrased another way, was to 'broaden' and 'deepen' its ties with its EU, Western European Union (WEU) and NATO partners, at a time of admittedly serious centrifugal tendencies in the Atlantic Alliance in the face of the strategic and ideological vacuum that had been created following the collapse of the Soviet bloc.

Greece's optimal defence and security profile for the foreseeable future can be visualised with the aid of a series of concentric circles (see Figure 10.1). The inner core of Greek security has been, and will continue to be, served by a healthy and competitive economy, functioning under conditions of free trade in an environment of strong and adequately tested democratic institutions backed by well-trained and equipped armed forces sufficient to maintain Greece's regional military balances.

The next circle represents the remarkable functional experiment of the EU which solidifies and supplements Greece's defensive/ deterrent/status quo stance. Needless to say, Greece's potential adversaries will think twice before attempting to challenge its territorial integrity, in the sense that they will be challenging, in addition to Greece, the gradually integrating EU of which it is a member.

Within the next concentric circle, there is a dotted line that circumscribes the WEU because there still remains some ambivalence as to the future structural fit of this recently resurrected organisation. The question that has yet to be answered is whether the WEU will evolve into the exclusive defence component of the EU or whether it will grow to house a greater number of member-states, thus serving as an inclusive European pillar of NATO. In either case,

Greece will be counting on the WEU to provide a segment of the value of collective security. Hypothetically, the WEU could assume quite substantial dimensions in the unlikely and undesirable contingency that United States policy-makers decided to opt for a neo-isolationist stance leading to a dramatic reduction of the American military presence in Central Europe and the Mediterranean.

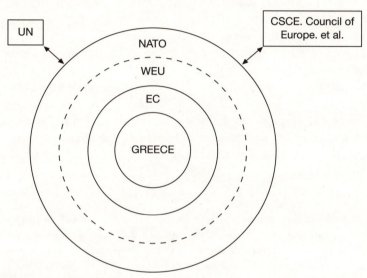

FIG **10.1 Greece's security profile**

Finally, in the next and most decisive circle, in terms of collective defence, we find NATO or the Atlantic community. As we shall see below, the maintenance of the institutions as well as the security and defence functions of NATO will remain the *sine qua non* for the creation of a post-Cold War order that can usher in decades of global peace and even prosperity for our planet. NATO, it should be remembered, offers the best mix of Atlantic solidarity as well as an intricate and long-proven set of procedures, command arrangements and facilities that can permit quick and effective multinational responses to UN authorised peace-keeping, peacemaking and peace-enforcement missions.

Figure 10.1 also refers to institutions with a wider membership, such as the CSCE, the Council of Europe, and the UN. These, also, could further enhance Greece's commitment to peaceful processes for the settlement of disputes.

Possible security scenarios

As we have indicated in the beginning of this essay the nature of the synergistic relationships between Greek policy-makers and their rapidly changing environments will continue to be subject to wider developments that will be taking shape both at the global and the regional (south-east European) settings as well as the domestic setting. The working assumption is that Greece, since 1974, has entered a trough of calm, permitting forecasts of stability (compared to the turbulence prior to 1974) in Greece's internal setting. If, for instance, the trend towards European unification continues unabated, one can predict that Greece's deeper integration into the Union will be part of the course. If, alternatively, following a renationalisation of EU member-states policies, there arise serious centrifugal forces that turn back the clock of European unification, then Greece will have to fend for itself as best as it can in a fluid, informal and quasi-anarchic international system; one reminiscent of conditions that existed during much of the nineteenth century or the war and inter-war periods of the twentieth century.

For heuristic purposes, the first part of this chapter will conclude by presenting three scenarios referred to as tolerable, undesirable and catastrophic respectively. The content and definition of security will vary from scenario to scenario and the rules and guidelines informing foreign policy behaviour of governments of small, medium and large European states will differ quite drastically in each case.

TOLERABLE SCENARIO: A GLOBAL CONCERT OF POWERS

Security definition: Security in the tolerable scenario is defined comprehensively to cover not only its core (territorial defence of a state through military capabilities), but also to include economic variables (free trade, free markets) as well as political freedoms and human rights protection (democracy).

Global Setting (major assumptions): (a) Permanent members of UN Security Council maintain a consensual environment on issues of peacekeeping, peacemaking and peace-enforcement; (b) major centres of economic power (US, EU and Japan) do not permit economic competition to spill over into the political sphere; (c) a grand strategy designed to reduce the gap between developed and developing States based on just and appropriate burden sharing is adopted; (d) a grand strategy on global environmental protection based on equitable distribution of contributions is put in place; (e) collective approaches to meet threats such as nuclear/chemical weapons proliferation, terrorism, narcotics and crime are adopted.

Regional Setting (major assumptions): (a) Inviolability of frontiers; (b) peaceful methods for dispute settlement; (c) consolidated democratic systems of governance; (d) economic interdependence; (e) fully protected human rights of minorities and other dual identity groups; (f) containment of racism and chauvinism (leading to ethnic cleansing).

Consequences: In such a system the security of individual Balkan States can be depicted in terms of institutional concentric circles similar to those in Figure 10.1 for the balance of the 1990s. The diagram in Figure 10.1 could be used to depict the security (comprehensive definition) for Bulgaria (also Rumania, Albania and component states of former Yugoslavia) as well as for Greece and for Turkey respectively.

UNDESIRABLE SCENARIO: RENATIONALISATION OF GREAT POWER POLICIES

Security definition: Security in this scenario is defined narrowly (in traditional fashion) in terms of territorial integrity and regime maintenance.

Global setting (major assumptions): (a) Disruption of the consensus among permanent members of the UN Security Council; (b) UN peacekeeping operations (as result of difficulties of the type encountered in Somalia and former Yugoslavia) follow a declining pattern; (c) major centres of economic power (US, EU and Japan) permit economic competition to spill over into political antagonisms; (d) nationalist, rather than collective, security policies are adopted by major powers and small/medium-sized states prevent the development of collective and comprehensive North–South and environmental protection strategies; (e) loosening and even dissolution of regional institutions such as the EU and NATO.

Regional setting (major assumptions): (a) frontiers challenged and/or revised on the basis of the principle of ethnic self-determination in an attempt to develop ethnically homogenous political entities; (b) a return to policies of short-term, shifting regional alliances; (c) solicitation of external patrons and Great Power interference in the regional and domestic affairs of regional states; (d) a proliferation of 'Bosnias' escalating into full-scale regional wars; (e) the rise to power of populist/authoritarian leaders/regimes; (f) pressures to reintroduce regional arms races including nuclear/chemical weapons proliferation; (g) rise of terrorism and/or guerilla warfare employed by defeated/dissatisfied groups, regimes *et al.*

Consequences: In such a system, security is a product of single-country arrangements based on so-called regional axes (e.g. a Muslim versus an Orthodox axis in the Balkans). Regional governments and opposition groupings solicit external support and guarantees (in return for influence accepted) from major powers who are, however, reluctant to assume the burden of exclusive spheres of influence of the pre-World War II or Cold War variety. From the standpoint of major powers, troubled regions are viewed as zones of indifference and benign neglect, if not outright non-involvement.

CATASTROPHIC SCENARIO: THE CLASH OF CIVILISATIONS

Security definition: Security in this scenario is understood in terms of solidarity within 'common culture areas' (civilisations) as defined in a recent controversial article by Samuel Huntington ('Clash of Civilizations', *Foreign Affairs.* Summer 1993).

Global setting (major assumptions): (a) Conflict is expected to take place at the border areas (fault lines) separating incompatible (in terms of cultural values) civilisations which, according to Huntington are the following: Western, Slavic–Orthodox, Islamic, Confucian, Hindu, Japanese, Latin American, and possibly an African civilization; (b) progressive isolation of the advanced, industrial, democratic West from the rest of the world, creating a new bipolarity (where religion substitutes for ideology) that Huntington describes as the 'West versus the Rest'; (c) given the projected alienation among Western, Slavic–Orthodox and Confucian–Islamic coalitions, consensual strategies (approved by the UN Security Council) regarding conflict management and prevention, economic development of the global South and global environmental protection are no longer feasible; (d) centrifugal tendencies (ethnic, autonomist and irredentist) grow in frequency and intensity within and between states throughout the globe; (e) international organisations at the global and regional level (e.g. UN, NATO, EU, CSCE) enter a declining path.

Regional setting (major assumptions): (a) Nationalist (chauvinist/populist) elites rise to power in most regional states; (b) authoritarian regimes are established either to prevent or to ride upon a popular wave of nationalism/irredentism; (c) new conflicts (e.g. Kosovo, Vojvodina), erupt with escalating involvement of South-eastern European states including Croatia, Hungary, Serbia, Albania, FYROM, Greece, Bulgaria and Turkey (in addition to long-suffering Bosnia); (d) new and lasting alliances, and attendant solicitation of external (Great Power) intervention, begin to develop as deeper and more dramatic lines are drawn separating Catholics from Orthodox Christians and both of them from Muslims in the Balkan region; (e) desperate/isolated movements and regimes begin engaging in economically damaging regional arms races and seeking non-conventional (nuclear/chemical) weapons capabilities in their attempt to put in place deterrent or pre-emptive bargaining strategies; (f) fanatic and revanchist waves of terrorism and/or guerilla warfare ravage the region.

Consequences: An atavistic reversion to the climate of the Balkan Wars (1912–13) period and the renomination of the Balkans as the powder keg of Europe, with parallel trends developing in the rest of the world. All unfolding in an environment in which nuclear weapons still predominate.

Part II – Greece's role in the Balkan transition

Part II of this chapter proceeds on the assumption that, of the possible post-Cold War international systems described above, the 'tolerable' scenario is most likely to obtain in the next two decades. However, in the relatively controlled environment which a global concert of major powers entails, Greece's room for manoeuvre is not going to be wide. Even so, it is possible to outline (in fact to recommend) a positive role for Greece in the process of democratic transition that the post-Communist Balkan societies are currently undergoing. Finally, this paper will conclude by addressing the Turkish challenge (as perceived by Greece) and by outlining a strategy that could lead, if adopted, toward the goal of *rapprochement* and reconciliation of the two Mediterranean adversaries.

The development of Balkan relations

As an EU member-state, Greece is committed to democracy, the protection of human rights, co-operative and institutionalised relationships and the peaceful means of settling disputes. It can therefore make a significant contribution to building peace and international co-operation in the Balkan area and in Eastern Europe more generally.

Towards Albania, Greece's policies should continue to be those of peaceful engagement, encouraging the process of transition to genuine political and economic democracy and the protection of the human rights of the Greek minority in Albania. The more advanced, pluralist and tolerant Albania becomes, the more the Greek minority, as an integral and lively part of the Albanian State, can play the role of a vibrant connecting-link. In the years ahead, Greece should strengthen its trade and investment links with Albania and should take the initiative in identifying joint Greek–Albanian infrastructural projects that can qualify for EU or other institutional support. Issues of mutual concern regarding the flood of economic refugees from Albania to Greece (estimated at about 250,000) should be subject to continuous consultation for mutually approved procedures for refugee reception, rehabilitation and eventual repatriation.

Greece's interests in former Yugoslavia would have been best served by the maintenance of the Federation (adjusted peacefully to suit the needs and interests of its constituent republics). It would also have been in Greece's interest to have witnessed a decentralised yet economically integrated Yugoslavia move toward the full implementation of political democracy, a market economy and gradual accession to the EU. As it is, the Federation's fragmentation has set off a domino effect which may yet prove regionally contagious and develop into a widespread epidemic. More specifically, Greece's interests have been directly affected by the collapse of the internal balancing effect of the old Federation. The successor State of FYROM, feeling vulnerable and isolated, has sought the support of other revisionist or potentially revisionist centres in the greater Balkan region (Turkey being among those heading this list). Given what now has become an irreversible process of Yugoslav disintegration, it is in Greece's best interest to develop good relations with all the new States that emerge from the ruins, and to facilitate their democratic transitions by recommending constructive policies for adoption by the EU.

The issue of recognition of a 'Slav Macedonian' entity can be resolved, provided the authorities in Skopje account for Greece's concern with the expropriation of the name 'Macedonia' which, from ancient times (the times of Kings Philip and Alexander), has been inseparably associated with Greek history, civilisation, tradition, culture and, of course, territory. On the other hand, it is becoming ever more apparent to Athens that the continued maintenance of a relatively weak (militarily) buffer state in the form of FYROM on Greece's northern borders is a far more attractive contingency than its partition and incorporation into either a Greater Albania, or a Greater Bulgaria and/or a Greater Serbia. It does not require much imagination to see the possibility that any 'partition process' would involve Albania, Bulgaria, Greece and Turkey in a dangerous and destructive general Balkan war.

Greece's relations with Bulgaria are currently quite good. Greece is second only to Germany as a partner of Bulgaria in terms of trade and investment. Moreover, there is the prospect of further improvement. Both countries are facing a potential revisionist challenge emanating from Turkey which, at times, presents itself as the protector and sole guarantor of Muslim populations well beyond the sovereign boundaries of the Republic of Turkey. The Cold War taboos limiting political, economic and security co-ordination across old bloc lines no longer operate.

To sum up, Greece is a member of the EU and has linked its destiny with this most remarkable transnational experiment. It is also a Balkan and a Mediterranean state. Greece can afford to assume a more energetic role in the formulation of a EU policy *vis-à-vis* the Balkans, something that has not been done adequately to date. In this respect, Greece should operate through the expanding mechanisms of the European Common Foreign and Security Policy. The admittedly thin structures of multilateral Balkan co-operation, which have been dealt a terrible blow by events in former Yugoslavia, could be eventually revived through the participation of Italy and Greece in new initiatives. These, of course, will only become feasible should a breakthrough to peace take place in former Yugoslavia.

In an analogous manner, other regional co-operation ventures, such as Turkey's Black Sea Initiative, also merit further support and collective participation. In order to act in this new fashion, Greece must throw off Cold War, Civil War and even pre-war memories and must also insulate its policies from corrosive manoeuvrings designed for internal partisan consumption. Greece needs to promote a policy package which commits the EU to assist the Balkans in its attempt to develop market mechanisms without serious socio-economic dislocations that might result in public unrest and gravitate toward violent conflict. Needless to say, effective economic development goes hand in hand with the transition to and consolidation of democratic institutions.

A new relationship with Turkey?

With respect to Turkey, one encounters the greatest challenges as well as opportunities in the Balkan cluster of Greece's bilateral relationships. The points of friction between Greece and Turkey are multiple and much ink has been used describing and analysing these problems as well as presenting the wide variety of Greek-oriented, Turkish-oriented and third-party perspectives. Difficulties include bilateral issues such as the delimitation of the Greek and Turkish portions of the Aegean continental shelf as well as Turkish complaints/claims regarding present and potential arrangements of Greece's territorial air space and territorial waters; defensive emplacements on the Greek islands of the Eastern Aegean and the Dodecanese islands; civil rights for the Muslim minority living in Greek Western Thrace; and present/potential command and control responsibilities within the framework of NATO. Greek complaints, in turn, begin with the continued Turkish occupation, since July 1974, of northern Cyprus; the emplacement of large Turkish amphibious forces on the western coast of Turkey; systematic violation of Greek minority rights in Istanbul and the islands of Imroz and Boskaada; and continuing Turkish pressures on the Oecumenical Patriarchate of Constantinople in Istanbul.

Regardless of the merits and demerits of the case made by each side, the central question that needs to be asked is whether Greece and Turkey, which have been involved in an undisguised Cold War since 1974, will be better off in a condition of protracted conflict as compared to entering into a new phase of mutual and active engagement and even co-operation. Unequivocally, the answer is that both countries would be much better off if they were to reach a final reconciliation – a new historic compromise – reminiscent of the Lausanne settlement of 1923.

The ingredients of a final compromise can only be based on the assumption that Turkey, in addition to Greece, adopts a West European profile. Greece since 1974 has developed durable and tested democratic institutions. It subsequently joined, irrevocably, the EU. Turkey is currently at the crossroads of choosing between a European and a Middle Eastern orientation. Like post-World War II France and Germany, Turkey and Greece can bury the geopolitical divisions of the past, accept and respect the territorial status quo that emerged after World War II, and resolve to deny the use of force in their bilateral relations.

No fundamental progress toward a comprehensive Greco–Turkish settlement can be made without a just and mutually acceptable solution to the prickly problem of Cyprus. For as long as the present situation in Cyprus continues (occupation of 37 per cent of the island's territory by the armed forces of Turkey), the Greek–Turkish dispute in the Aegean, which could otherwise become eminently manageable, will be marred by Greek fears that Turkey will be encouraged to proceed further in the Aegean if its behaviour in setting up the partitionist prototype of Cyprus is called into account.

A genuine settlement of the Cyprus problem (which is today ripe for a solution given the recent breakthroughs in the Israeli–Palestinian and Northern Ireland conflicts) would exclude *Enosis* ('Union' of Cyprus with Greece) and *Taksim* ('Partition' of Cyprus into Greek and Turkish segments). The historic compromise, therefore, calls for independence of a federal, bi-zonal and bi-communal state along the lines of the Makarios–Denktash (1977) and Kyprianou–Denktash (1979) agreements.

The federal State of Cyprus that emerges from an agreement between the Greek- and Turkish-Cypriot communities will be given an excellent chance to survive and prosper if, at the time of its new birth, the 'Federal Republic of Cyprus' were to become simultaneously a member-state of the EU and NATO. EU membership, together with genuine collective guarantees (including those of Greece, Britain and Turkey), demilitarisation (except for the British base areas), and a UN or NATO commanded multinational police force (until mutual confidence is securely established), will allow the Cypriots to forge a more permanent unity based on all the rights, duties and freedoms that democracy provides. A genuine settlement of Cyprus, however, cannot rest on a premise equating (in terms of shares of territory, GNP, parliamentary and executive powers) the 80 per cent of the Greek-Cypriots with the 18 per cent of the Turkish-Cypriot minority community.

A much needed historic compromise between Greece and Turkey in the Aegean must rest on two general and two operational principles of foreign policy behaviour. The first principle involves the mutual denunciation of the use of force by Greece and Turkey (for example, by signing a non-aggression pact). The second general principle is that Greek–Turkish disputes in the Aegean should follow the road of peaceful settlement involving time-tested methods such as bilateral negotiations and, in case of deadlocks, conciliation, good offices, mediation, arbitration and adjudication.

The two operational principles reflect Turkish and Greek interests respectively. For the benefit of Turkey, it must be understood that the Aegean cannot be transformed into a Greek lake. For Greek peace of mind, the Aegean cannot be partitioned or subdivided in a fashion that enclaves Greek territories (Eastern Aegean and the Dodecanese Islands) into a Turkish zone of functional responsibility or even joint responsibility.

For heuristic purposes only, one among many alternative strategies leading towards (or permitting) a comprehensive settlement of Greek–Turkish disputes should be outlined. It begins, as stressed above, with the assumption that a mutually acceptable settlement of the Cyprus question has been achieved. Further, the strategy rests upon the two operational principles discussed above: to wit the Aegean neither becomes a Greek lake nor is it apportioned in a way that enclaves Greek territories into a Turkish zone of functional responsibility.

Following the steps of the proposed strategy, the thorny issue of the Aegean continental shelf will once more become subject to bilateral negotiations. In the absence of mutual agreement, issues will be submitted to arbitration or to the International Court of Justice for final resolution. Alternatively, both Greece and Turkey could agree, following the prototype of the Antarctic Treaty, to freeze the issue of continental shelf delimitation for a number of years, reserving the right to press their respective claims at the end of the treaty period. Needless to say, an 'Antarctic approach' would gain additional appeal if one could assume that there are no significant and profitably exploitable oil reserves in the Aegean region. Further, the opportunity costs involving unacceptable Aegean environmental costs (caused by oil spill) should be taken into consideration, given the fact that both Greece and Turkey are heavily dependent on thriving tourist industries to help balance their payments.

Three ways of bypassing the thorny issues of Turkish challenges to Greece's 10-mile territorial air limit (in effect since 1931) and to the potential of extension of Greece's territorial waters and territorial air from the present 6 and 10 miles to the generally accepted 12-mile limit could go as follows:

a) Both Greece and Turkey would agree to 12-mile limits (for both territorial waters and territorial air) for their mainland territory and to 6-mile limits for islands belonging to Greece and Turkey in the Aegean (excluding Crete and Rhodes that will have 12-mile limits).

b) Greece settles for a 10-mile limit (for territorial waters and territorial air) formally declaring its commitment not to make any further extensions in the future.

c) An 8-mile limit for territorial sea and air is accepted as a universally agreed upon regime in the Aegean.

The potentially explosive issue of minorities in Greece and Turkey should follow a dual rule. First that minority protection should not lead to claims by either side calling for boundary changes; and secondly that minorities within each country should be treated as well as each side might expect that affinity ethnic groups should be protected in third countries, thus meeting the highest standards set in the international community.

Finally, in an era favouring arms control, arms reduction and confidence building measures, Greece and Turkey would be best advised to begin a series of mutually balanced force reductions (MBFRs) involving their land and sea border areas in Thrace and the Aegean. A mirror image reduction or the removal of offensive weapons from potential front lines would go a long way toward reducing the chances of the outbreak of armed conflict as well as relieving the hard-pressed economies of both countries from the heavy burden of high military expenditures.

Last but not least, Greece and Turkey, as well as other Balkan States, should embark on the much needed task of MBPR (mutually and balanced prejudice reduction), whether prejudice is manifested in hostile press commentaries, textbooks, literature, theatre, movies, sport and other forms of social and cultural expression.

Following a potential grand settlement, both Greece and Turkey would increase significantly (in textbook-style neofunctionalist fashion) their trade, tourism, investment and joint ventures at home and abroad. Greece would also abandon its policy of conditionality regarding Turkey's accession strategy to the EU and would, in fact, seek to facilitate Turkey's entry. Put simply, a European Turkey will be for Greece a much easier neighbour to live with than an isolated, fundamentalist and militaristic one.

Concluding remarks

Ultimately the state of relations between countries is a product of attitudes and perceptions of ruling elites and general publics. Looking at the Balkans in its long and adventurous history, one can see clear manifestations of conflicting visions longing for a Greater Albania, a Greater Serbia, a Greater Bulgaria or a Greater Rumania. The Greeks still preserve the memory of Alexander's Macedonian Empire and the 1000-year Byzantine Empire. The Italians can look back to the centuries of the Roman Empire. The Turks have even more recent memories of great prowess that had accompanied the Ottoman Empire. The collective challenge is to contain these territorially overlapping and potentially irredentist visions which add up to a highly explosive formula.

References

Abramowitz, Morton (1993), 'Dateline Ankara: Turkey After Ozal', *Foreign Policy*, 91, 164–181.

Amstrup, Niels (1976), 'The Perennial Problem of Small States: A Survey of Research Efforts', *Co-operation and Conflict*, 11, 163–182.

Asmus Ronald, Richard Kugler and Stephen Larrabee (1993), 'Building a New NATO', *Foreign Affairs*, 72:4, 28–40.

Buzan, Barry (1983), *People, States and Fear: The National Security Problem in International Relations* (Brighton, Wheatsheaf Books).

Carlsnees, Walter (1992), 'The Agency-Structure Problem in Foreign Policy Analysis', *International Studies Quarterly*, 36, 245–270.

Chipman, John (ed.) (1988), *NATO's Southern Allies* (London, Routledge).

Constas, D. (ed). (1991), *The Greek–Turkish Conflict in the 1990s* (New York, St Martin's Press).

Couloumbis, Theodore (1983), *The United States, Greece and Turkey; The Troubled Triangle* (New York, Praeger).

——, Theodore and Thanos Veremis (1992), *The Southeast European Yearbook 1991*, (Athens, ELIAMEP).

East, Maurice (1973), 'Size and Foreign Policy Behaviour: A Test of Two Models', *World Politics*, 35:3, 464–487.

Ermides, P. and A. Egyptiades (1993), 'Albania, Bulgaria, Rumania. Today's Economic and Commercial Environment', *Organization for the Promotion of Experts*, (in Greek) Office of Northern Greece.

Fox, Annette (1969), 'The Small States in the International System', *International Journal* 4, 751–64.

Glaser, Charles (1993), 'Why NATO is still Best: Future Security Arrangements for Europe', *International Security*, 18:1, 5–50.

Gurel, Sukru (1993), 'Turkey and the Region – A New Role in a Changing Environment', *Nato's Sixteen Nations*, 4, 79–81.

Halliday, Fred (1987), 'State and Society in International Relations: A Second Agenda', *Millennium: Journal of International Studies* 16:2, 215–229.

Handel, Michael (1981), 'Weak States in the International System' (London, Frank Cass).

Hermann, Charles (1990), 'Changing Course: When Governments Choose to Redirect Foreign Policy', *International Studies Quarterly*, 34:13–21.

Hermann, Charles, Charles Kegley Jr, and James Rosenau (eds.) (1987), *New Directions in the Study of Foreign Policy* (Boston, Allen and Unwin).

Holl, Ottmar (ed.) (1983), *Small States in Europe and Dependence* (Vienna, Braumuller).

Hollis, Martin and Steve Smith (1990), *Explaining and Understanding International Relations* (Oxford, Clarendon Press).

Holsti, Kalevi (1982), *Why Nations Realign: Foreign Policy Restructuring in the Postwar World* (London, Allen and Unwin).

Katzenstein, Peter (ed.) (1978), *Between Power and Plenty* (Madison, University of Wisconsin Press).

Katzenstein, Peter (1984), *Small States in World Markets* (Ithaca, Cornell University Press).

Kazakos, P.s and C. Ioakimides (eds.) *Greece and EC Membership Evaluated* (London, Pinter 1994).

Keohane, Robert (1971), 'The Big Influence of Small Allies', *Foreign Policy*, 2, 161–182.

Korany, Bahgat (1983), 'The Take-off of Third World Studies: The Case of Foreign Policy', *World Politics*, 35:3, 464–487.

McGowan, P. J. and K. P. Gottwald (1975), 'Small State Foreign Policies', *International Studies Quarterly*, 19, 469–500.

Moon, Bruce (1983), 'The Foreign Policy of the Dependent State', *International Studies Quarterly*, 27:3, 315–340.

Petersen, Nikolaj (1988), 'The Security Policies of Small NATO Countries: Factors of Change', *Co-operation and Conflict*, 23, 145–162.

Pijpers, Alfred *et al.* (eds.) (1980), *European Political Co-operation in the 1980s: A Common Foreign Policy for Western Europe?* (The Hague, Nijhoff).

Psomiades, Harry and Stavros Thomadakis (eds.) (1993), *Greece, the New Europe and the Changing International Order* (New York, Pella).

Rothstein, Robert (1968), *Alliances and Small Powers* (New York, Columbia University Press).

Sens, Allen (1994), 'The Security of Small States in Post-Cold War Europe: A New Research Agenda', *Working Paper No 1, Institute of International Relations* (The University of British Columbia).

Skidmore, David and Valerie Hudson (eds.) (1992), *The Limits of State Autonomy: Societal Groups and Foreign Policy Formulation* (Boulder, Westview Press).

Stuart, Douglas (ed.) (1988), *Politics and Security in the Southern Region of the Atlantic Alliance* (Baltimore, The John's Hopkins University Press).

Vayrynen, Raimo (1971), 'On the Definition and Measurement of Small Power Status', *Co-operation and Conflict*, 6, 91–102.

Waltz, Kenneth (1979), *Theory of International Politics* (Reading, Massachusetts).

Abramovitz, M. 174
Act of Accession 35, 39, 41
Aegean 112, 153, 155, 172; *see also* Cyprus,
       Turkey
Afentouli, I. 52
Agricultural Bank of Greece (ATE) 50
aid, EU to Greece 5, 25–6, 35, 39, 53–4, 55,
       69, 76
Albania 7, 18, 22, 27, 112, 134, 135, 137,
       143, 152, 157, 166, 168, 169,
       173
Albanians 98; *see also* minorities
Alesina, A. 82, 91
Alexandris, A. 115
Alivizatos, N. 127
allogeneis 118
Alogoskoufis, G. 24, 25, 85, 90, 91
Alpe-Adria Association 133
Ames case 138
Amstrup, N. 134
Anastassiadis, Th. 52
Anastopoulos, I. D. 50
Aranzo-Ruiz, G. 111
Areios Pagos 119, 127
Arvanites 101, 112
Asmus, R. 174
asynchronic Europeanisation 34–52 *passim*
'Ataturkist approach' 172
Athens Stock Exchange 67
autarkic Europeanisation 34–52 *passim*
Austria 85, 133, 137
Automatic Wage Indexation (ATA) x, 79

Badinter Arbitration Commission 134
Baker, James 135
Baldwin, R. E. 91, 92
Balkans 3, 8, 13–16, 17–23, 44, 131–41,
       142–6, 152–3, 155–7, 166, 168–70
   EU role 132–4, 137–8, 144–5
   Greek policy 8, 17–23, 26–9, 44, 131–41,
       142–6, 152–3, 155–7, 168–70
   US role 132–4, 137–8, 155–7
Banac, I. 140

Bank of Greece 85–8
Belgium 5, 6, *62*, 75, *77*, 85
Blinkhorn, M. 111
Boskaada 170
Bosnia 13, 28, 131–41 *passim*, 168
Brown, S. 158
Brussels 9, 19, 27, 42, 142, 144
Bulgaria 13, 113, 114, 123, 136, 143, 145,
       159, 166, 168, 169, 173
   Bulgarian language 100
Buzan, B. 174
Byzantine tradition 46, 173

Capie, F. H. 91, 92
Capotorti 95, 96, 110, 126
Carlsnees, W. 174
Casruny, A. W. 51
Catholics, in Greece 98, 121, 127
cement industry 41
census, Greek 98–9
Chipman, J. 174
citizenship, in Greece 118–19
Civil War, Greek 15, 19, 161, 162
'clash of civilisations' 167
Clinton, Bill 14, 140, 156, 157
Clogg, R. 28, 29, 49, 52
CNN 19
Code of Citizenship 118–19
Cohen, R. 140
Cold War 3, 7, 13, 14, 15, 17, 143, 148, 150
Colonels' dictatorship, Greek 19, 35, 58,
       161
Common Agricultural Policy 5
Common Foreign and Security Policy
       (CFSP) x, 137, 170
communism 15, 21; *see also* Cold War,
       USSR
Community Support Framework (CSF) x,
       42
Conference for Security and Co-operation
       in Europe (CSCE) x, 108, 165, 168
conservatism, in Greece 18–19, 36, 112
Constantine, King 142–3

Constantinople 103, 115, 170
Constas, D. 50, 174
Convention of Constantinople 102
Couloumbis, T. 148, 150, 158, 159, 160–75
Council of Europe 96, 108, 116, 126, 165
Council of State, Greek 120, 121, 122
Courakis, A. S. 70
Crete 127
Cristodoulakis, N. 91, 92
Croatia 28, 131–41 passim, 168
    Croats in Germany 133
    recognition 133–4
Curry, F. C. 140
Cviic, C. 140
Cyprus 7, 18, 19–20, 59, 112, 146, 148–9,
        153–5, 162–3, 170–3
Czechoslovakia 133, 143

De Grauwe, P. 70, 71, 92
Del Giovane, P. 83, 91
Delors, J. 133
    'Delors package' 40, 42
Denktash 171
Denmark 8, 9, 62, 133
Diamantouros, N. 52
Dimitras, F. 111
Dimitras, P. 112
Dornbush, R. 84, 90, 92

East, M. 174
economic performance, Greek 5–6, 24–6,
        37, 53–71, 54; see also Greece,
        economic performance
    and EMU 72–91
    inflation 72–82, 74, 82–5, 83
Egyptiades, A. 174
Eleftherotypia 45, 52
enosis 171
ensomatosis 46
Ermides, P. 174
d'Estaing, V. Giscard 18
ethnicity 96–7; see also minorities
ethnos 14, 118
Etzioni, A. 141
European Court of Human Rights 124
European Monetary System (EMS) x, 89
European Monetary Union (EMU) x, 6, 8,
        24, 55, 65, 70, 72–91
    convergence criteria 72–3, 76–7, 77–8,
        83–4, 90
    convergence programme 84
    inflation and 72–82, 74, 82–5

European Political Co)operation x, 7,
        37–8
European Trade Union Confederation
        (ETUC) 11
European Union (EU) x, 166, 167
    aid 5, 25–6, 35, 39, 55–4, 55, 69, 76
    in Balkans 132–4, 137–8, 144–5
    effect on Greek administration 38–9,
        42–3
    effect on Greek democracy 38, 40–1
    effect on Greek economic policy 37, 39,
        53–71, 72–91
    effect on Greek foreign policy 37–8
    Europeanisation, of Greece 33, 34–52
    infringing of laws, by Greece 6–7, 37
    Integrated Mediterranean Programmes
        (IMPs) 37, 39–40, 42, 54
    joining, of Greece 10–12, 35–9
    'multi-speed' 3, 6, 16
    Single European Act (SEA) x, 8, 18
Europeanisation, of Greece 33–52
    asynchronic 34
    autarkic 34–5
    problems of 40–4
    process 34–40
Evdoridis, G. I. 92
Exchange Rate Mechanism (ERM) x, 88
Eyal, J. 142–6

farmers, Greek 66, 68
Fatouros, A. 50
Featherstone, K. 3–16, 49
Finland 137
Flynn, N. 70, 71
foreign policy
    EU 132–4, 137–8, 144–5
    Greek 160–75
        re Albania 168–9
        re Balkans 3, 8, 13–16, 17–23, 131–41,
            142–6, 152–7, 168–70
        re Bulgaria 169–70
        re FYROM 169; see also FYROM
        re Skopje 169; see also Skopje
        re Turkey 10, 13, 17, 18, 22, 27, 39,
            103–7, 112–19, 122, 124, 135,
            45–6, 148, 149–50, 152, 153–5,
            161, 162, 170–3
        re US 10, 14, 17, 20, 134–5, 147–59,
            161, 165
        security profile 164–8
    Turkish 154–5, 159, 168, 170–3
    US 134–5, 138–9, 151, 155–7

Former Yugoslav Republic of Macedonia
  (FYROM) x, 7, 9, 14, 17, 19–20, 27,
  44, 100–1, 112, 113, 134, 135–6,
  137, 138–9, 143–6, 152, 157, 163,
  168; *see also* Macedonia, Skopje
  needling Greece 145, 157, 163, 168
  trade embargo 7–8, 22, 139
Fox, A. 174
France, 5, *62*, 102, 133, 171
Frangakis, N. 7, 16, 49, 50

Gaddis, J. L. 158
Gagauz 99
Gastello-Branco, M. 91, 92
Gensher, H. D. 133–4, 135
Gensher-Colombo plan 38
Georgakopoulos, T. 51, 70, 71
Germany 5, 7, *62*, 133–4, 171
Gianaitsis, T. 49
Gillespie, R. 50
Gjidara, M. 110, 111
Glaser, C. 174
Glenny, M. 140
Gligorov, K. 20, 113, 143
Gottwald, K. P. 174
Gow, J. 140
Greco-Turkish War 99, 103, 161
Greece
  Act of Accession 35, 39, 41
  aid from EU 5, 25–6, 35, 39, 53–4, *55*, 76
  and Balkans 7–8, 13–16, 17–23, 26–9,
    131–41, 142–6; *see also* Albania,
    FYROM, Serbia
  census 98
  citizenship 118–19, 142–3
  clientelism 25, 41, 45–6, 67
  conservatism 18–19, 36, 112
  constitution 118–27
  economic performance 54–71, 72–91
    passim
    Bank of Greece 85–8
    budget deficit 63–7, *74*, 75–6
    GDP 57–61, 62–70 *passim*, 73, *74*,
      75–91 *passim*
    industrial relations 56
    inflation 72–82, 82–8
    liberalisation 85–8
    PSBR *63*, 63–5, 75, 82
    public expenditure *54*, 57–61, *62*,
      65–6, 67, 68–9, 82
    revenue 57–61, *62*, 65–6, 67–8
  elites 34–5

and EMU x, 6, 8, 34, 55, 65, 70, 72–91
  convergence criteria 72–3, 76–7, 77–8,
    83–4, 90
  convergence programme *84*
  and disinflation 78–9, 82–8
  and exchange rate policy 80–1, *81*, 83,
    85–6
  financial liberalisation 85–8
  and inflation 72–82, *74*, 82–5, *83*
  and wage policy 79–80, *81*
and EU 3, 4–13, 17–23, 24–9, 33–52,
    53–71, 71–92, 142–6, 157, 163,
    165
  joining 10–12, 35–9
  and PASOK 36–7, 39, 43, 56, 60–1
  splits on 44–5
Europeanisation 34–52
  problems of 40–4
fiscal policy 53–71, 72–91
  budget deficit 63–7, *74*, 75, 76
  disinflation 82–8
  EU effect 37, 39, 53–71, 72–91
  GDP 57, *62*, 62–70 *passim*, 73, *74*, 75–91
    passim
  'hard drachma' 76, 80–2, 89
  industrial relations 56
  inflation 72–91
  interest rate policy *81*, 81–2, 84–8
  New Democracy 61
  PASOK 56, 58, 60–1
  pensions 56, 64, 75, 82
  privatisation 56–7, 68, 85
  PSBR *63*, 63–5, 75, 82
  public enterprise 37, 40–1, 56, 65
  public expenditure *54*, 57–61, *59*, *62*,
    67–8
  public sector employment 65–6, 66–7,
    68–9
  public sector inefficiency 66–7, 76–8
  revenue *54*, 57–61, *58*, *59*, *60*, *62*, 67–8
  role of state 55–7
  tax 58, 66, 67–8, 75
    evasion 66, 67–8, 75
    farmers' exemption 66, 68
  wages 78–80
foreign policy 3, 7, 17–23, 26–9, 37–8, 39,
    44, 131–41, 142–6, 152–3, 160–75
  Albania 168–9
  Balkans 3, 8, 13–16, 17–23, 131–41,
    142–6
  Bulgaria 169–70
  EU effect 37–8

FYROM x, 7, 9, 143, 17, 19–20, 27, 44,
    100–1, 112, 113, 134, 135–6, 137,
    138–9, 143–6, 152, 169
  security profile 104–8
  Skopje 7, 9, 13, 18, 20, 22, 27, 135, 145,
    153, 156; *see also* FYROM
  Turkey 10, 13, 17, 18, 22, 27, 39,
    103–7, 112–19, 135, 145–6,
    148–50, 152, 153–5, 161, 162
  USA 10, 14, 17, 20, 134–5, 147–59,
    161, 165
human rights 13, 22, 102–16
infringement of EU law 6–7, 37, 39, 40–1
international criticism of 4–5, 17, 19, 24,
    117, 142, 144
language 122–3; *see also* Slavophones,
    Turcophones
Macedonia 14, 19–20, 100–1; *see also*
    FYROM
Ministry of the National Economy 11, 42
minorities 95–127
  consitutional protection 117–27
  definition of 95–6, 110
  international protection 95–6, 101–16
national identity 13–14, 17–23, 26,
    95–116, 117–18
Orthodox Church 15, 19, 21–2, 46, 97,
    120–1, 122–3, 167
PASOK x, 4, 7, 36–7, 39, 43, 49, 52, 56,
    60–1, 142, 149, 163
policy planning 42
Prime Minister's authority 11
privatisation 40–1, 56–7, 68
public administration 38–9, 42–3
public enterprise 37, 40–1, 56, 65–7
relations with Turkey 10, 13, 17, 18, 22,
    27, 39, 103–7, 112–16, 119, 135,
    145–6, 148, 149–50, 152, 153–5,
    161, 162
relations with USA 14–15, 17, 147–59
religion 15, 19, 21–2, 46, 94, 120–2; *see
    also* Orthodox Church
security profile 104–8
state, boundary of 40–1, 45–6, 55–7, 65
underdog culture 46–7
Grilli, V. 82, 84, 92
Gros, D. 76, 85, 92
Gross Domestic Product (GDP) x, 57ff
Gulf War 150, 154
Gunther, R. 25, 29
Gurel, S. 174
Gypsies 98, 100, 113

Haftendorn, H. 158
Halliday, F. 174
Handel, M. 174
Harvie, C. 49
Heald, D. 70, 71
Hellenes 97, 111; *see also* Greece, national
    identity
Helman, G. B. 141
Heraclides, A. 140
Hercules 37
Hermann, C. 174
Hexagonale 133
Hoffman, S. 49
Holl, O. 174
Holland 133
Hollis, M. 174
Holsti, K. 174
Hudson, V. 175
Hungary 168
Huntingdon, S. 167

Iaos 118
Iatrides 158
Ifantis, C. 147–59
Imbros 22
Imroz 170
inflation, Greek 72–82
Institute of Economic and Industrial
    Studies 50
Integrated Mediterranean Programmes
    (IMPs) x, 37, 39–40, 42, 54
International Monetary Fund (IMF) x, 20,
    74, 92
Ioakimidis, P. C. 10, 11, 33–52, 174
ipokootita 126
Ireland 54, *62*, 85
Israel 26
Istanbul 107, 116, 170
Italy 5, 6, 9, *62*, 72, *77*, 85, 89, 91, 102, 103,
    133, 170
ithageneia 126
Izetbegovic 138

Japan *62*, 102, 166
Jehovah's Witness 13, 99, 121–2
Jenkins, S. 140
Jews, in Greece 98, 122

Karamanlis, C. 4, 162
Karamoulis, N. 91, 92
Kathemerini 52
Katseli, L. T. 51

Katzenstein, P. 174
Kazakos, P. 49, 50, 51, 52, 174
Keohane, R. O. 49, 151, 174
Kitromilides, P. 111
KKE (Communist Party of Greece) x, 8, 12, 44
Kokkinakis 124, 127
Konidaris, I. M. 127
Korany, B. 174
Kosovo 168
Koufka, K. 115
Kouloumbis, Th. 51
Krasner, D. S. 151, 158
Krauthammer, C. 140
Krugman, P. R. 91, 92
Kucan, M. 133
Kugler, K. 174
Kurds 159
Kutsovlachs 114
Kyprianou 171

Ladrech, R. 33, 49
Lafazani, D. 113
Larrabee, S. 174
League of Nations 104–5
Leonardi, R. 49
Lesser, I. O. 154, 158
Loizides, I. 70, 71
London Protocol 102
Luxembourg 7, 62

Maastricht Treaty 11, 17, 20, 22, 24, 42, 55, 72–3, 77, 85, 88; see also EMU
Macedonia 14, 19, 22, 100–1, 113, 134, 136, 163; see also FYROM, Skopje
Major, John 143
Makarios 171
Makrydimitris, A. 50, 52
Malinverni, G. 110
Maravegias, N. 49
Marks, G. 51
Masciandaro 82
McCaskill, C. W. 159
McGowan, P. J. 174
metapolitefsi 147
Metaxas regime 121, 124
Michalopoulos 9, 72–92
Miller, L. B. 159
Mills, T. 91, 92
Milosevic, S. 134
Minaidies, S. 127
Minford, P. 91, 92

minorities, in Greece 95–127, 170–3
   Albanians 98
   Arvanites 101
   Catholics 98, 101, 121, 127
   constitutional protection 117–27
   definition of 95–6, 110
   education of 106, 116, 122, 124
   European Convention on Human Rights 107–8
   freedom of religion 120–2
   Gagauz 99
   Gypsies 98, 100, 113, 119, 124
   international protection 95–6, 101–16
   Jehovah's Witnesses 13, 99, 101, 108, 121–2
   Jews 98, 103, 122
   and language 122–3
   Muslims 13, 98, 99, 101, 102, 103–7, 113–14, 119, 120, 122, 123, 124, 125, 167
   Old Calendarists 99
   Pomaks 98, 100, 113, 119, 123, 124, 125
   Protestants 98, 101, 127
   relations with Turkey 103–7, 112, 113, 114, 115, 116, 119, 145, 170–3
   Slavo-Macedonians 99, 113
   Slavophones 19, 21, 23, 26, 98, 100–1, 108, 113
   Treaty of Lausanne 100, 102, 103–7, 114, 161, 171
      Articles 103–4
   Treaty of Sèvres 102–3, 113–14
   Turcophones 98, 99, 108, 109, 113, 116, 119, 120, 122, 124
   Vlachs 1–3, 98
Minority Rights Group 23, 112
Mitsokakis 6, 21, 153, 157
Mitsos, A. 49
Moon, B. 175
Moura-Roque 70
Mouzelis, N. P. 49, 51
Muftis 106
multi-speed Europe 3, 6, 16
Murdoch, R. 18, 19
Muslims 13, 98, 99, 101, 102, 103–7, 108, 109, 113, 119, 120, 122, 167
mutual and balanced force reduction (MBFR) x, 173

Negreponti-Delivani, M. 90, 92
Netherlands 62
New Democracy (ND) x, 11, 21, 41, 44, 61,

142, 149
New Zealand 85
Nickles Amendment 134
North Atlantic Treaty Organisation (NATO)
        x, 14, 17, 20, 27, 137, 151, 155,
        163, 164, *165*, 166, 167, 170, 171
Nye, J. S. 151, 158

OECD 66–7, 71, 74, 78, 83, 92, 162
Old Calendarists 99
omogeneis 118
Organisation for the Reconstruction of
        Europe (OAE) x, 37
Orthodox Church 15, 19, 21–2, 46, 97,
        120–1, 122–3, 167
Ottoman Empire 26, 99, 102, 173
Owen, David 156

Pan Hellenic Federation of Agricultural
        Cooperatives (PASEGES) x, 11
Pan Hellenic Socialist Movement (PASOK) x,
        4, 7, 8, 36, 43–4, 49, 52, 56, 58,
        60, 142, 149, 163
    and Church 21–2
    EU effect on 11–12, 36–7, 39, 43–4
    foreign policy 14, 21–2
Papademos, L. 24, 29, 90, 92
Papageorgiou, F. 51
Papandreou, Andreas 4, 7–8, 12, 14, 21, 22,
        50, 149, 157, 158
Passas, A. 50
Paterson, W. E. 50
Pazartzis, P. 112, 114, 127
Pentzopoulos, D. 111, 115
Petersen, N. 175
petroleum industry 41
Pettifer, J. 14, 17–23
Pfaff, W. 141
Philhellenism 18
Pijpers, A. 175
Pindos Mountain 103
'Pinheiro Package' 137
Politiki Anoiksi 21
Pollis, A. 14, 16, 125, 126
Pomaks 98
Portugal 5, 6–7, 25, 54, *62*, 161
'praetorian zone' 161
Pretenderis, I. K. 52
Price, P. W. R. 70, 71
Pridham, G. 50
protectionism 47
Protestants, Greek 98

Provopoulos, G. 71
Psomiades, H. J. 50, 51, 92, 175
Public Sector Borrowing Requirements
        (PSBRS) x, 63

Ratner, S. R. 141
Rhodes, R. A. W. 49
Romany 113
Rothstein, R. 175
Roumeliotis, P. 49
rousfeti 45
Rouzakis, C. L. 13, 50, 117–27
Rumania 113, 133, 173
Russia 138, 140

Sadik 116
Samaras, Andonis 134, 135, 153
Samaras, Antonio 21
SEB (Confederation of Greek Industries) x,
        43
seigniorange 84–5
Sens, A. 175
Serbia 131–41, 168, 173
Seremetis, D. B. 52
Seventh Day Adventists 122
Shaw, M. 110
Shehadi, K. S. 141
shipping industry 41
Simitis, C. 52
Single European Act (SEA) x, 8, 38, 40, 85
Skandamis, N. 50
Skidmore, D. 175
Skopje 7, 9, 13, 18, 20, 22, 27, 135, 145, 153,
        156; *see also* FYROM
Slavo-Macedonians 99
Slavophones 19, 21, 23, 26, 98, 100, 113,
        136
Slovenia 28, 132, 133–4
Smaghi, L. Bini 83, 91
Smith, M. 159
Smith, S. 174
Sotiropoulos, D. A. 52
Sotitellis, G. 126
Soysal, M. 154, 159
Spain 5, 25, 54, *62*, *77*, 133, 161
Spanou, K. 52
Spinelli Plan 38
Spraas, J. 24, 29
Stavros, S. 13, 95, 117–27
Stearns, M. 159
Stefanou, C. 49, 51
Sterns, L. 158

Stuart, D. 175
Summers 82, 91
Svolopoulos, E. 115
Sweden 137
Swinburne, M. 92
Synaspismos 8, 44

Tabellini 82
Thessaloniki 22, 127
Thomadakis, S. B. 50, 51, 52, 92
Thrace 13, 100, 103, 106, 112, 113, 115,
        116, 119, 122, 124, 135, 153
Thygesen, N. 76, 85, 92
Tirana 22, 23
Tito 132
Tonge, D. 50
Treaty of Athens 114
Treaty of Bucharest 113–14
Treaty of Lausanne 100, 102, 103–7, 114,
        161, 171
    Articles 103–4
Treaty of Neuilly 114
Treaty of Sèvres 102–3, 113–14
Tridimas, G. 53–71
Truman, President 148
Tsinizelis, M. J. 10–16
Tsoulakis, L. 24–9
Tudjman, Franjo 134
Turcophones 98, 99–100
Turkey 10, 13, 17, 18, 22, 27, 39, 103–7,
        112, 113, 114, 115, 116, 119, 135,
        145–6, 148, 149–50, 152, 152–5,
        161, 162
    foreign policy 154–5, 159, 168, 170–3
Tuschhoff, C. 158

underdog culture, in Greece 46–7
Union of Industries in EC (UNICE) x, 11
United Kingdom 8, 9, 10, *62*, 133, 142
United Nations 110, 111, 116, 146, *165*, 166,
        167, 168
    Charter 105
    Covenant on Civil and Political Rights
        97, 111
    Declaration on the Rights of Persons
        belonging to National or
        Ethnic, Religious and Linguistic
        Minorities 96, 108–9

International Court of Justice 105
    Secretary General 102, 114
    Sub-Commission of Minorities
        Resolution 95–6, 110, 126
United States of America 14, 17, 20, *62*,
        147–59, 165–8
    in Balkans 134–5, 138–9, 155–7
    global agenda 151
Urwin, D. W. 50
USSR 14–5, 143, 148; *see also* Cold War
Ustasha Croats 132

Valinakis, Y. 50, 140, 159
Vance, Cyrus 156
Vayrynen, R. 175
Venice Commission for Democracy
        through Law 96
Venizelos, E. 113, 116
Veremis T. 13, 111, 131–41, 142, 159
Verney, S. 4, 16, 50
Vlachs 98, 103, 113, 114
Vorio Epirot 22
Vozvodina 168

Walker, V. 50
Wallace, H. 29, 49
Wallace, W. 49, 51
Wallden, S. 28, 29
Waltz, K. 175
Warsaw Pact 163
Webb, C. 49
Wessels, W. 49
Western European Union (WEU) x, 164, *165*
'West vs Rest' 167–8
Wohlstetter, A. 140
Wood, G. E. 91, 92
Woolcock, S. 159
World Bank 20
World War I 102, 161
World War II 102, 161

Yannas, P. 160–75
Yannopoulos, G. N. 49
Yugoslavia 13, 18, 21, 27, 131–41, 143–6,
        152, 166
    history 132

Zhirinovski, V. 138